Andean Aesthetics and Anticolonial Resistance

Bloomsbury Studies in World Philosophies

Series Editor:
Monika Kirloskar-Steinbach

Comparative, cross-cultural, and intercultural philosophy are burgeoning fields of research. *Bloomsbury Studies in World Philosophies* complements and strengthens the latest work being carried out at a research level with a series that provides a home for thinking through ways in which professional philosophy can be diversified. Ideal for philosophy postgraduates and faculty who seek creative and innovative material on non-Euroamerican sources for reference and research, this series responds to the challenges of our postcolonial world, laying the groundwork for a new philosophy canon that departs from the current Eurocentric sources.

Titles in the Series:
Andean Aesthetics and Anticolonial Resistance, by Omar Rivera
Chinese Philosophy of History, by Dawid Rogacz
Chinese and Indian Ways of Thinking in Early Modern European Philosophy, by Selusi Ambrogio
Indian and Intercultural Philosophy, by Douglas Berger

Andean Aesthetics and Anticolonial Resistance

A Cosmology of Unsociable Bodies

Omar Rivera

BLOOMSBURY ACADEMIC
LONDON · NEW YORK · OXFORD · NEW DELHI · SYDNEY

BLOOMSBURY ACADEMIC
Bloomsbury Publishing Plc
50 Bedford Square, London, WC1B 3DP, UK
1385 Broadway, New York, NY 10018, USA
29 Earlsfort Terrace, Dublin 2, Ireland

BLOOMSBURY, BLOOMSBURY ACADEMIC and the Diana logo are trademarks
of Bloomsbury Publishing Plc

First published in Great Britain 2022
This paperback edition published 2023

Copyright © Omar Rivera, 2022

Omar Rivera has asserted his right under the Copyright, Designs and Patents Act, 1988,
to be identified as Author of this work.

For legal purposes the Acknowledgments on pp. ix–x constitute an extension of
this copyright page.

Series design by Louise Dugdale
Cover image © Olga Kurbatova/Getty Images

All rights reserved. No part of this publication may be reproduced or transmitted in any form or
by any means, electronic or mechanical, including photocopying, recording, or any information
storage or retrieval system, without prior permission in writing from the publishers.

Bloomsbury Publishing Plc does not have any control over, or responsibility for, any third-party
websites referred to or in this book. All internet addresses given in this book were correct
at the time of going to press. The author and publisher regret any inconvenience caused if
addresses have changed or sites have ceased to exist, but can accept no responsibility
for any such changes.

A catalogue record for this book is available from the British Library.

Library of Congress Cataloging-in-Publication Data
Names: Rivera, Omar, author.
Title: Andean aesthetics and anticolonial resistance : a cosmology of unsociable
bodies / Omar Rivera.
Description: London; New York: Bloomsbury Academic, 2021. | Series: Bloomsbury studies in
world philosophies | Includes bibliographical references and index. |
Identifiers: LCCN 2021023398 (print) | LCCN 2021023399 (ebook) | ISBN 9781350173750
(hardback) | ISBN 9781350173767 (ebook) | ISBN 9781350173774 (epub)
Subjects: LCSH: Aesthetics–Andes Region. | Indian cosmology–Andes Region.
Classification: LCC BH221.A53 R58 2021 (print) | LCC BH221.A53 (ebook) | DDC 111/.85098–dc23
LC record available at https://lccn.loc.gov/2021023398
LC ebook record available at https://lccn.loc.gov/2021023399

ISBN: HB: 978-1-3501-7375-0
PB: 978-1-3502-7322-1
ePDF: 978-1-3501-7376-7
eBook: 978-1-3501-7377-4

Series: Bloomsbury Studies in World Philosophies

Typeset by Deanta Global Publishing Services, Chennai, India

To find out more about our authors and books visit www.bloomsbury.com and sign up
for our newsletters.

Para Christina y Aurelio; and in memory of my father, Miguel Rivera, who taught me about architecture and politics.

Contents

List of Figures	viii
Acknowledgments	ix
Introduction: "Marginal" Theorizing of Anticolonial Resistance	1

Part I Cosmological Aesthetics

1	From Elemental Poetics to Cosmological Aesthetics	37
2	An Approach to Andean Aesthetics	62

Part II Embodiments of Resistance

3	Visions of Resistance	91
4	After-Bodies	115
5	Resistant Gestures	128

Part III In Company

6	Ana-topia (in Dialogue with María Lugones)	145
7	*Aísthesis* (in Dialogue with Enrique Dussel)	161
Conclusion: Turns and Departures		178
Notes		193
Bibliography		209
Index		223

Figures

0.1	Omar Rivera, *Intihuatana*	21
1.1	Photographic reproduction of the oil painting by Emilio Pettoruti, *Día Tranquilo*	45
1.2	Photographic reproduction of the oil painting by Emilio Pettoruti, *Temporal*	46
1.3	Emilio Pettoruti, *José Carlos Mariátegui* (portrait)	47
1.4	Photographic reproduction of the watercolor by Emilio Pettoruti, *Vieja Puerta*	49
1.5	José Sabogal Diéguez, *India del Collao*	53
1.6	Photographic reproduction of the oil painting by José Sabogal Diéguez, *Procesión de Taitacha Temblores*	55
2.1	Omar Rivera, *Tambomachay*	63
2.2	Omar Rivera, *Echo Stones*	67
2.3	Julia Navarrete, *Sín Título*	79
2.4	Omar Rivera, *Kenko*	86
2.5	Staged photograph by Omar Rivera, Edwin Quispecuro Nina, Richard Peralta, *Kenko Altar*	87
2.6	Julia Navarrete, from the Interstices series, *Sín Título*	87
3.1	Martín Chambi Jiménez, *Wiñay Wayna, Cusco 1941*	93
3.2	Martín Chambi Jiménez, *Queromarca Woman with Child in the Study, Cusco Approximately 1925*	94
3.3	Aliza Nisenbaum, *La Talaverita, Sunday Morning NY Times*	104
3.4	Laura Aguilar, *Clothed/Unclothed #16*	113
3.5	Laura Aguilar, *Center #73*	113
5.1	Liliana Wilson, *Bearing Witness*	140

Acknowledgments

This book was born co-teaching a study abroad seminar on Inka architecture and colonial art with Patrick Hajovsky, an art historian, in Cusco, Peru. In dialogue with him and with Richard Peralta and Edwin Quispecuro Nina, two local artists and faculty at the Universidad Nacional Diego Quispe Tito, I began to explore the intersection between Andean aesthetics, phenomenology, and possibilities of embodying anticolonial resistance. Rather than attempting a political mobilization of indigeneity (something that is beyond my knowledge and capacities), I focused on the kinds of physicalities (including sense perception, affects, and memory) that can emerge from an aesthetics of light, water, and stone, and on how these physicalities can illuminate resistances to colonial and modern social oppressions. The artworks of Peralta and Quispecuro Nina in particular inspired this exploration and showed me that it did not have to be a project of a historical recovery of a pre-colonial lineage, but an aesthetic engagement with the here and now of pre-colonial, colonial, modern, and global lives that occur simultaneously in Cusco and beyond. I have presented parts of this book at the Collegium Phaenomenologicum and benefited from discussing it there. I am thankful to Charles Scott, Nancy Tuana, Bret Davis, and Anne O'Byrne for these opportunities. I have also been fortunate to have the support through dialogues and invitations of Alejandro Vallega, Daniela Vallega-Neu, Ted George, and Kristi Sweet. Under the encouragement of Nancy Tuana, I immersed myself in decolonial feminism, which informs the second and third parts of the book in ways that I did not anticipate at the beginning. This book would not have been possible without the help of two research assistants: my former student Cat Kelly, who carefully went through the first draft of the whole manuscript and identified much work to be done, and Rachel Cicoria (currently a PhD student at Texas A&M), who helped me finalize the manuscript, polish the ideas, and gather the images. Among the artists that I discuss, I am grateful to Liliana Wilson, Aliza Nisenbaum, and Julia Navarrete in particular. Oscar Chambi, the Director de Patrimonio del Archivo Martín Chambi, helped me find photographs that fit well with my discussion. I wrote the majority of this book at LLILAS-Benson at the University of Texas, Austin, during a year-long residency with the support of the ACLS Burkhardt Fellowship.

Above all I thank Christina, who encourages me to pursue challenging philosophical paths and who, like me, is always eager to return to Cusco and the Sacred Valley.

Introduction

"Marginal" Theorizing of Anticolonial Resistance

In Andean settings resistance has been conceived as part of a *pachakuti* or an overturning of the cosmos.¹ Echoing Luis Alberto Reyes, I find that the following observation by José María Arguedas sheds light on this: "the struggle is not only spurred by economic interests; other deep and violent spiritual forces set the parties ablaze, which are agitated with implacable force, with an incessant and unavoidable exigency" (Cited by Luis Alberto Reyes, 2008: 286).² Perhaps the "implacable force" of anticolonial resistance—the aspect of it that cannot be traced back to specific liberatory intentions, critical deliberations of determined revolutionary subjects, or to reactions to particular injustices—could be that of the cosmos or *pacha*, specifically as it is manifest in processes of generation, destruction, and creation, in the transitions between day and night, the seasons, sickness and health.

For example, in the sixteenth century the widespread indigenous rebellion of *Taki Oncoy*, or the "sickness of song and dance," roused forms of resistance that sought to propitiate a cleansing cosmic turn—an ineffable destruction and rebirth that could not be the expression of reform or opposition to the colonial order. From a sensibility informed by Latin American and Latinx aesthetic traditions, I retroactively view *Taqui Oncoy* as invoking ritualized and physical dispositions that override dominant inhabitations of manageable social and political resistances (articulated by both oppressors and liberators), embodying instead a form of cosmological resistance that lets go of investments in development, progress, and the calculable redemption of the oppressed.

I understand the "propitiatory" character of *Taqui Oncoy* to show that resistance does not need to abide by expectations of intelligible and protagonist agencies, such as those that reflect dominant social logics and structures of power or inflate the liberatory role of theorists engaged in social critique. At the same time "propitiatory resistance" does not arise spontaneously from the social positionality of the oppressed. Instead it is formed and maintained through aesthetic practices cultivated communally. These practices harness physicalities (such as affects, modalities of perception, and memory) and allow for unsettling inhabitations of colonialist social orders that unleash alternative socialities within concrete contexts of modern/colonial oppression. I see in these resistant propitiations ways of situating possibilities of critique that are attentive to the social complexity of the manifestations of forms of power with colonial roots, and avoid both monolithic critical perspectives and attachments to clear social differentiations, including those of oppressor and oppressed, or of oppressing and resisting.[3]

Taqui Oncoy's ritualized and cosmological resistance was deemed irrational by colonial authorities, as if it were the work of the devil. This kind of colonial indictment can also be elicited by Arguedas's words in the twentieth century. Aren't the "violent spiritual forces" of the struggle something to be feared if they are not intelligible from familiar economic and social orders, and from critiques of them? Shouldn't resistance be ultimately transparent in its motivations and projections, and in its being framed by clear dichotomies of oppressor/oppressed and oppressors/liberators? Isn't there a responsible and proper way to resist, and shouldn't resistance be itself a social project with sensible values and forms of accountability? If resistant subjects remain illegible, unsociable, wouldn't they be just vehicles of violence and barbarity?

The analyses in this book do not share in the spirit of these questions. They, rather, take a path that could be easily dismissed as "cultural," "spiritual," and "ethnic," as "irrational," or "emotional"—namely, a path that may appear to be politically esoteric and even irrelevant. I take seriously, however, the possibility of a cosmological basis for a resistance that arises in physicalities and social forms that can't be exhausted by dominant social articulations of identities (even oppressed ones) and economies, even by dominant social differences legible in view of oppressive and liberatory possibilities. Specifically, I explore resistance arising from an immersion in affective and other physical registers attuned to the cosmos or *pacha*, rather than in physicalities disciplined and intelligible within colonially managed socialities. I am interested in resistant irresponsible and unsociable bodies, and study in them a physical realm where a destructive/generative cosmos and the resistant/oppressed find joint rhythms that build up toward an "incessant and unavoidable exigency" to transform social orders.

At the background of my discussion are recent developments in Latin American art history, anthropology, and archeology.[4] These inform my aesthetic approach to pre-colonial, colonial, and modern architecture, artworks, and rituals, without restricting it to modern, Western notions of fine art, and art criticism. On this basis I offer a "cosmological aesthetics" that sheds light on sense perception, affects, postures, and other bodily enactments that decenter modern/colonial elucidations and inhabitations of social formations, even liberatory ones.[5]

At the same time, I do not aim at recovering authentic, non-Western modes of being. I do not intend to represent "indigenous" bodily experiences and feelings operative in movements of anticolonial resistance. The turn to the Andes in this book is prompted by complex, situated junctures of anticolonial resistance in a number of diverse historical and geographic contexts—where the clear demarcations between oppressed/oppressor, oppressor/liberator, and human/non-human are forged and contested—rather than by a commitment to cultural authenticity as inherently resistant. In other words, Andean indigenous lineages are not being claimed, elucidated, or legitimized by my discussion. Following Gloria Anzaldúa, I attempt, then, to stay away from the pervasiveness of colonialist interests and appropriations in some theorizations of anticolonial liberation. She notes, for example: "The essence of colonization: rip off a culture, then regurgitate its white version to the 'natives'" (2015: 48).

Instead, Andean aesthetics and cosmologies become relevant for my analysis because they can reveal ways of sensing, feeling, and remembering that, as I have suggested, are oriented toward belonging to the cosmos as *pacha* rather than only to socialities (including social identities and the character of their relations) that support colonial lineages of exploitation and dehumanization. This approach illuminates various physical possibilities of anticolonial resistance that are not restricted to or representative of "indigenous" cultures.

Anzaldúa is a defining presence in this book with regard to its theoretical positioning. Her term "*mestizaje* theories" is applicable here:

> Theorists of color are in the process of trying to formulate "marginal" theories that are partially outside and partially inside the western frame of reference (if that is possible), theories that overlap many "worlds." We are articulating new positions in these "in-between," Borderland worlds of ethnic communities and academies, feminist and job worlds. . . . In our *mestizaje* theories we create new categories for those of us left out or pushed out of the existing ones. We recover and examine non-western aesthetics while critiquing western aesthetics; recover and examine non-rational modes and "blanked out" realities while critiquing rational, consensual reality; recover and examine indigenous languages while critiquing the "languages" of the dominant culture. And we simultaneously combat tokenization and appropriation of our literatures and our writers/artists. (2009: 137)

My discussion is "marginal," that is, it attempts to transgress Western frames of reference and reductive presentations of modern/colonial socialities. In particular, it explores possible and concrete inhabitations of the social without falling prey to the influence of the colonial, social distinction between the human and the non-human.[6]

With this end in view, my theorizing happens at the borders between Andean cosmologies, phenomenology, hermeneutics, and decolonial feminism. It does not take itself to belong to one of these "sides." It, rather, seeks to remain in both theoretical and lived tensions (such as those within academic spaces, museums, colonial churches) so as to provide sensuous schemas that make room for the expression of marginalized bodies with unsociable resistant potentials. "Cosmological Aesthetics" and "Afterbodies" are two of such schemas that I develop in this work. Through them my marginal or *mestizaje* theorizing creates leeway at concrete theoretical and social borders, and thus gives an unstable ground for examinations and recoveries of suppressed modes of sensing, thinking, and remembering. In these impure and unstable margins, projects of tokenization and appropriation have difficulty taking hold.

In addition to the frame of "marginal theorizing," this book relies on a particular understanding of social formations as "modern/colonial" (which I draw from Aníbal Quijano and María Lugones). This determination of the "modern/colonial" involves the organization of social identities, like race and gender, by a capitalist economy that cannot completely settle into the wage-labor/capital relation, giving rise instead to a number of heterogeneous social and economic orders. In view of this heterogeneity, I am interested in the tense social formations that arise with the imposition of social identities as manageable and calculable, and of specific hierarchies and models of power that continue colonial legacies in their differentiation between the human and non-human. These tense socialities involve a contextually shifting yet efficacious double social formation. It includes both a sphere of sociality (including normativity, normalization and transgression) that coincides with the "human," and a socially unintelligible non-human sphere where dispensable colonized lives come to pass without the support of dominant "modern/colonial" social orders. This book's tracing of anticolonial resistance delves into physical inhabitations of the "non-human" sphere as they destabilize the social support of "human" socialities, and participate in the formation of socialities with alternative articulations of power, such as those that operate in alignment with cosmological (rather than strictly "human") orders.

In this introduction I interpret Luis Alberto Reyes's study of *Taki Oncoy* in order to shed light on his statement that *pacha* or the cosmos was the "subject of the revolution." I also offer a preliminary elucidation of my uses of the terms "physicality" and "aísthesis," and analyze *pacha* phenomenologically, all of which illustrates the "marginal" orientation of this book. I end with brief chapter overviews and a statement on the scope of the discussion.

Theorizing Resistance through *Taki Oncoy*

Toward *Pacha* as the "Subject of the Revolution"

Even though I won't focus on *Taki Oncoy* in the following chapters, there are some aspects of this early movement that orient this book's analyses of a cosmological resistance on the basis of Andean aesthetics. As I noted, it would be a mistake to conceive of *Taki Oncoy* as articulated in opposition to, that is, as reactive and derivative from, colonial oppressive structures, as participating in a collision of two social orders, cultures, worlds that moves toward a transformative resolution of a power differential. This oppositional framing of resistance fits within colonialist perspectives and projections, especially with regard to their investments in extermination, exploitation, development, and conversion. Reyes puts it well:

> The interpretation of the indigenous struggles for emancipation is usually enunciated from perspectives that are external and incidental, perspectives on the significance that these struggles had for European or creole interests, or for the indigenous reaction in terms of immediate concerns, namely, the confrontations and the challenges that the presence and domination of the invaders implied. (2008: 285)

The vision of resistance as oppositional is here connected not only to colonialist dichotomizing perspectives on the oppressor and oppressed but also to a narrowing down of what counts as indigenous resistance, namely, its reduction to reactive and immediate confrontational movements.

Reyes emphasizes *Taki Oncoy*'s non-reactive stance:

> In its resistance, it did not invoke the gospels against the abuses of the mayors, priests, and *encomenderos*. It did not get tangled up in legal demands as the *curacas* did, who questioned the Spanish due to their inconsistencies with respect to the Christianity they professed. It also did not argue, as the indigenous chroniclers did, that the values and gods of the Inkas were similar to those of Christianity, and ought to be respected for that reason. (2008: 287)

I don't take Reyes to mean that these kinds of acts of resistance and questioning of colonial powers are insignificant. The issue he points to, rather, is that if resistance is reduced to such acts, then it is intelligible *from* and *for* colonialist perspectives (including social, religious, economical, and gendered perspectives), since it occurs within the purview of the colonial system and its projections. In this sense, resistance would appear to be a striving for a social and political stage that is continuous, even if dialectically so, with colonialism. Resistance would be, then, a movement in which assimilation, development, progress, and socialization are at play; the latter meaning a process of recognition through social identification, and of validation of contributions to the reproduction and development of colonialist social orders (even if under a liberatory guise).

In order to understand *Taki Oncoy* as a different kind of resistance, I interpret Reyes suggesting a transition: from resistance as socialization, to the cosmos or *pacha* as a physical force of resistance. He states:

> The movement [*Taki Oncoy*], according to the known testimonies, did not put forth demands for the reparations of particular injustices . . . it looked for justice as a cosmic compensation. The subject of this revolution were not the officers, the women that conducted the rites of *Taki Oncoy*, or the prophet of the movement, Juan Chocné, but *Pacha* [the cosmos]. (2008: 286)

At first it seems that, rather than instigating resistance, *pacha* as the subject of revolution is obscurantist, a fatalistic passivity, a disempowerment of the oppressed, and a denial of the possibility of willing oppression out of existence. Reyes explains, however, that evoking *pacha* in this context allows for discerning a movement of generation, destruction, and creation that involves both oppressors and oppressed, and for joining transformations that cannot be anticipated from either of these positions. This constitutes an anticolonial resistant disposition for which oppressive structures appear as already passing, so that there is no need to instigate resistance (either through theory or ideological praxis) since it is always already there, effervescing in everyday concrete places, yet not as a willed act owned by oppositional rebellious masses.

Resistance as "Propitiation" (Beyond the Action/Passivity Dichotomy)

Identifying *pacha* as the "subject of the revolution" does not reduce the resistant-oppressed to passivity. I suggest, rather, that at issue here is an affective, postural, perceptual inhabitation of the cosmos as sweeping social and political forms toward destruction. This is a finding of oneself and of one's community already practicing resistance, which requires a mode of physical sentience that is not predominantly volitional, one that seems to be at play in the "sickness of song and dance."

This sentience is not a doing but a physical turning, and this turning is a "propitiation." Reyes writes:

> The mystical-revolutionary movement of *Taki Oncoy* is a propitiatory rite of cosmic transitions. . . . The rites of *Taki Oncoy* evoke and propitiate the conflict and the alternations that are the plot of the life of the cosmos. Beyond the positions that, in the different conflicts between men, are at play, there is a latent background that holds the conflict, that stimulates it. (2008: 288–9)

The meaning of "propitiate" in this statement is key to move beyond the dichotomy of action/passivity as it bears on resistance. "Action," including resistant action, is recognizable as such in terms of dominant social intelligibilities, or related intelligibilities forged by liberatory movements and their academic and activist gatekeepers. "Passivity" means that which is unrecognizable as action in this sense. To move beyond this dichotomy is to recognize that under what seems like "passivity" there is a form of resistance that does not fit the framework of action because it does not draw solely from available social intelligibilities enforced by oppressors and liberators.

Here I am approximating the mode of resistance Lugones calls "active subjectivity." She states: "What I mean by 'active subjectivity' . . . has no such presuppositions, no ready-made sense within which our actions and intentions can be made congruent with our domination" (2005: 7). I refer to Lugones at this point because she helps me understand the meaning of Reyes's "propitiation." I interpret it as inhabiting a dominant and oppressive sociality so that its structural determinacy appears illusory and insufficient for the articulation of resistant intentions. Propitiation is also finding leeway that allows for inhabitations of socialities in which bodies disciplined by colonialism/modernity are released from postural, affective, perceptual, and memorial impositions that align them with their oppression. Such alignments are manifest in the perceptual racialization of bodies, nostalgia, resentment, and the repression of anger, among other physicalities. I also find that propitiatory resistance is fostered in aesthetic forms, especially when their ritual dimensions are evoked.

"Propitiation" involves sensing, from released physicalities, limina, tensions, resistances within modern/colonial socialities. This includes sensing social fractures that signal the destruction, generation, and creation of structures of oppression as they are swept by the cosmos. I am referring here to resistant inhabitations of concrete spaces with entrenched social architectures (such as academic institutions, museums, corporations). A cosmological sentience of "conflict and alternations," in Reyes terms, makes the leeway within these social architectures apparent. To resist is to "propitiate," but these words do not intend actions at this juncture, but a form of physical and aesthetic enactment of a cosmic "background" that stimulates "conflict."

Resistance as "propitiation" does not "do" anything, but enjoins the intensification and charge of a conflictive atmosphere that is apparent not ideologically or theoretically, but physically.[7] Bodies, for example, that are next to each other in a rite or strike can feel differently, even suspending the usual dispositions toward authority, rationality, the law, and death. In this physical transformation the space of plazas and streets can be re-inhabited. The concreteness and situatedness of this inhabitation energize a conflictive atmosphere, rather than abstract communication of theories or the staging of debates. I am not suggesting that the articulations of demands don't matter, but that there is a physical situatedness that pre-determines and informs the understanding of those demands and the modes in which they come to be mobilized as resistant.

I include in this physical situatedness hearing dominant counter narratives and letting them impact one's affective and cognitive bearings, reacting to the enticement of assimilation, as well as feeling pressure to adopt oppositional stances entrenched in identities. Related to the latter, I note as well the response of the oppressed to the imposition of social identities on their bodies by liberatory movements in order to articulate political demands. *Taki Oncoy*, especially in Reyes's interpretation, seems to have been a movement attentive to this physical dimension that situates and brings one to a communicative, practical, and strategic field, setting into play alternatives to oppositional framings of resistance and to what is understood as proper political and liberatory acts.

Abstracted from this physical dimension, the field of liberatory politics is too narrow, and too determined by the dichotomy of action/passivity, to exhibit the physical, cosmological, "propitiative" resistance I am interested in. Resistance as "propitiation" belongs to a prior field of affective, postural, and perceptual transformations, one that modernity/colonialism suppresses in order to trap the resistant-oppressed in having to say, feel, and act without the support of the cosmos as a background. Without the cosmos "that holds the conflict, that stimulates it," the resistant-oppressed would be disembodied revolutionaries.

Appearances of Oppression

At stake in the physical dimension of resistance I am analyzing is how structures of oppression are taken on not just cognitively but, above all, bodily. In particular, I focus on whether the oppressed assume structural oppression as exhaustive, being left paralyzed, finding no possibility of resisting except on the basis of the bodily inhabitation of socialities and institutions aligned with the very structures that oppress them. This paralysis can be enforced both by dominant interests and by critiques of oppression that present oppression as "inescapable" (to borrow María Lugones's phrasing).[8]

I find Kusch's work on Andean indigenous thought to be helpful at this juncture. He puts forth two modes of addressing a crisis. One is through "externalization," by which he means objectifying a situation so as to render it manipulatable and resolvable in ways that are pre-articulated, known in advance. This response to a crisis fits within the frameworks of "action" and "passivity" I discussed earlier. It is also a response assailed by an inescapable sense of oppression, by feeling that resistances can only come to pass through affects, actions, deliberations, values, and socialities that are set up in advance and that ultimately contribute to the preservation of domination.

The second mode of addressing a crisis engages it through the heart or *chuyma*. "Externalization" is affectively supported by feelings of safety tied to self-certainty and the execution of actions. *Chuyma*, instead, is a movement toward safety through a complex affect that finds balance in the instability or "seminality" of the cosmos. *Chuyma* senses an "así" or "thusness" in a simultaneity of generation, destruction, and creation, which is manifest in psychological and emotional states, immediate and concrete situations, larger socio-political contexts and environmental events. The spread of the heart through these different cosmic scales can reach a sense of transhuman centeredness, stillness, and simply sitting, while enduring transformations and rebirths. Kusch calls this "estar."[9]

Similarly to Lugones, I draw from Kusch in order to think through the possibility of resistance beyond the active/passive dichotomy. *Estar* is a physicality that retreats from the imperative to "act," and is able to sustain the loss of the pre-articulated support of dominant socialities. In this retreat, I suggest, the possibility for physical inhabitations of concrete situations beyond the single purview of domination and oppression comes to pass. *Estar*, then, can in my view happen as a physical transformation that is not fulfilled in an action as much as in charging a socio-political atmosphere that "propitiates" conflict. This charging or energizing emanates from postures, affects, perceptions, and infuses the articulation of demands as if the cosmos or *pacha* were the "subject of the revolution." This atmosphere of resistance dispels the appearance of oppression as absolute, exhaustive, and inescapable, and allows one to take on domination as embedded in a cosmic movement that entails turns and overturns. Yet, the oppressed as determined by domination also succumb to this movement, undergoing unprecedented physical metamorphoses.

Ukhu Pacha[10]

In *estar* I find a retreat into a physical/cosmic realm that can enable resistance beyond the "action/passivity" dichotomy. I understand this realm to be *ukhu pacha*, the underworld. Reyes describes it as "associated with . . . a primordial disorder, the night, the past and future rebirths" (89). *Ukhu pacha* is the interior of the body as well as the depth of the cosmos where it undergoes destructions and re-births. "Destructions and rebirths" are not continuous processes, but involve leaps, ruptures. I capture this cosmic discontinuity as generation and destruction, *and* creation. With the addition of creation, I underscore that destruction does not lead to generation, and vice versa, as in a circular process. Destruction and generation of the cosmos occur simultaneously, without being clearly differentiated, which comes to pass as lack of determination or an emptiness. For this reason, in *ukhu* the cosmos can be conceived of as transpiring in and emerging from emptiness, as creation.

The cosmic leaps of *ukhu pacha* bring about a dissemination of human-centered time in its progressivism, and developmentalism, as well as in its circularity and calendric patterns, in its return to a self that becomes more habitual, disciplined, (self) knowledgeable, or even in its ecstatic opening of a moment of decision and of truth as resoluteness. This cosmic region, then, empties out intentions that project on a pre-articulated field of social and political orders. It empties out "action" and the ground of its intelligibility, especially as it is configured in modernity/colonialism.

Ukhu pacha is apparent to a physical sentience, and within memorial, gestural, and affective registers. Reyes approaches it in view of affects, through a differentiation of modes of suffering in particular, namely, of *pena* (sorrow) and *dolor* (pain). He interprets the colonial play or *wanka* that narrates the encounter between the Inkas and the Spanish, and the capture and death of Atahualpa: *Atau Wallpaj P'uchukakuyninpa Wankan*. He connects pain to the guilt of Pizarro, the conquistador. Feeling guilty, Pizarro's pain is "the suffering of a lonely man, author of his regrets, responsible for the evils that befall the earth" (2008: 281). His guilt does not release him from the field of actions, where the significance of them returns to a self and is pre-articulated socially and morally.

The princesses that mourn Atahualpa's death feel a sorrow "that is a cosmic suffering... that extends to animals, mountains and rivers... sorrow takes shelter in the lap of the world" (2008: 279). Sorrow does not entail the concentration of pain in the individual, but a mode of abandonment into the destructions and rebirths of the cosmos. Pain is an affect that through localization re-enforces the configuration of the self as a "doer," as the source of crises and their resolutions. Sorrow, on the other hand, does not return to a self because its cosmic shelter in *ukhu pacha* means that the destruction it faces involves both the situation one is in and one's own sense of self. *Ukhu pacha* is the region, then, where new bodies, and the selves configured by them, await us. This loss in sorrow, like the cosmos, is destructive and creative, but not developmental or progressive. It is not a mental realization but a reshaping of one's physicality, a re-ordering of one's bodily bearings, including those of the inhabitations of oppression.

The difference between pain and sorrow corresponds to the one between a resistance of "action" (the one intelligible in the context of modernity/colonialism) and a propitiative or cosmological resistance. Colonizing and liberatory gazes expect the dehumanized and the oppressed to be in pain; that is, pain makes oppression intelligible for them. They can only see resistance from pain, as the expression of men moved by a sense of responsibility and indignation, seeking to right the wrongs. Resistance from pain confines resistant agents to the field of action.

The sorrow of the oppressed, instead, is not intelligible in colonialist registers. When bearing witness to the suffering (including one's own suffering) of the oppressed that is not reduced to pain, that is, when pain is revealed to be sorrow, there is a physical shift that propitiates the destruction of both an oppressive order and the oppressed as determined by that order. This shift is invisible in the field of action where pain renders the oppressed transparent. It ushers in physical configurations that are not disciplined into responsibility, and anticipates a turn of the cosmos, a *pachakuti*.

Reyes suggests mapping these sufferings onto resistance. Pain is connected to "the usual methods of the native cuzqueño *curacas* and chroniclers: to confront the priests, the landowners and other Spanish authorities with their own principles and values" (2008: 281). While sorrow appears to "a different vision of the conquest that emerges in testimonies about *Taki Oncoy*, where indigenous suffering and the Spanish domination are explained by turns in cosmic emergencies and declinations" (2008: 282).

The meaning of the name "the sickness of song and dance" becomes clear at this juncture. Reyes points out that Andean rituals seek to access a state of sickness as a purification that brings one closer to a cosmic and sacred origin. More precisely, sickness (*Oncoy*) reveals that the "protagonist of all conflicts, and the one to resolve them" is death. In other words, sickness reveals that one has always been "livingdying," just as the seminal cosmos: destroying, generating, re-birthing, and emptying out the difference between destruction and creation.[11] About song and dance (*Taki*), Reyes states that they "fulfilled the function of establishing reality... Songs and dances brought about the consummation of the revealment of new events" (2008: 289). On this basis, I interpret *Taki Oncoy*, the "the sickness of song and dance," as establishing the sentience of the simultaneity of cosmic destruction and creation, of *ukhu pacha*, in the concreteness of the "here and now" (which is one translation of *pacha*). This establishment characterizes *Taki Oncoy* as a movement of resistance and not of "action," a turn in physical sentience that, invisibly and atmospherically, propitiates the overturning of domination. Reyes emphasizes that in this establishment of *pacha* as the subject of resistance, there are no redemptive moral values (referring to the absence of a responsible self), "yet one can ascertain and critique the ignorance of the powerful who do not notice the fragility of their position" (2008: 289).

Delimitations of Cosmological Resistance

There is something disappointing about situating resistance in a field where volition, oppositionality, and action are not mainly at play, especially given the expectations that resistance be seen, and its effects be clear. Lugones dissipates these expectations by connecting them to modernity/colonialism and its preservation. In other words, the demand that resistance be reduced to action is a mode of oppression. It denies the oppressed the possibility of resisting or, more precisely, the possibility of finding themselves already resisting in their everyday, in the concrete inhabitation of institutions that exclude them, in their range of affectivity, in their sorrow. In the modern/colonial context the demand that resistance be only action puts resistance a step removed from the physical situatedness of the oppressed, and obviates the physical aspects of both oppression and resistance.

Lugones makes a clear turn to this field of resistance in a way that echoes my discussion:

I dismiss the modern Western notion of agency—the ground of individual responsibility—in favor of a more contained, more inward, sense of activity of the self in metamorphosis. Like in a cocoon, the changes are not directed outward, at least not toward those domains permeated by the logics of domination. (2005: 86)

This aspect of Lugones's theories of resistance is in dialogue with Kusch, his notion of "estar" in particular. She relates this notion not only to the "seminal" movement of the cosmos, but also to a way of taking on the appearance of oppressive systems. In particular, the cosmic simultaneity of generation, destruction, and creation fractures this appearance as both exhaustive and univocal, coherent. I suggest here that the cosmic "background that stimulates conflict" reveals oppression as being "multiple," fluid, contextual, irreducible to a single principle or origin, and, thus, impossible to be simply opposed.[12]

In other words, there is no pure oppression, and no pure resistance. This points to a mode of taking on domination that arises from a multiple resistant physicality that undergoes fragmentation along with the breakdown of oppressive structures. This fragmentation configures resistance as physically metamorphic, and as connected to a sentience that is in-stilled while in transformation. In this in-stillness, or "estar," new figurations of postures, affects, and perceptions arise, released from the hold of the processes through which bodies are disciplined by modernity/colonialism.

I suggest drawing an analytic distinction between resistance and liberation. Liberation involves entering in the field of action, strategy, and effective communication. It is oriented toward the actualization of actions and the transformation of social, political, and economic structures. Without resistance, as I have elucidated here, however, liberation remains disembodied, abstract, and only in the realm and intelligibility of "action." Resistance, in my view, situates liberation. It brings the body forth into the field of action, complicating it, decentering it, and localizing it, with unruly affects, sexualities, ways of perceiving, postures and embodiments of race and ethnicity, revealing multiple and impure oppressions and resistances, while liberation seeks to articulate a political program. These two moments, liberation and resistance, are implicated and in tension with one another, and a full-fledged theory of liberation cannot resolve this tension but, in my terms, can bring the cosmological to bear on the liberatory. If this tension is not sheltered, movements of liberation draw from the social and political intelligibility of domination and become machines of socialization and exclusions that target the oppressed, their bodies in particular. In this book I delve into the physicality of "cosmological resistance" in its relation to aesthetics, and defer the study of the tensions between resistance and liberation.

Physicality

Physical Sentience

The term "physical" in this text (and the related terms "physicalities," "corporealities," and "bodies") entails a sentience of and within posture, spatio-temporal bearings, affects, memory, and sense perception.[13] I focus on how this sentience discloses the way one is situated in concrete, localized environments, a situatedness that pre-determines understanding and self-understanding. In particular, physicalities can disclose one's situatedness within architectures of social relations, including power dynamics. They sense one's orientation and disorientation in these social architectures, and also their configurations and de-configurations, their emerging and passing, and the different bodily dispositions that arise in and after such transitions.

This physical sentience is not submitted to self-conscious processes of a self-certain subject, and does not seek resolute actions that show the subject's power. Yet, it senses (mostly affectively and spatio-temporally) corporeal attachments to and detachments from such subjective formations and actions. Through anxiety it can sense the sudden loss of social support and intelligibility that guide actions and validate values. Through *machariska* (a mode of fright) it can sense the forced, colonial/modern submission to expectations of self-certainty, mental and physical ability, affective clarity, transparency of purpose, responsibility and moral judgment. I single out these two affects because they allow me to center on the possibility of a physical sentience that destabilizes the social architectures, and the corresponding subjective forms, of colonialism/modernity. These are physicalities that—like Anzaldúa's shadow beast—can resist without relying on the figuration of a modern subject.

Physical sentience is a kind of knowing, or a *sentipensar*, even though it does not conform to dominant Western epistemic expectations, such as self-consciousness, clear communicability, and conceptuality. *Sentipensar* happens, rather, through the physical attentiveness to the way social architectures (that hold histories, cultural values, and senses of identity) situate one's pre-judgments in the articulation of understanding. It senses the complexity and fluidity of this situatedness, and the localized transformations of one's pre-judgments. In other words, the sentience I am focusing on is an epistemic determinant insofar as it allows one to attend to how one arrives at knowing by taking in situational factors (such as sensing institutional presences and histories, the ways in which our interlocutors inhabit social identities, and the sensuous allocation of epistemic authority, among others).

I am not pointing to deliberate, rhetorical strategizing, but to postures, involuntary memory, affects, and perceptual habits that condition knowledge formation at a pre-reflective level, and to the awareness that accompanies them, which allows for receptiveness to and interaction with one's concrete situation.[14] In this respect, physical sentience maximizes the range of intelligibility and of possible things to say about the "here/now." This sentience of how one arrives at socially mediated understanding can also garner the power of situated silence and incommunicability. By this I mean a holding back or stillness that can make room for modulations of one's and others' physical bearings, a letting go of bodily dispositions that support pre-judgments, and a draw to the formation of different ones, at the threshold of speech and knowledge.

The Social Architectures of Colonialism/Modernity

The explorations of physicality in this book mostly center on this modality of silence and the sentience that happens with it, and show possibilities of dispelling and disseminating how social architectures anchor one's self-understanding, especially as these architectures are forged within a colonial/modern, global order. I turn, then, to social architectures characterized by the enforcement of the difference between the human and non-human.[15] This difference allows for the exploitation of the oppressed and is articulated in terms of enmeshed social differences, such as race, gender, and ability. It is also contingent and its application is localized and flexible, variably instantiated in terms of tones of skin color, levels of education or assimilation, intersectional formations, and perceptual encodings of socialities.

These multifarious instantiations of the difference between human and non-human make it seem as if it had no concrete grounding, being, thus, ephemeral. It appears as a spectrum rather than a difference, something that can be crossed, which gives the illusion that the oppressed can be socialized, or socialize themselves, into humanity. The indeterminacy of designations of humanity, however, does not constitute a social continuity. It, rather, creates a shifting border populated by those for whom their humanity could be taken away at any moment on the basis of social categorizations. It is important to make a distinction between the arbitrary dispensation of humanity that at times includes and excludes the same person or group of people, and the possibility of socialization. The accumulation of valued social markers, such as a college education, wealth, or even familiarity with socially progressive terminology, may appear to facilitate socialization, but all those markers can be denied, relativized, contextualized so as to reveal that one's entrenchment in the non-human category remains.

In this respect, colonialism establishes social determinations that render the colonized dispensable, that is, unable to contribute to the preservation and development of the socialities that are managed in order to sustain the colonial/modern global economic order (even if this order relies on the labor of the colonized). More succinctly, it initiates social determinations that exclude people from the social by deeming them non-human. Colonialism results, then, in two modalities of the a-social. The transgression of social norms, including the inhabitation of identities, can arbitrarily and contextually place one within the "human" or within the "non-human" categories. The former allows for reintegration and reform via socialization, for the latter socialization is foreclosed because non-humanity is not something one sheds.

The complex entanglement of social determination and colonial dehumanization means that socialization never gives access to "humanity." In particular, socialization in the context of colonialism/modernity cannot be an inclusion of the non-human into the social via new forms of social recognition, since such recognitions are always, even if in varying ways, invested in dehumanization. At the same time, processes of socialization can disguise their involvement with dehumanization through promises of assimilation, education, development, modernization, progress, and even of belonging to movements of liberation, promises that can be enticing to the oppressed. This convoluted character and appearance of socialization adds to the disorientation of being at the border where humanity feels like it is just out of reach.[16]

The Physical Parsing of the Difference between the Human and Non-Human

I delve into social architectures formed under modernity/colonialism, and into the viability of socialization within them, because the kinds of physical sentience I focus on parse the involvement of socialities with the differentiation between the human and non-human: parsing, for example, ways of seeing where this difference is at play racially, postures that hold bodies ambivalently toward assimilation, the gaze of those that look like oneself yet seem supported by the very socialities one experiences as oppressive, and insidious spatial sensibilities that assume the occupation of space to be neutral and univocal despite the lived experience of the repression of "ethnic" inhabitations within everyday places.[17]

This parsing involves one's whole body, *sentipensando*, drawing from a sentience of and in physicalities that may breach the inhabitations of modern/colonial socialities but do not ultimately abide by their basic orientations and purpose. This is a sentience that situates affects, perceptual experiences, and memorial processes, letting bodies undergo border realignments with social architectures with a sense of attachment to their transformative possibilities and detachment from how these possibilities may be ultimately inhabited. These attachments/detachments give leeway for the manifestation of unexpected dimensions within dominant articulations of concrete and social space, together with bodies that inhabit them. They also situate ways of interpreting and speaking, shaping bodies that give bearings to language. At the same time, physical leeway allows for bringing other bodies in, physically, into surprising domains.

In this leeway, affects can amplify their range. In Lugones's account, for example, anger can be a demand for social recognition, a way of keeping dominant social expectations at bay, and an opportunity to let different bodies arise even within "one" body so as to disseminate the disciplining that bodies, especially those of the oppressed, are subjected to in colonialist spaces (like educational institutions, religious buildings, museums). In terms of sense perception, it is possible to glean ways of seeing within concrete spaces that modulate normalized vision, including the loosening of structures of visuality enforced by colonialism in its construction of racial identities (I am drawing here from Alia Al-Saji's and Enrique Dussel's work on the perception of race).[18] Posture, by which I mean a basic sentience that is responsive to the available enmeshed spatial and social bearings within particular places, is also affected by leeway: embodiments of confidence by being supported by one's environment can suddenly go away in a transformation of corporeal bearings, and oppressed bodies are brought to different postures through body art and fashion.[19]

In such physical enactments the difference between the human and non-human can lose its definitive hold as a difference, which is not the same as saying that those deemed not human are allowed to be human. This entails, instead, the possibility of re-inhabiting the contingency of the designation "human" in modern/colonialist orders in ways that are indifferent to humanization as socialization, and of encountering physicalities that can form new kinds of seeing, feeling, remembering, and even socialities (if this word can be freed from its modern/colonialist determination). This amounts to inhabiting concrete spaces and their social architectures at a physical border that is and is not of the articulation of the socialities defined by the difference between the human and non-human, even breaching them, but without being incorporated into their oppressive sense.

Aísthesis

Aísthesis happens with physicality. Through it, posture, affects, spatio-temporal bearings, and perceptions sense from a depth of body that is not oriented toward the objectification of sensuousness. Physicalities sense situatedness, leeway of/ in place, the weight of and release from socialities, the disseminations of time in memory. Moreover, "aísthetically" the senses withdraw from the delimitations of entities, and see, hear, touch non-objectifiable phenomena. I include here the elements (light, earth, water) that draw the senses toward transitions and transformations (the play of light and shade, earthquakes, the transubstantiation of water) that manifest the cosmos as "seminal" (destructing, generating, creating) in ways that cannot be reduced to spheres under human control. In this book, I access cosmological resistance through *aísthesis*, in particular through the senses and their exposures to the elements.

I am interested in sensing the bodies, postures, and affectivities of the oppressed, in the ways habits of seeing are operative in entrenching racist views and internalized, for example. As Dussel's analysis of the "ugly" shows, the oppressed are habitually seen as overdetermined and fully fitting within dominant social parameters (identities, behavioral norms, appearances), effectively appearing as objects.[20] I suggest (as I explore in the first two parts of this book) that attending to the way elements are perceived can shed light on perceptual modifications that release the appearance of the oppressed from the socialities imposed on them.

Something similar happens in view of "action." That is, there is a sensing of "action" in which it appears as intelligible within a pre-articulated field of social values, which allows one to call an action "proper" or "responsible" (these perceptions continue to follow visual and affective cues). This sensing extends to resistance, including actions that resist in ways expected within dominant registers of values, resistant actions pre-articulated either from oppressive positionalities or liberatory ones invested in determining who is a resistant agent and what counts as resistance. At the same time, the oppressed, especially in colonial/modern contexts, where they are deemed non-human, can engage in resistant practices that are invisible or that appear as irresponsible from established socialities. Cosmological resistance fits in this latter kind of resistant practices, and can be sensed through a praxical *aísthesis* that does not rely on a background of pre-articulated social intelligibility.

Aísthesis also includes the sense of being sensed, especially as a transformative potency. One is not only sensed by oneself and other "humans," but by animals, buildings, and landscapes, and this being sensed leads to physical shifts (affective reorientations, for example). *Aísthesis* is most pronounced and felt in moments of sensing and being sensed, and it cultivates a form of alertness that is akin to the intensity of the anticipation of being touched. When *aísthesis* is charged with this kind of anticipation, it broaches, in my terms, the field of *aesthetics*.

I am drawing here from Alejandro Vallega in order to revisit the term "aesthetics" and free it from its overdetermination within the history of Western philosophy. He returns to ancient Greek philosophy to recollect that "*Aesthesis* for the Greeks has to do with bodily experience and with affect and sensibility" (2014: 198). He finds in aesthesis the process of *mimesis*, which, in my view, connects to my determination of awareness of sensing/being sensed. He writes:

> "Mimetic" here means able to mimic, to copy. Furthermore, this ability is inseparable from the very life of the mind or soul and of the city, since citizens, slaves, women, children, and strangers find their place in the world not only through arguments and politics but also in the sense of being they encounter in the Greek theater. To copy is to represent in the form of a confrontation with our limit. And this limit is met in the Greek theater through the experience of *katharsis* . . . a confrontation with chance, the uncontrollable, the unexpected, the uncanny, that which is strange beyond measure. (2014: 198)

I am not trying to re-claim an "authentic" meaning of aesthetics here, but I want to note the resonances between my discussion so far and the ancient Greek emphasis on physicality and *mimesis* as a transformative confrontation with one's limit, which is a form of purification via exposure to the uncontrollable.

These aesthetic experiences echo with the way death is ritualized in *Taki Oncoy*, that is, through catharsis via transgression, destruction, rebirth, through a sensing/being sensed that resituates one's bodies. Indeed, in the case of *Taki Oncoy* the colonial context entails an aesthetic field that has to be approached from the dehumanized position of the oppressed, and from a resistance to being socialized. This a consideration absent from the Aristotelian approach to tragedy. The meaning of *katharsis* or purification can be also challenged from this perspective, and dispossessed of socializing aims. Furthermore, the "uncontrollable" or "uncanny" in *Taki Oncoy* is not an existential dimension, or an ensouled event, but a cosmological one in which the very delimitation of the human or *anthropos* is a limit to be confronted.[21]

Reyes complements Vallega's point in reference to the play of the capture and murder of Atahualpa and to Taki Oncoy: "in Western culture tragedy gradually parted ways with the fatality of divine causes in order to reach the freedom of human motivations. It shrunk from cosmology to subjectivity" (2008: 282). That is, gradually Western tragedy underwent an affective transition from sorrow to pain, from cosmological forms of agency to human "action," and, in this way, I suggest, the frame from which both aesthetics and resistance comes to be seen and understood is reduced. In the Andes, however, *aesthetics* does not quite undergo this transition, and rituals and artworks retain a resistant force that is of *pacha*.

Pacha and a De-Westernizing Phenomenological Opening

Reflections on Seminality and Emptiness

By "cosmos" I refer to the Andean notion of *pacha*, which has an array of connotations: the here and now, the universe, the relations between all entities, and also a mode of physical sentience or *senti-pensar*.[22] So *pacha* is not a collection of objectifiable entities and, in fact, withdraws from epistemologies that separate a subject from an object, and the mind from the body. Moreover, *pacha* is the source of stability (the seasons, the fertile earth, the movement of the stars) but also of overturns or *pachakuti* (cataclysms like floods, earthquakes, pandemics). This duality means that in *pacha*, like in day and night, entities turn and come to be through what they are not, that they are and are not what they are at the same time.

In Andean ontology, this does not lead to a dialectical resolution but to a blur (which Rivera Cusicanqui calls *ch'ixi*), a kind of border movement of transitions, leaps, non-consequential transformations. This blur cannot be conceptualized but, going back to Kusch, it can be sensed as an "así," or a simple "thus," which is a form of "seminality" (in which moments of generation, destruction, and creation are entangled and simultaneous). Echoing my earlier discussion, another way to approach the "así" is to think of it as emptiness, a "where" where nothing comes to its own or fully disappears, an emptiness that does not belong to the dichotomy between being and non-being. *Pacha* "is" both the sentience of this seminality and emptiness and the seminality and emptiness.

It, as Rivera Cusicanqui and Kusch suggest, happens physically, in bodies that are and are not "ours," including affects, postures, sense perceptions, and in a sentient layer that is different from the one oriented toward the objectification of sensation.

Experiencing the Intihuatana: A Brief Phenomenology of Pacha

The "sundial" stone or "Intihuatana" lies at the highest point of the sacred sector in Machu Picchu (see Figure 0.1).

It is exposed to the sky by an upward thrust that heaves not only its imponderable weight but also that of the ancient city and the mountain where it rests. This thrust manifests an uncanny vertical spacing that articulates this Inka site. It also evokes architectural forms that join schemas of heights and depths emanating from the surrounding mountains. To be primarily drawn into vertical space, something that is inevitable in this built environment, has a disorienting effect. The viewer cannot sensuously or intellectually synthesize this verticality. The simultaneous upward and downward openings of space are irreducible to one another and constitute distinct spatial spheres. This makes massive mountains, like the ones holding and surrounding Machu Picchu,

Figure 0.1 *Intihuatana*, Omar Rivera, 2019.

spatially incomprehensible. Andean cosmologies and languages seem to capture this irreducibility and doubling of space by identifying two elemental cosmic regions that are equally primordial: *hanan pacha* is a space facing the sky, and *ukhu pacha* faces the earth. At first sight, *intihuatana* belongs in *hanan pacha*. As stone, however, it pulls toward the earth.

Calling the Intihuatana a "sundial" intrumentalizes this sculpted Inka stone. It is true that it draws from the sky calculations of movements of the sun, and that these calculations predict the seasons, which in turn makes possible agriculture. There would not have been an Inka society without the practical knowledge of the *intihuatana*. Yet, following Kusch, the directionality of Andean, indigenous "thinking" includes the reverse. One could say that it also begins with the "here and now," as in springs and land, and reaches toward cultivated food, and families and communities nourished by it, toward festivals and social forms; reaches toward calendars coded in the skies, and toward the *intihuatana* that lets the sun reflect on in-stilled stone rhythmically, marking the elemental, seminal possibility of all these interwoven, harmonic layers of life.

The *intihuatana* is more than a "sundial." It joins the rhythmic opening to the cosmic spacing of the sky, or *hanan pacha*, that is manifest with an elemental stillness that holds back from a world of human aims, even if it encompasses all of life. It gathers modes of physicalities that, rather than being solely oriented toward objectifying and calculating the environment, take a step back into the stillness of the sky from which the movement of the sun becomes apparent, a stillness that points to the "this is it," or "así," of the cosmos in its elemental simplicity and insignificance.[23]

Sensing the "así" of the cosmos or *pacha* is not simply a matter of looking up toward the sky. It is elicited by walking through and taking in the architecture of Machu Picchu. It buds as one traces the contours of the city toward the summit where the *intihuatana* lies. Suddenly, the elemental architecture of a city held by the sky allows for sensing with one's whole body the weaving and re-weaving of reciprocities among communities and their environments, making explicit intricate, non-calculable relationalities between everyday life and the rhythms of the seasons and of the upper celestial movements. The architecture of Machu Picchu allows for a constant, situated recreation or *poiesis* of the cosmos that does not transcend the sensuous and leads to the joy of being enveloped by the elemental embrace of the sky. In this moment of the "así," cosmos becomes sense and sense becomes cosmos. Yet this moment in its concreteness is always only an instance; it has to be renewed. It is, in Quechua, on the verge of a *kuti*—a *pachakuti*.

Reaching the *intihuatana* requires walking up a serpentine set of stairs that climb a steep hill. Every turn on the way seems to have been carefully studied so that, from an edge, one faces toward the side of the city that appears to be falling, as if run over by an avalanche of stone. This means that prior to encountering the sacred stone at the peak, one is already elementally assailed by a feeling of vertigo, drawn by the downward pull of the earth. When one reaches the *intihuatana* as a site of cosmic sense and sensing, one is not only exposed to the way it opens to the sky. Its weight is most apparent as part of a hill sculpted in stone that drags one toward an abyss. The massive stone is not simply the scene for the play of light. It radiates stonelight.

Stone is related to the vertical spacing that faces the earth, or *ukhu pacha*. There are different ways to conceive of this cosmic region. It is the underworld, the space of the interior of the earth, the space of caves and the source of natural springs. It is a place *of* and *in* hiding that eludes the sunlight and the sky or *hanan pacha*. As a primordial region, *ukhu pacha* shelters a secret cosmic order that is in-stilled, petrified, yet waiting, and that is the negative or flipside of the one illuminated by the sky or *hanan pacha*. Both of them in their interrelation, however, are the cosmos or *pacha*. *Ukhu pacha* is a face of *pacha* that could turn at any point. Always at the edge of a cosmic turn or *pachakuti*, the cosmic face of joy and harmony attuned to the rhythms of the sky could be reversed, turned upside down, leaving the inhabitants of the cosmos disoriented—in a *pachakuti*, since *kuty* not only means "instance," but also "turn." More precisely, *pachakuti* connotes that every instance of the cosmos can also be a cosmic upturn; and it does not denote a movement that overpowers the cosmos, but a movement of the cosmos itself. Even though *ukhu pacha* permeates all of *pacha*, there are particular places close to this cosmic region, like caves, which can be *huacas* or shrines. As Kusch notes, *ukhu pacha* is a "place for weeping." It is a place of sorrow rather than pain.

Ukhu pacha is the cosmic region toward which things fall, stones in particular. This stone fall is reflected in the side of Machu Picchu visible from the stairs toward the *intihuatana*. Evoking stones falling as in cataclysmic avalanches, the whole city is permeated by a cataclysmic architecture. It presents its built environment as destroyed not only by falling enormous rocks from the mountain peaks but also by earthquakes in which the earth breaks open. *Ukhu pacha* spreads a spacing at the edge of a *pachakuti* that, as Kusch notes, includes "earthquakes, lights in the sky, monsters, sicknesses, or wars" (2010: 132).

The relationship between *ukhu pacha* and stone is essential to understand this cataclysmic cosmic face. One can picture a massive stone falling down the side of an

Andean peak, as part of an avalanche perhaps, its force coming to a standstill at the lowest point of a valley. At this moment the stone gathers itself back into stillness, a redundant petrification of stone. It shelters, then, the stillness of a cosmos about to undergo transformation. The relationality of the two faces of the cosmos, *hanan* and *ukhu pacha*, comes forth in terms of modulations of stillness. The stillness of *hanan pacha* or sky reveals patterned, harmonic movements, that of *ukhu pacha* or earth reveals transformation, destruction, and regeneration. *Pacha* or cosmos is both sky and earth; but is also neither because sky and earth are distinct from one another. Pacha is both each and neither at the same time. This is the impossible relationality between sky and earth that is sheltered in a pervasive cosmic stillness.

The stillness of the sky allows for patterned movements that give reliability, the stillness of the earth petrifies movement so as to potentialize cosmic transformations; the sky irradiates harmony, the earth overturns this harmony so that another cosmic face of the sky—the one sheltered in *ukhu pacha*—emerges in an instance of reversal or "kuti" as a transformative leap in and of the cosmos. Between sky and earth there is a tense, vertical oscillation held by an elemental, encompassing cosmic stillness of simultaneous collapse and renewal. This generates a rhythm that is joined by a sensuous, affective, and postural physical sentience that can endure, in an instance or turn, irreducible patterns of harmony and destruction. This is not a sentience of "our" bodies, but of the bones that give us posture, the eyes that give us sight, and the lungs that pause in fright.

A rhythm emerges precisely at a pivoting moment in which harmony turns into destruction and destruction into renewal, when the two cosmic forces of sky and earth become almost undifferentiated. This makes untraceable a beginning in and of *pacha*. At this juncture, the sentience of the "así" or the "this is it" becomes more explicit than when it appears only in terms of the sky. Kusch states: "No doubt Kuty is related to seeing the así of the world. This is centrally what distances indigenous thinking from ours" (2010: 115). Being sensuously open to the torn stillness of sky and earth, teetering between joy and sorrow, the sensing of the constantly recreated and renewed cosmos, tracking the everyday to the stillness of sky and earth, enacts and is rhythmically given to the cosmos as the space-time of destruction, transformation, and creation, or, in Kusch's terms, of "seminality."

From this perspective the *intihuatana*, as the gathering of stone and light, of earth and sky, is not of sky and not of earth, but of the space for their blurring and distinction; that is, where the sentience of the "así" I have just described comes to pass. The name for this third cosmic spacing or face, architecturally rendered in the stone buildings of Machu Picchu, is *kay pacha*, the "here/now" one cannot avoid having to deal with. In *kay pacha* the "seminality" of the cosmos is most manifest, the ways in which earth and sky reciprocate and dispel one another are apparent. For this reason, *kay pacha* is not populated by objects but by a set of relations that undergo harmony and destruction at the same time, constituting entities that cannot be objectified because they are always interwoven with other entities that support them and lead to their overturning or flipping. In *kay pacha* one is always on edge.

"What" is, then, the cosmos or *pacha*? Nothing, but it is also not the absence of something. It is a silent "así," but not the silence that is a step toward sound. Like the silence after an earthquake, it simply is "thus." It is emptiness without relation to fullness. It is the emptiness of porosity, and of leeway as a spacing that appears from nowhere. It is where memories go after they are lost. It is the indiscernible emptiness that allows for weaving and knotting but also for unweaving. This knotting through nothing, or (k)notting, is what allows one to be and not be part of a social fabric, to be and not be an identity colonially manufactured for capital gain. It is also the (k)notting that renders human spheres insignificant in their embeddedness in the cosmos as a seminal fabric that is destructing and regenerating with indifference to the human/non-human distinction.

The following chapters hone in on this conception of cosmos as seminal and (k)notted through an aesthetic approach that reveals its physical instantiations in artworks, sense perception, memory, imagination, and spatio-temporal bearings. They also elucidate resistance in the tension between these cosmic physical instantiations and colonialist/modern enforcements of capitalist, global subjects through the institutionalization of art and art criticism, the visual construction of oppressed identities, the configuration of social forms and values on the basis of the distinction between the human and non-human, and the imperative that resistance happen through processes of socialization that cover up this distinction.

From the perspective of Andean cosmologies and aesthetics, colonialism/modernity is the attempt to deny *pacha*, namely, to deny the "seminality" of the cosmos, the stillness that encompasses the reciprocity and mutual destruction of sky and earth, and the (k)notted relationality of the here/now or *kay pacha*, in order to enforce an objectifying sense of a present under human control and in processes of development. I note that colonization, including the modern world born out of it, is thought in the Andes as a *pachakuti*, since it brings with it a new ordering of the cosmos through an overturning. Yet it is a particular kind of *pachakuti*, that is, one that denies the cosmological, physical backing that would allow one to undergo it by sensing its "seminality," that is, its destruction and overturning.

In particular, colonization leaves one under the illusion that its impact can only be understood and addressed from instrumentalizing epistemic stances and progressivist dispositions, that the way out of it needs to draw from the subjective, social, and political constructions it enforces.[24] Consequently, colonialism/modernity conceals its belonging to cosmic processes of generation, destruction, and creation, making it seem that its overcoming is a matter of "human" agency. It veils cosmological resistance, namely that, as Reyes puts it, the subject of the revolution is *pacha*.

Another Sense of Earth

If one is not willing to destabilize dominant frames of Western philosophy, the phenomenological sense of *pacha* may be lost. John Sallis's work on the elementals, sky, and earth, in particular, attains this destabilization. In fact, in the chapter "The Elemental Turn" in *The Return of Nature* he offers a phenomenological study of the elements that is relevant to my upcoming analyses. In that text, the departure from Western metaphysics is marked by the turn to the elements. Sallis states: "Having thus dismantled the very frame of the classical turn, this thought to come will shift its focus to the elemental in its distinction from—and its relation to—natural things. The ancient order of intelligible and sensible (*noetón kai aesthetón*) will be replaced by the dyad of elements and things" (2016: 76).

This difference between "elements" and "things" is at the center of this book. By "things" I understand entities that acquire significance in a context of relations with other things, a context that constitutes the field for the unfolding of human interests and actions. I emphasize that this field is not only rendered intelligible by causal relations and pre-articulated possibilities to fulfill tasks, but also by social determinants endowing orders of values that inform human projections and senses of fulfillment. Colonialism/modernity aims to fix this field in order to enhance its calculability. In this sense, the difference between the elements and things can become operative in an anticolonial philosophy, going beyond the purview of Sallis's work.

I underscore two aspects of Sallis's treatment of the elements that help define the trajectory of the upcoming chapters. First, he lays out different ways of understanding the difference between elements and things. All of them entail, in my view, elementals as phenomenal movements of dissemination and configuration of things, movements that are not reducible to thingly processes but belong, rather, to the possibility of their appearing in the first place (movements of shining and reflecting light, for example). In distinction from things, the elements enabling the appearing of things are "encompassing, indefinite, gigantic, and peculiarly one-sided" (2016: 80).

At risk of simplifying Sallis's extensive analyses, I emphasize that these elemental traits refer to a volatile phenomenal expanse that is structured differently than that of things. In particular, the modality of distance (and space) between oneself and things, their appearing through sides and horizons, their abiding by a human scale, are all phenomenal determinants of things that submit them to the goals of human actions, and that do not apply to elemental appearings. Furthermore, the elements not only enable the appearing of things but also dispossess things from their anchoring in definite articulations of significance that allow them to offer a side or face. They disempower instrumental dispositions and corresponding modern/colonial configurations of subjectivity and agency.

This discussion is applicable to the sky as the elemental source of light. Sallis's study of Monet's *Haystacks*, for example, provides a careful analysis of light as an elemental force that bestows a "shining through which appearing occurs." Sallis, then, turns to the elements as involved in the coming to appear of things, rather than as objectifiable phenomena. For him, the difference between elements and things gives an opening to attend to the precise articulation of the structure of thingly phenomenological concretions. Light, for example, in its elemental difference, effuses a vibrancy that blurs the sides and horizons through which things are gathered.

Alejandro Vallega hones in on this moment in his essay on Sallis's work "Freeing the Eye." Light provides a kind of hovering or, in terms that I develop later, in-stillness that holds both the configuration and dissemination of things as they appear. He departs from Sallis by reversing the emphasis of the phenomenological analysis toward dissemination. He writes: "the vibrancy in the gathering occurs at the same time with a disseminating movement that, if engaged as such, may bring us to engage the visible in its originary cosmological arising movement" (Vallega forthcoming).

Furthermore, he goes on to make explicit what he means by a cosmological arising movement: "Visibility is not only a matter of unity. Seeing happens simultaneously with a unifyingdisseminating movement, as the vibrant flickering of livingdying, through the delicate and fragile upsurge of presence" (Vallega forthcoming). Attending to the disseminating power of light, allows for encountering the elements as a simultaneous phenomenal gathering and disseminating, and this simultaneity is the elemental manifestation of the cosmos in its "seminality" and, ultimately, emptiness (that is, "unifyingdisseminating" or "livingdying").

At this juncture, Vallega is thinking of *pacha*, and of the elemental as a manifestation of it (in this case through light and the visible). In the upcoming beginning chapters, I draw from the phenomenal relationship between *pacha* and the elements to set up a discussion of ways in which "human" and objectifiable orders come to be disseminated at the level of sense perception, focusing on Inka stonework and architecture as a "cosmological aesthetics." This allows me to show that Sallis's elucidation of the difference between elements and things, and Vallega's departure from it, uncover physical, sensuous enactments that can destabilize prevalent Western philosophical frameworks, as well as the colonial/modern disciplining of bodies and the objectification of sensuousness. This book begins, then, with a phenomenological, de-Westernizing opening converging with anticolonial, resistant physicalities (including affects and posture, as well as sense perception).

A second aspect of Sallis's phenomenological analysis of the elements relevant to this book concerns the earth. His treatment of sky and earth as elementals, and of the "enchorial" space that subtends them, resonates with Andean cosmology, with the dimensions of *hanan pacha* and *ukhu pacha* in particular. In *Elemental Discourses* Sallis brings forth sky and earth as bounds of a kind of space that is different from space in its modern configuration, a kind of non-objectifiable space. It is a space, however, where "all the things and events that matter to humans take place" (2018: 112). He draws a distinction, then, between the space of the subject/object dichotomy and of instrumentalization, on the one hand, and the spacing of the elementals, on the other hand. In terms of the latter (and building on Vallega's interpretation just discussed), Sallis is attentive to it as a field in which the elementals are involved in the appearing of things, rather than focusing on tracing the way elementals disseminate things, dispelling their phenomenal structures (sides, horizons, scale, and others).

This difference in emphasis, in my view, shows that Andean cosmology of sky and earth does not quite fit within Sallis's orientation toward elementals, as it draws from Western phenomenology and ancient Greek philosophy. There is a parallel between *hanan pacha* and Sallis's treatment of the sky as a source of light, as the expanse in which things come to be seen as what they are, and as that which sustains vision and enables thinking. He quotes the *Timaeus*:

> [the god bestows vision upon us] in order that, by observing the circuits of *nous* in the sky we might use them for the revolvings of thinking [dianoesis]

within us, which are akin to those, the disturbed to the undisturbed; and by having thoroughly learned them and partaken of the natural correctness in their calculations, thus imitating the completely unwandering circuits of the god, we might stabilize the wandering revolvings in ourselves. (2018: 115)

In Andean cosmology the sky or *hanan pacha* is taken as the same kind of source of ordering and intelligibility, even if the upward aspiration toward it, the desire to reach mind or *nous* across an unbridgeable difference is not marked. In fact, the Western fascination with flight, with reaching toward the stars, is not as definitive in Andean cosmic sensibilities. The reason for this, I suggest, has to do with the difference in the conceptions of *ukhu pacha* and the earth in its predominant phenomenological determination.

Sallis builds on Husserl in this respect: "the earth is not a mere place for things but rather is the ground (*Boden*) on which things can have a place and on which human endeavors can be carried out" (2018: 112). The earth supports all human life, but is in itself not objectifiable as an element that let's things be available, at hand, in the first place. This granting of ground for the human is quite different from *ukhu pacha*, which also refers to the earth. I find that in Andean cosmology, close attention is paid to the stillness of stone/earth, and to its double meaning of support and of cataclysmic potency. The earth is at the same time the most stable and the most destructive, *ukhu* being the cosmic region of this "seminality" or "livingdying" of the cosmos. This is where a de-Westernization of phenomenology suggests itself.

In Sallis's discussion one is taken to the threshold of this de-Westernizing turn. He remains with Husserl when he states, for example, "[to] the earth, we are by nature bound. Even when the age old dream of flight is realized, the earth remains the basis, the ark, from which and back to which flight is undertaken" (2018: 113). The earth is the base of thinking as flight toward the stars, it is where one takes off from, one could even say, that which binds the human to nature, and to human nature. *Ukhu pacha* provides such a base in its configuration as *pachamama*, which is also a non-objectifiable granting of stability and the possibility of the demarcation of the human (even if this granting is not the result of a human intention).

Yet, *ukhu pacha* is also the realm of *pachakuti*, the unleashing of cataclysms in which all orders are turned upside down, even those supported by *pachamama*. It would be difficult to affirm that humans are by nature bound to *ukhu pacha* in this sense, since *pachakuti* is indifferent to human interests; in fact, it unravels the human, flattening it out within immense cosmic relations that render it insignificant and ephemeral. Insofar as Western phenomenology remains tied up to Husserl's notion of earth, *ukhu pacha* will remain partly within its purview. This partiality curbs the inquiry into a mode of thinking that cannot project toward the sky because it lacks the stability of earth as ground, or into the ways in which such thinking is involved in the demarcation of the human (that is, in its assumption of ground, shelter, abode). These are, however, precisely the kinds of inquiry that are relevant in an anticolonial turn in phenomenology, and in the exploration of the relationship between cosmos and resistance I undertake.

Sallis's phenomenological work, as I noted, is at the threshold of this turn. Revisiting Plato's allegory of the cave, where the philosopher walks back into the darkness, he brings phenomenology toward the earth, as if returning from the sky. His elucidation of *chora* as the space of sky and earth, and as the spacing of the elementals, offers a recognition of irreducible errancy and impropriety in the very manifestation of things. The *chora* is not directly "phenomenal," it is invisible, yet it is at play in the articulation of things as sensible and, ultimately, as intelligible. Sallis even relates the *chora* primarily to the earth. And more recently, his analysis of the cosmos is perhaps resonant with *ukhu pacha*; the cosmos being beyond the sky, it shelters the possibility of "altering the bond to the earth" (2016: 113). Yet, *pachakuti* is not an elemental movement that can be assimilated into the movement of the appearing of things. It may, in this sense, not be of phenomenological concern. The destruction that it unleashes is ultimately of a different order than movements in which things appear or disseminate; even as it instigates phenomenal disseminations. *Pachakuti* entails the undoing of Husserlian earth and of the sky above it. *Pacha* is related to emptiness, seminality, sorrow, stillness, "the sickness of song and dance," and, as I intend to show, to physicalities of resistance.

The Itinerary

This book consists of analyses of physicalities attuned to the cosmos or *pacha*, including sense perception, affects, memory, imagination, and spatio-temporal bearings. I attend to ways they destabilize modern/colonial formations (patriarchal, racist, ableist formations) of responsible, able, and socially valuable subjects, including agents of liberation. Through these transgressions, unsociable bodies breach clear demarcations of social/human identities and do not abide by the systemic exigency to preserve a modern/colonialist global order based on them. Anticolonial resistance, in this respect, is not an action intended to negate oppressions. It is the tensions and frictions between the bodily disciplining of modern subjects (including investments in disembodied rationality, self-certain agencies, the suppression of affects, and the fixation of social identities) and cosmological physicalities.[25] In this sense, resistance emerges as an atmospheric charge within and between bodies, emanating from specific, spatial inhabitations of dominant socialities. Artworks can reveal these unsociable physicalities of resistance, but only through the suspension of conceptual and social modern/colonial framings of what counts as art and the experience of art.

The first part, "Cosmological Aesthetics," traces a movement away from the containment of artworks and aesthetic experiences in colonialist institutions (such as museums), and toward their emplacement in relation to landscapes and elemental settings. In this aesthetic flight, the rootedness of bodily experience in cosmological phenomena becomes apparent in a way that challenges the assumption of anthropocentric worlds, especially as configured by modernity/colonialism. In order to uncover an "elemental poetics," Chapter 1 links Gloria Anzaldúa's aesthetics with a discussion of the Latin American avant-garde in Mariátegui's works and his journal *Amauta*. On this basis, Chapter 2 develops a "cosmological aesthetics," focusing on Andean aesthetic lineages beginning with Inka stonework. This chapter is the aesthetic foundation of the rest of the book: it begins to show physical instantiations of the cosmos, especially as spatio-temporal bearings and sense perception, by a comparative study of Inka architecture, and an analysis of contemporary Peruvian painting. The chapter hones in on the concept of a visible cosmological past, or *ñaupa pacha*, that recurs throughout the book.

The second part, "Embodiments of Resistance," is a sustained study of cosmological physicalities of resistance, building on modes of sensing and sensuousness made explicit through "cosmological aesthetics." These are physicalities that embody *pacha* in different ways, and articulate themselves in spaces of tension and physical transformation, fracturing social structures that enforce modern/colonial oppression built on the difference between the human and non-human. Chapter 3 develops sense perception as a resistant physicality, specifically as an embodiment of the visibility of cosmological time that decenters the force and normalization of racist vision. In this respect, I focus on the racialization of resistant bodies on the part of gatekeepers to movements of liberation, revealing aesthetic practices in which the oppressed end up oppressing the oppressed. In the face of this form of oppression, I turn to Lugones's decolonial feminism in order to find alternative ways of seeing resistant bodies. This chapter includes my central articulation of cosmological resistance and its relation to aesthetics.

In Chapter 4, I move away from sense perception toward spatio-temporal physical bearings, including posture, affects, and memory. On the basis of these three physicalities, I develop the embodiment of stillness, drawing from Kusch, Lugones, Anzaldúa, and Viveiros de Castro. Stillness is not structured agentially or within a linear temporality. It, rather, establishes a physical relationship with the cosmos, being both detached from its specific instantiations in processes of generation, destruction, and creation, and drawn to these processes in their potency for transformations and destabilization of dominant social embodiments. In Chapter 5, I explore specific instantiations of "in-stilled" bodies and their ability to engage a corporeal imagination (drawn from Anzaldúa), including language and silence, gesture, and bearing witness to the suffering of the oppressed. In this chapter I make explicit cosmological physicalities resisting the enforcement of social forms based on the difference between the human and non-human, and relating to the suffering of the oppressed, which leads to forms of resistance that do not capitalize on their suffering, and are "unsociable."

The third part, "In Company," brings my discussion of cosmological resistant physicalities to everyday peopled places, like churches and markets, and to concrete encounters with the corporealities of oppressed others, with their faces and dignity. In addition to this immersion in the everyday, this part also provides critical engagements with Lugones and Dussel. Chapter 6 is a phenomenological study of space from the perspective of resistant physicalities rather than normalized and able ones. Through an analysis of postural imagination, as well as of the architecture of a colonial Andean Church and the rhythms of markets, I bring forth charged atmospheres of resistance that irradiate from oppressed bodies. The chapter also offers a critical reading of the notion of worlds in Lugones in view of the physical rhythms of the everyday. Chapter 7 is dedicated to an interpretation of Dussel from the perspective of "cosmological aesthetics." I mark ways in which my focus on physicalities of resistance makes me depart from his ethics of liberation, even if his recent determination of *aísthesis* brings our projects close to one another.

In the first section of the conclusion I revisit the connection between "cosmological aesthetics" and resistance, and return to the theme of an elemental dimension in lineages of Andean aesthetics. The second section is dedicated to Vallega's departure from Dussel's ethics and aesthetics in relation to my own. These two sections mark a transition from cosmological resistance to an ethics of liberation rooted in cosmology, the latter being beyond the purview of this book.

I close this introduction noting the limited scope of this work, namely, the articulation of possible physical sites of anticolonial resistance on the basis of interpretations of Andean aesthetics and cosmology. As I noted earlier, this work does not focus on liberatory interventions guided by anticolonial political programs, on representative movements of indigenous resistance, or on the political implications of the difference between resistance and liberation that undergirds my analysis. Its narrow scope helps me articulate, however, a dimension of anticolonial resistance that tends to be overlooked when liberatory theorizing is framed by modern/Western philosophical concepts such as agency, identity, self or subject, and development or progress. I am not suggesting that these concepts are useless. Rather, I maintain that their applicability has to be delimited and contextualized, especially in light of marginalized cultures and cosmologies embodied by the resistant-oppressed in colonial and postcolonial contexts.

In my discussion, for example, the notion of "self" is not particularly useful to reveal the physical enactments that I theorize. In particular, the notion of "self" can carry investments in socialization, in moments of decision and self-transparency, and in temporalities that are productive of self-knowledge at the expense of abstracting from conflicting cultural lineages of the oppressed. These investments can muddle the articulation of cosmological resistances as I study them in this book. This is not to say, however, that the notion of "self" has to be discarded. I anticipate that in the transition from anticolonial resistance to liberation, especially when entering a field in which communication, action, and responsibility are efficacious, notions of self may be appropriate to articulate political phenomena. In postcolonial contexts, I am interested in the "self" as it arises in the tension between modern/colonial social enforcements guided by the difference between human and non-human, and cultural embodiments and non-modern socialities of oppressed and colonized cultures. In other words, I approach the "self" as it arises in the resistive conditions I analyze in this study, rather than as a theoretical assumption and an unchallenged "reality" that precedes and grounds resistance. These paths of study, however, exceed the purview of this work.

The risk I underscore with this reflection on the self is that the connection between living resistingly and the cosmos can be lost in theory, so that the origin of resistance appears to be a matter of self-oriented and socializing processes that are complicit with colonialist interests. At this point, a theoretical lapse can trigger mechanisms of oppression at the intersection of academic production and liberatory movements, reinforcing modernist conceptions of resistance.

For this reason, I question the tendency to leave unchallenged modern/colonial conceptualities and socializations when theorizing anticolonial resistance, and I reveal modes of resisting that may be invisible from them, especially those informed by suppressed cultures, like Andean ones. This gesture on my part is not a romantic recovery or instrumentalization of an indigenous past, but attentiveness to the ways non-Western cosmologies can be at play in the formation of resistance in fractures within colonizing forms of dehumanization.

The denial of the embodied resistances of the oppressed, including rituals and other cultural practices, as well as affects, and ways of seeing and moving, compounds their oppression even when it comes from well-intentioned and active-oppressed revolutionaries. Moreover, extending the range of our capacity to theorize, see, and reveal resistance beyond familiar philosophical frameworks (as when one ventures into cosmology and physicality) may allow for new sights, and for more ready encounters with the structures of modern/colonial oppression in their precariousness, at the verge of a cataclysm.

Part I
Cosmological Aesthetics

1

From Elemental Poetics to Cosmological Aesthetics

An elemental poetics is hard to fathom, especially if one attends to the most basic meaning of *poiesis*, namely, to give shape, to turn something into something else, to make or produce. Water, light, and stone do not readily let themselves be made into something; especially when one thinks of them as ocean, river, or lake; as sky; and as mountain or earth. The way the elements challenge human projects, objectifications, and instrumentalizations, however, does not mean that they are simply "beyond" or "outside" a human sphere. They at the same time belong and do not belong to the realm of human interests, intentions, histories, and other forms of meaning making. They belong and do not belong to human "worlds."[1] Certainly, there is no building without earth, even if only as ground. And one could argue that light is the source of lived time, of the possibility of agricultural calendars, for example, as when it is reflected on stone in the *intihuatana*. Yet the elements also show an insistence indifferent to human care. This ambivalence makes it difficult to articulate the poetic force the elements exert on "worlds." When stone is poetized, carved, for example, how is the human "world" affected by the way stone resists the chisel? Or, how is the human "world" poetized by the elements in their indifferent insistence (or resistance)?

I bring to bear these questions surrounding an "elemental poetics" on modernity/colonialism,[2] which are interrelated processes that make the human "world" absolute.[3] By this I mean that they enforce a difference between human and non-human, so as to see the non-human (nature, slaves, indigenous peoples, and other social identities) as for the sake of the human; as an instrument for the reproduction of a manageable world born with colonialism and fulfilled in global capitalism. When the human "world" is rendered absolute, the sway of the elements is also repressed and denied, and "nature" emerges as an object within it. There is a tension, then, between modernity/colonialism or the human absolute and the ambivalence of the elements in their indifferent insistence.

I am referring not only to the way modernity/colonialism seeks to exploit the elements and reduce them to "nature," to integrate them into an economy as resources and energy, but also to the possibility that the elements in their unsettling ambivalence shed light on sensuous and physical modalities of resisting the social, political, and economic violence and oppression currently waged by a global order. Specifically, I propose that the indifferent insistence of the elements can elicit aesthetic experiences (conditioning sense perception, spatial and temporal embodiments, and affects, especially in relation to a cosmos that does not fit the human "world") that shape resistant embodiments without deriving them from within a modern/colonial "human" sphere (from self-conscious subjectivity, instrumentalizing dispositions, able bodies, and administered socialities submitted to the interest of capitalist economic forms). I am also suggesting a shift from modernist notions of revolution[4] to "elemental" forms of resistance that arise from colonized bodies beyond the purview of colonial determinations of who and what counts as human.

In this respect, this book brings together a "cosmological aesthetics" (explored in the second chapter) and anticolonial resistance through the study of artworks, sense perception, racial embodiment, and corporeal involvements with the elements and the cosmos. In this chapter, I focus on my notions of "geo-aesthetics" and "elemental poetics," drawing from Gloria Anzaldúa's aesthetics. The center of my analysis is the friendship between the socialist revolutionary theorist José Carlos Mariátegui and the Argentinian painter Emilio Pettoruti.[5]

Anzaldúa's "Geo-Aesthetics" and Elemental Poetics

Anzaldúa provides an entry point to understanding elemental poetics, including a "geo-aesthetic" de-centering of dominant modern/colonial institutions as the proper sites of "art." The relevant text for my discussion is "Invoking Art" in *Borderlands/La Frontera*.[6] I am interested in the distinction she draws between "invoked art" and "Western art." This distinction is the basis for her critique of a model of aesthetic experiences cultivated by museums, art critics, and high-end galleries, rather than those worked out by Western philosophers (even if these are related).[7] In this model, the viewer must recognize "technique" and identify "schools" as a condition of appreciating or "witnessing" fine art. She also finds this model to belong to the colonialist legacies of modernity, and calls for a decolonizing of aesthetics.

Anzaldúa states:

> The aesthetic of virtuosity, art typical of Western European cultures, attempts to manage the energies of its own internal system such as conflicts, harmonies, resolutions and balances. It bears the presences of qualities and internal meanings. It is dedicated to the validation of itself. Its task is to move humans by means of achieving mastery in content, technique, feeling. Western art is always whole and always "in power." It is individual (not communal). It is "psychological" in that it spins its energies between itself and its witness. (2015: 68)[8]

There is a self-containment of artworks that is here related to modern Western art housed in museums. It involves a separation between an inside and an outside of the work. The inside of the work is the site for technique, the convergence of sensual orders with meaning, the bridging of feeling and interpretation. Most strikingly, perhaps, "great works" hang in museums so as to show an exemplary "inside." The standard from which their technique is judged seems reflected in the works themselves; they validate themselves. Beyond their meaning and sensuousness, they are self-fulfilled, autonomous, masterful—they dictate how they have to be experienced, they overpower their outside "witnesses."

The term "psychological" in Anzaldúa's statement refers to an aesthetic process in which the viewer is turned into a passive "witness," being both subjectively (that is, affectively, socially, and cognitively) constituted and controlled by the foregrounded artwork in a museum. "Technique," then, does not mean only skill, but a particularly modern aesthetic that disempowers the viewer and allows artworks to be accepted as part of larger mechanisms for the disciplining of subjects that belong to modern/colonial socio-political orders and institutions. In this respect, Anzaldúa writes: "The 'sacrifices' Western cultures make are in housing their artworks in the best structures designed by the best architects; and in servicing them with insurance, guards to protect them, conservators to maintain them, specialists to mount and display them, and the educated and the upper class to 'view' them" (2015: 90). Museums, and their academic and financial networks, institutionalize the modality of aesthetic power Anzaldúa finds in Western art, and create viewers as sensuous receptors of dominant social norms and histories, entangled with and legitimized by particular notions of what counts as "fine" art and what must be included in art history. In this way, artworks become part of a movement through which the human world becomes absolute; humans are sources of artworks that, through technique, in turn become their masters and makers. This reinforcing circularity is mobilized politically, socially, and financially as a global project invested in totalizing Western culture as if it coincided with the sphere of the human, and in subsuming the earth and the peoples rendered non-human to its interests.

This operation is, then, exclusionary. It corresponds to the construction of a global class through the colonial suppression of artforms that do not fit within the purview of technique, mastery, and the museum industry, and the dehumanization of the people who make, ritualize, and celebrate such artworks in their houses, communities, and other marginalized cultural and social environments. This double, socially constructive and oppressive, movement is perhaps most manifest in the colonialist appropriation of art by global elites. Anzaldúa explains:

> Modern Western painters have "borrowed," copied, or otherwise extrapolated the art of tribal cultures and called it cubism, surrealism, symbolism. . . . Whites, along with a good number of our own people, have cut themselves off from their spiritual roots, and they take our spiritual art objects in an unconscious attempt to get them back. (2015: 90)

"Borrowing" art from the colonized for the sake of producing "-isms" to be parsed in terms of style and technique forces marginalized cultures into a colonialist aesthetic circulation that constitutes Western modern subjects and spreads with the global institutionalization of art.[9] In other terms, an essential part of the establishment of a modern/colonial order is to deploy the "art of tribal cultures" in order to make the "human" world absolute and dismiss and dehumanize any relationships with natural environments, landscapes, elements, and the heavens that are not circumscribed within such an absolute. I interpret this dismissal to be part of the "cutting off of spiritual roots" that draws Westerners to tribal art in the first place.[10] The "borrowing" of tribal art by "-isms" is, then, a form of self-reinforcing entrapment within a manageable "world" forged by colonialism, modernity, and capitalism.

I call "geo-aesthetics" the analysis of aesthetic phenomena that de-center the modern West as a defining source of a global mode of aesthetic experience of artworks, and, thus, contributes to destabilizing both the human "world" built on colonial demarcations of the human and non-human and its corresponding oppressive socialities. "Geo-aesthetics" is not simply the recognition that "art happens everywhere" or that non-Western cultures "also" produce art. It is not a call to include "indigenous art" in museums. It involves the dismantling of technique, of the mastery and autonomy of the artwork, of the passivity of its witness, of the desperate "borrowing" of the exotic, and of the corresponding aesthetic and historical processes of subject formation that help sediment the global rule of the West.

In this respect, Anzaldúa's "invoked art" is an important "geo-aesthetic" notion. She writes:

> When invoked in rite, the object/event is "present"; that is "enacted," it is both a physical thing and the power that infuses it. It is metaphysical in that it "spins its energies between gods and humans" and its task is to move the gods. This type of work dedicates itself to managing the universe and its energies . . . Invoked art is communal and speaks of everyday life. It is dedicated to the validation of humans; that is, it makes people hopeful, happy, secure, and it can have negative effects as well, which propel one toward a search for validation. (2007: 89)

The performance or enactment of "invoked art" is a different aesthetic process than passive witnessing. It does not belong to an object or a subject, and it is not the mastery of one over the other. For this reason, the presence of the invoked artwork is not a form of autonomy and self-validation that overwhelms and constitutes a passive witness; it does not impose an exclusive history and sociality.

Rather than making the human world absolute, "invoked art" spreads out toward divinities and the cosmos, establishing continuities between spheres of existence rather than wielding the difference between the human and non-human. This spreading weaves these spheres of existence through reciprocities: they move one another in a process in which cosmic energies are managed. I understand "human validation" as participation in this managing process, a validation that comes from the cosmos itself and makes "people hopeful, happy, secure" yet without instrumentalizing or objectifying dispositions. This validation takes root in everyday experiences of a full present: smells, landscapes, the safety of the habitual, even breathing, can carry with them a validating sense of cosmic connectivity. "Invoked art" also brings about a "negative effect" that I interpret as a cosmic sense of loss, of undergoing events, like cataclysms, that cannot be resolved through human projects and capacities, instances in which one reaches toward validation by the cosmos through rites and other aesthetic enactments.

"Invoked art" arises as a performative practice from the quotidian rhythms of colonized peoples. It does not render the human "world" absolute, it does not fit in museums and art galleries, it is not "psychological," and it is not part of a colonialist, expansionist mechanism. It is an aesthetic process that cannot be "borrowed." At the same time, attempts to "borrow" can still be made as insidious extensions of a colonialist/modern aesthetics.[11] Differentiating "invoked art" from borrowed art can be difficult.

One of the tasks of "geo-aesthetics" is this differentiation. It involves attending to "invoked art's" relation to the "earth" as its proper site, rather than to a museum setting for example. Anzaldúa explains: "White America has only attended to the body of the earth in order to exploit it, never to succor it or be nurtured in it. Instead of surreptitiously ripping off the vital energy of people of color and putting it to commercial use, whites could allow themselves to share and exchange and learn from us in a respectful way" (2007: 90). For her, this exploitative attitude is an aesthetic issue and an issue of a colonialist determination of the human, one that becomes clear from the "geo-aesthetic" perspective of "invoked art."

The "body of the earth" is not a fetishized or romanticized notion of a pristine earth untainted by human activity. It is, rather, a transhuman weave of reciprocities that can both give support to communities or threaten them cataclysmically in a way that exceeds the illusions of control pertaining to modern conceptions of human subjectivity and civilization. The "body of the earth" is manifest in the ambivalence of the elementals I discussed earlier, their belonging and not belonging to human "worlds." "Invoked art" hovers in this ambivalence as the search for cosmic validation, which is denied in dominant modern/colonialist aesthetics. For the latter, the earth is the stage for the unfolding of human history, a stage which is constituted by the non-human realm. In modern/colonialist aesthetics, "nature," as well as colonized cultures, histories, and racialized lives are understood as resources for the sustenance of the human "world." I propose a "geo-aesthetics," then, both as a de-stabilization of the West as the center of the global institutionalization of art and its appreciation, and as an aesthetic turn toward the earth as an interconnected, cosmic body rather than as a natural resource. I find Anzaldúa to be engaged in this double gesture.

Similarly to "invoked art," the notion of "elemental poetics" I develop in this chapter is "geo-aesthetic." Its ambivalence, its being at the border of a human "world," is a portal toward an aesthetic enactment of the "body of the earth." Departing from Anzaldúa and inspired by Andean stonework, in the rest of this chapter I attend to an elemental aesthetic dimension that continuously upsets the modern/Western notion of art Anzaldúa identifies. In particular, "elemental poetics," like when the stone resists the chisel, perseveres as a poetizing of the human "world" that transforms it so as to shed its absolute character. In this way, technique and the "-isms" recede as aesthetic frameworks while the "body of the earth" comes forth as both a supportive and cataclysmic force, triggering the need for a cosmic validation of the human that destabilizes the colonialist project of modernity.

Mariátegui's Problem with "-isms"[12]

> You should clarify further your views on the -isms. That is, that in art they are not important. Just like schools are not important . . . . I have never wanted to make, because I don't believe or feel it, a work of cubism, futurism, etc . . . for this reason I am only concerned with values, volumes, compositions and colors, in short, with "realizing" without "theorizing." (Emilio Petorutti, "Letter to Mariátegui," 1927)

Mariátegui (1894–1930) rejected the reduction of artworks to the expression of "-isms" (like cubism, expressionism, futurism) because it forces them into a defined historical stage within the development of global capitalism from colonialism. For him, through this reduction the spirit of creativity may be contained, controlled, erased, as part of a process through which a dominant modern/colonial socio-political order appears as a comprehensive and inescapable unfolding totality. In my terms, the "-isms," and their emphasis on technique, are social forces that curb the spirit of creativity as part of the enforcement of an absolute human "world." He seems wary, for example, of the ways museums, academics in the arts and humanities, and art galleries, sediment "-isms," so that institutionalized art becomes historicized and co-opted by tendencies to conserve global political and social systems.

For him, then, safeguarding the spirit of creativity by challenging the "-isms" and their institutionalization, by undoing the frames through which art is understood and defined, sold and exhibited, is part of an anticolonial and anti-capitalist revolutionary activity. In this sense, the spirit of artistic creation converges with the spirit of revolution, which explains Mariátegui's interest in the avant-garde as both an artistic and political movement. At the same time, artists can be seduced into making a work of cubism, futurism, and so on due to a desire for belonging to a historical stage. Mariátegui thinks of these artists as not creative but decadent, complicit with political stasis and conservatism.

Art and its "-isms" are a field of struggle between decadent and creative spirits, sometimes even in the same artwork, a struggle that allows for the enforcement of social, economic, and political control or for the possibility of revolution.[13] When Mariátegui studies artworks he diagnoses their spirit, which brings him to the recognition of the modern/colonial West's decadence in its investment in, in my terms, an exhausted and exhaustive human "world." He approaches Latin American art with the intent of finding in it the manifestation of an aesthetic form that eludes categorization within a school or technique. This approach defines the character of his journal *Amauta* as an avant-garde network between artists from Peru, Argentina, and Mexico. I trace this exploration of a Latin American avant-garde, exceeding perhaps the purview of Mariátegui's own texts. My discussion does not intend to defend or critique him. My aim is much simpler: to learn to see art with him without relying on the scaffolding of "-isms."

The "Aesthetic Burden of the Past" and Reclaiming the Italian Landscape in Painting

> I am a man who wished to see Italy without literature. With his own eyes and without the ambiguous and captious lens of erudition. . . . In order to love the Italian landscape, in order to feel its beauty integrally and originally, I had to isolate myself a little from its excessive celebrity. Otherwise I would not have been able to comprehend it, to love it. I have found it to be pedantic, classical, academic like a humanities professor. I have felt it too illustrious, too glorious. (Mariátegui, 1975: 123)

During his years of political exile, Mariátegui struggled to see beauty in the Italian landscape. This may come as a surprise since Italian lakes and hills, and the medieval towns nested by and on them, are readily seen as, and assumed to be, beautiful. Mariátegui, however, shuns a beauty determined by celebrity, and frees his senses from a recognition of beauty dictated by what one is supposed to see, experience, and feel in the Italian countryside. For example, Mariátegui lets go of the ways vision is overdetermined by erudite immersion in historical sources that frame the presence of landscapes as settings for momentous events. He refuses to be swayed by literature's power to endow mountains and rivers with intimate and familiar atmospheres and bucolic scenes. For him, Italy's excessive history and culture have become an aesthetic burden, composing seemingly inescapable touristic spectacles.

The aesthetic burden of the past is manifest in different ways. Mariátegui observes that new things appear old as soon as they are enveloped by the Italian scene, and every place is a stage where an eternally rehearsed story plays out (1975: 123). The past affects the senses and even the imagination. While sitting in ordinary places, for example, one cannot help but think of all the people who have also been placed there as if by historical fate, or wonder whether a literary master or critic has already captured one's present emotions. The Italian landscape is a scene. Mariátegui states, "ocean, sky, mountains and trees . . . it all seems to me scenographic" (1975: 123). In other words, the landscape has become the closed setting for history, for human plots and protagonists, for layers of stories built on stories. The past can turn landscapes—mountains, sky, rivers—into a stage for a human spectacle and "world." A determination of what counts as "human" is implicit here, informed by colonialist, racist, and excluding constructions of others, and by instrumentalizing dispositions toward nature. A kind of theatricality results from this, burdening Mariátegui's eyes.

Art, and writing about art, as well as museums and galleries, are not exempt from enforcing this kind of burden and theatricality. Yet Mariátegui longs for an agony of images that struggle with word and story, teasing the possibility of non-scenographic landscape paintings: that is, paintings that cannot be reduced to being a backdrop for human scenes and speculations. This is the context for the inclusion of Emilio Pettoruti's work in *Amauta* (1926), together with a discussion of his Italian landscapes by Sanin Cano. How does the painting of *Lago da Garda*, for example, teach us to see beyond the theatrical? How does it break through historical frames and erudite lenses? Cano is helpful here.

Figure 1.1 Photographic reproduction of the oil painting *Día Tranquilo* by Emilio Pettoruti, 191?, 14.7 x 12 cm. Positive on paper. José Carlos Mariátegui Archive.

Figure 1.2 Photographic reproduction of the oil painting *Temporal* by Emilio Pettoruti, 1921, 15.9 x 11.5 cm. Positive on paper. José Carlos Mariátegui Archive.

He notes the "softness of tones, the placidity of the environment" as well as "a tonal vacillation, and an evanescent and tenuous coloring" (Sanin Cano 1926: 22). In the painting, tonality and coloring through broad brush strokes allow for unexpected transitions and disintegrations between mountains, lakes, and cloudy skies. They blend in an elemental presence hovering over and diminishing fields of vanishing human traces. The placidity of the image has to do with the way our sight settles in an elemental plane (of earth, water, sky) where human history is dispossessed of its aesthetic prerogative.

Pettoruti's Italian landscapes show this elemental plane that overpowers the human centeredness of history and literature. In *Día Tranquilo* the placid environment of Lago da Garda is enhanced through a play of light on earth and water. When the light hits the lake, water turns into a cosmic mirror that reflects not only the mountain but the buildings resting on its side. This reflection has the effect of in-stilling the image as a whole, at the same time that it relegates the human to a spectral presence and a light echoing.

In *Temporal* clouds are gathered with a centripetal force that pulls on the image. The mountains seem to be facing the clouds as they are submitted by stormy weather to a dynamic play of light that makes them crumple and fold, throwing senses of distance, and other dimensions, into disarray. In this way *Temporal* creates an atmosphere that is distant and indifferent to human intervention.

Escaping Categories of Art and an Exhibit in Rome

Pettoruti's Italian landscapes disclose and evoke a creative sensibility that eludes the delimitations of realism, cubism, futurism, and all other "-isms." This is a sensibility that exceeds overarching art historical narratives and the hold of academic gatekeepers over the display and criticism of art. Mariátegui develops this theme in a short text on Pettoruti. It begins with a story of the friendship between these two Latin Americans in Italy. Mariátegui recalls inviting Pettoruti to leave Rome and go to his villa in Frascati:

Figure 1.3 *José Carlos Mariátegui* (portrait), Emilio Pettoruti, 1921, oil on canvas, 63x51.5 cm. Col. Museum of Art of Lima, Peru. All Rights Reserved Pettoruti Foundation—www.pettoruti.com.

I was resolved to kidnap Pettoruti for a month in the villa. My invitation was strengthened by a decisive argument: "In Rome there is only the exhibit; in Frascati the cherries have bloomed." In Italy cherries signal the springtime. Pettoruti allowed himself to be kidnapped with pleasure: "Let's escape from these horrible paintings. Let's go toward the cherries." In the villa in Frascati he started to paint my portrait. He announced his purpose to take with him the whole landscape in a few brush strokes. However, the spring and the villa irresistibly lured one into idleness. (1975: 14)

The exhibit Pettoruti was happy to escape from was the first Biennial Exhibit of Rome, whose "horrible paintings" included his own work. Mariátegui understands this escape to be a rejection of the institutionalization of art, of the reduction of artistic creativity to trends and academic categories. It is also a departure from Rome as both a historical and mythical place.

I suggest that the exchange between Mariátegui and Pettoruti shows a shared creative sensibility that would rather go "toward the cherries," and leave behind layers of words, theories, interpretations that weave art into sedimented histories, socialities, and political orders. This sensibility involves the retreat of a creative impulse that finds itself stunted when it becomes a spectacle to be staged and analyzed. It also strives for a loss of protagonism and of pre-determined purpose. This is a refusal to be encoded into academic positions and cultural transactions, into schools and techniques, that render artistic creation and artworks historical, the testament of an epoch, and the expression of a nation or culture. Such a creative sensibility is not invested in being in a scene. After the announcement of his creative inspiration, Pettoruti becomes idle instead. The blossoming cherries and Mariátegui's company freed him from having to enter the stage. It is perhaps appropriate, then, that Mariátegui's portrait remained incomplete, not only as a testament of friendship but also as a refuge for the Peruvian critic allowing him to remain holding blank pages, as if having been relieved from writing.

Trees

Works like *Lago da Garda*, *Día Tranquilo*, and *El Temporal* are remarkable in the Italian context because they not only show an elemental landscape indifferent to the staging of history but also shelter an anti-scenographic creativity and sensuousness within the artist and the viewer.[14] They are image and refuge, and relieve one from the aesthetic burden of the past and from the sterility of museums and galleries. I imagine Mariátegui finding refuge for his creative spirit in these paintings, and allowing himself to become exposed to images in an elemental plane of a beauty that is not meant to be exhibited and rendered academic or touristic.

Mariátegui's admiration for Pettoruti's paintings as refuge is reflected in a discussion of trees in and as landscapes. He recognizes in the Argentinian painter

> the admirable sense for the plastic worth of trees. Pettoruti is a great lover of trees. His eyes know how to discover in oaks, olives, cypresses, the most untold and marvelous gestures. Trees are, perhaps, his preferred motif. His strong pantheism is epitomized in this beautiful preference. (Mariátegui 1970: 89)

Figure 1.4 Photographic reproduction of the watercolor *Vieja Puerta* by Emilio Pettoruti 1926, 16 x 11.1 cm. Black and white paper support. José Carlos Mariátegui Archive.

An olive tree, for example, grows in folds, warps, and knots, creating unprecedented forms and disorienting dimensions, being able to offer a sight of unruly movement even in its stillness. Due to this kind of growth, a Roman portal is enveloped by branches while tree roots deform its base subjecting it to a slow ruination. In this way the portal appears bereft of its world, dispossessed of its past, through an elemental process of growth and destruction without a scene. The painted trees warp vision, not letting the senses settle in a human "world" or epoch.

When Mariátegui sees Pettoruti's trees in his landscape paintings, he finds an artform that not only retreats to an elemental plane of non-human-centered events but also shows growing knots that twist this plane like a canvas, creating a proliferation of folds, crevices, orientations, and shadings that cannot constitute a single scene to be perceived. In this way, through trees, Pettoruti shows the elemental forces of landscapes expressed as an unruly and unwieldy cosmic fabric. Moreover, such twisting trees embody Pettoruti's own creativity. By the statement "his strong pantheism is epitomized in this beautiful preference," Mariátegui means that Pettoruti's artistic spirit has the force and shape of trees, belonging to no one order, human or divine, ambivalent to social worlds and histories, and to the framings of art within exhibits like the first Biennial Exhibit of Rome. With Pettoruti's work, one senses the cosmos as an immense and volatile sphere in which human events are not privileged.[15]

Futurism and a Latin American Avant-Garde[16]

Mariátegui's rejection of what I call the "aesthetic burden of the past," and of the related network of museums and galleries, leads him to be interested in Italian futurism. He would agree with these lines in Marinetti's first *Futurist Manifesto*:

> daily visits to museums, libraries and academies (those cemeteries of wasted effort, calvaries of crucified dreams, registers of false starts!) is for artists what prolonged supervision by the parents is for intelligent young men, drunk with their own talent and ambition. (1909: 23)

And he would not categorically object to "we want to demolish museums and libraries" or to "we want to deliver Italy from its gangrene of professors, archaeologists, tourist guides and antiquaries" (1909: 23). In my view, Mariátegui agrees with Marinetti on the diagnosis of the sickness, namely, the "aesthetic burden of the past." Yet they disagree on the kind of creative spirits and artworks that overcome it.

It is possible to understand their disagreement on the basis of artistic principles. Marinetti exalts the beauty of speed in technology, and calls for artworks that adhere to this thesis: "Time and Space died yesterday. We are already living in the absolute, since we have already created eternal, omnipresent speed" (1909: 23). Mariátegui interprets the effect of this thesis in painting: "the futurists center on this issue: that movement and light destroy the materiality of bodies" (1909: 23). I find Umberto Bocioni's *Dynamism of a Cyclist*, 1913, representative of this. The burden of the past is overcome in futurism through a pure speed that undermines space and time as framing definite historical scenes. The cyclist is not in a scene. His uncontained body stretches out almost to the point of disintegration and non-recognition. This anti-scenographic image is delivered through the appearance of sheer motion.

Assuming Mariátegui's perspective, however, this image retains some of the burden of the past, namely, an attachment to historical protagonism. In the painting a human form appears stretched out by speed, yet retaining the aggression of a machine. A body is suggested by hard, bold lines that break through a more placid surface. This body has the decisiveness of a military force going to war, even if there is no reason or context for it. *Dynamism of a Cyclist* is an absolute exaltation of human action and work as forging the future through the destruction of background. The omnipresence of speed turns, then, into the expression of power for power sake. For Mariátegui this futurist's rejection of the past is ultimately unsustainable as distilled aggression, and cannot but be manipulated and instrumentalized for political purposes, like Italian fascist nationalism. At this point futurism becomes an "-ism."

I suggest that the catastrophic case of futurism's cooptation by fascism was an important incentive for Mariátegui's tracing of a "Latin American" avant-garde, one that is mostly implicit in his writings and, above all, in the journal *Amauta*. In my view, some of its tenets include (1) that "the aesthetic burden of the past" is both an aesthetic and politically oppressive phenomenon, yet overcoming it can become the spiritual basis of authoritarian and nationalist politics, (2) the avant-garde must not reduce human history to a series of rehearsed scenes and must not fit artworks within "-isms," like cubism, impressionism, and so on, yet its task, however, is not to dissolve space and time, as in Italian futurism; and (3) the avant-garde, as the expression of creative and revolutionary spirits, can instead be oriented by the aesthetic and political task of de-centering history (not erasing or destroying it) in its sedimentation into "stages" through aesthetic and political interventions that undermine investments in historical univocity and protagonism. In my discussion so far, such interventions are manifest in paintings like Pettoruti's, in the way his paintings intervene in the perception of Italian landscapes, rendering human scenes spectral through the effect of an elemental plane of sense expressed through imagings of earth, sky, and water; plays of light; and tree-like forces that twist and turn the canvass, warping one's entrenched modern/colonialist vision.

"Latin America" can be thought of in terms of the elemental forces suggested in Pettoruti's landscape painting. These forces cannot be subtracted from nor integrated within histories staged by and for those deemed human. This kind of elemental realm is vast in Latin America, and includes silenced, racialized lives and cultures in addition to landscapes. As Mariátegui's economic analyses show, Latin America is not articulated in cumulative historical stages,[17] but is constantly being de-centered and thrown off track by what I am calling here the "elemental." There is no Latin American historical scenography, and the term "Latin America" means, if anything, the destabilizing force of such an absence. Isn't this a fertile soil for an avant-garde art that counters the "aesthetic burden of the past"? Almost at its inception, José Martí imagined Latin America as a tree, with its roots not in history but in "nature": that is, a "nature" that is not opposed to, within or outside of history, but operates with a certain elemental ambivalence to history's staging, always crossing its borders. In this sense, Martí imagines Latin Americans as "natural men" (2004: 33).[18]

The Paradoxes of a Socialist Indigenismo and the Agony of Sabogal's Images

Part of the persisting violence of colonialism in Latin America is the attempt to fit an array of heterogeneous and simultaneous cultures, epochs, temporalities, economies, into one historical logic of social and political development,[19] which re-enforces the dehumanization of colonized peoples. To put it in my wording, colonialism seeks to suppress the non-scenographic character of Latin America, attempting to forcibly turn it into a stage for a dominant Euro-American historical unfolding disguised as a human "world." This attempt is not only political, social, and military, but also academic and aesthetic, including the importation of "-isms" to frame Latin American artistic production and sensibilities. It, however, fails, since there is always an elemental excess to the colonial project. This is manifest most of all in the irreducibility and resilience of indigenous cultures and knowledges and their cosmological relations to their landscapes that, through processes of adaptation and mixing, elude the purview

Figure 1.5 José Sabogal Diéguez, *India del Collao*, 1925, Oil on canvas, 70,5 x 60,3 cm. Hochschild Correa Collection. Photography: ARCHI, Archivo Digital de Arte Peruano, Daniel Giannoni.

of colonialist systems and its historical scenographies. I interpret the elemental or cosmological as the site for "indigenismo" as an avant-garde amalgam of aesthetics and anticolonial resistance.[20]

Indigenismo involves not only the manifestation of a critical consciousness arising from indigenous histories (which for Mariátegui is an indigenous socialism), but also the aesthetic sheltering of a creative spirit which originates from a marginal or border elementality that can destabilize the historical unfolding of colonial/modern economic, social, and political systems. Socialist indigenismo, however, agonizes from at least two paradoxes: those of "representation" and "exoticism." First, indigenista images have to be interruptive of colonialist historical stagings without simply introducing an indigenous presence into the scene.[21] This is a delicate balance that shows the danger of representation or of what Anzaldúa calls "borrowing." By this I mean the risk of inventing an indigenous identity connected to a supposed pre-Columbian past, an invention tied to conservative forms of nationalism that Mariátegui deems "pasadistas": that is, drawn toward, longing for, a pure pre-colonial past with a petrifying nostalgia. Mariátegui calls this kind of artistic style "picturesque."[22] Second, indigenista images must maintain their exteriority, emphasizing the non-assimilability of the oppressed within the social logics that oppress them. This maintenance is essential for the possibility of resistance, yet exteriority cannot be the affirmation and fetishization of difference, which turns into an "exoticism" that petrifies indigeneity. One way to think of these paradoxes is that in a socialist indigenismo, indigenismo cannot be an "-ism": that is, a constant technique and thematic of representation, or a school that constitutes itself around the exoticism of indigenous cultural practices. As I have stated before, becoming an "-ism" is a way of entering the scenography of history, which in this case has harmful aesthetic and political consequences.

This is the context for my approach to Sabogal's paintings.[23] In his article on Sabogal, Mariátegui praises the Peruvian indigenista for understanding the plasticity of an indigenous aesthetic, rather than falling into the representative or the "picturesque." Moreover, Sabogal, he states, is not part of an "-ism," he resisted the emphasis on schools prevalent in Europe, and developed his own artistic temperament. I agree with Mariátegui, but to an extent. I see Sabogal's work as ambivalently showing the agony of indigenista images haunted by representation and exoticism. Or, in my terms, I sense in his artworks an elemental dimension that broaches the limits of a colonialist/modern absolute world, opening limina for the emergence of resistant aesthetic forms. Is the *India del Collao* a folkloric representation? Is her posture passive and her attitude nostalgic? Or is this an image that resists nostalgic frames of indigeneity, energizing a will to transform entrenched socialities? Is la *Procesión de Taitacha Temblores* an anthropological study of an oppressed culture that has assimilated into the religion that oppresses it? Or, is Christ in the background a disempowered God left behind by rebellious masses?

I see, then, in Sabogal's works indigenista images in agony. Yet I also think that their conflicts and tensions are perhaps a way of manifesting the dissemination of history by elementality, something that itself cannot be captured in an

From Elemental Poetics to Cosmological Aesthetics 55

Figure 1.6 Photographic reproduction of the oil painting *Procesión de Taitacha Temblores* by José Sabogal, 1927, 9.1 x 7.7 cm. Black and white paper support, José Carlos Mariátegui Archive.

image, and requires creative spirits like Pettoruti and Sabogal as painters, and Mariátegui as a revolutionary.

Pettoruti's Mosaics

Indigenismo as avant-garde, then, is an aesthetic spirit more than a technique: a creative, even resistant, spirit. This spirit stands in contrast to the decadence

Mariátegui finds in Europe, especially in the convergence of Italian futurism and fascism. It also does not have to be contained in a way of doing art, and can be generative of unprecedented artforms, like those that remain close to the elements. This brings me back to Pettoruti's landscapes, to his cosmic trees, and to how they relate to his mosaics, one of which was featured in *Amauta*. He writes about them in a letter to Mariátegui, explaining them as a new artform rather than a derivative of painting:

> I have tried to free myself, as much as possible, of all the old prejudices, of all theories. None of my mosaics has a flat surface . . . their surfaces are completely undulating, which gives more contrast to the work, salience, forming infinite arabesques of lights and lines . . . they move together with the light of every passing day . . . mosaics must defy water, sun and, above all, time. (1926: 1)

Pettoruti adds that every one of his stones is not only unique, but uniquely placed by him. This is an art that does not abide by a form or technique, participating in elemental patterns and rhythms that withdraw from the relevance of historical scenes. His mosaics defy water in the richness of their reflective surfaces, and the sun in the playful scattering of light they reflect. Embedded in the contingencies of the environment, every mosaic is what it is once. For this reason they are not staged. All this, I think, is the manifestation of a joint aesthetic and revolutionary spirit. That is, if one thinks of revolution as a unique, flashing event that comes from the borders of human history and refuses to be framed, staged, accumulated. This is one form of avant-garde aesthetics. I hope it is clear by now that the avant-garde does not have a single form or theory attached to it, at least not in Mariátegui's and Pettoruti's view.

Can we think of Pettoruti's mosaics as having a sort of indigenista aesthetic? If one recalls the Inka walls in Cusco, where unique stones reflect light so as to create an effect of gushing water or even a river, a cosmological aesthetics comes to view—perhaps just beyond the reach of Mariátegui's avant-garde, indigenista imagination.

Toward an Andean Cosmological Aesthetics

I noted earlier that "geo-aesthetics" has two interrelated aspects, the decentering of modern Western aesthetics, and the turn toward the earth; both amounting to a challenge of the closure of a human "world" and the colonialist interests and institutions that secure it. I have followed Mariátegui and Pettoruti in view of the first aspect, but my analysis so far has not completed the turn toward the earth. My discussion of elemental poetics so far engages the ambivalence of the elements in relation to the human "world," and begins this turn. The issue however is to shift toward an earthly *aísthesis*, and, thus, re-engage and disrupt modern Western aesthetics norms from a different sensibility, even from a different body, one that Anzaldúa intimates when she discusses the "validation of the human" as a search for joining the "body of the earth," the reciprocities of the cosmos in both their supportive and cataclysmic instantiations. Once this turn is effected, "geo-aesthetics" leads to a "cosmological aesthetics," where the traces of the human "world" become fainter in the happenings of elemental aesthetic events. I finish this chapter pursuing this turn in the Andean context, which I develop more fully in Chapter 2.

The influential essay "The River around Us, the Stream Within Us: The Traces of The Sun and Inka Kinetics" by Tom Cummins and Bruce Manheim foregrounds a pre-colonial Andean "elemental poetics" in which the elements shape human environments. This involves an "aesthetic that takes light and liquid, hardness and softness as sources of expression and casts them in various guises across skies and landscapes, buildings and bodies" (2011: 6). "Elementals" are expressive in themselves, and can take on new forms, when light reflects on stone, for example. I maintain that an "elemental poetics" is manifest in this metamorphic capacity.

In terms of "elementals" as aesthetic forms, and referring to Kubler, Bataille, Neruda, and others, the text reads: "Neither they nor the first Spaniards could see . . . that a crafted, created world was so animated that those who lived it, inhabited it, could sing it aloud, such that the hard stones were experienced as turbulent rushing waters" (2011: 6). For those who could not see (Inka stonework and architecture specifically) there is an assumed correspondence between a "crafted world" and the technical use and mastery of stone as an inert building material. In this respect, the pressing questions elicited by Inka built environments (like the megalithic Sacsayhuaman) are about construction and technique. This is a set of concerns that has dominated speculations about Inka engineering and architecture.[24] With respect to stone as material, the emphasis here is on force upon stone, on its submission and objectification. This technical interest occludes the possibility of relating to stone as an element beyond subject-object structures of thinking, sensing and making: as resisting the chisel.

"Animacy," in the Andean context, is a cosmological principle that interrupts this technical comportment and sheds light on aesthetic phenomena without fitting within modern Western aesthetic frames.[25] It is not the projection of a human form of life upon all things. It means, rather, that things (including human beings) are given to metamorphoses through the alteration of their placement in an interrelated and reciprocal cosmos. Stone, for example, can be experienced as "turbulent rushing waters." And, as it is evident in Andean collective memory, they can also become human. These transformations are possible because the cosmos or *pacha* is a dynamic and mutable system of relations between things and people out of which their significance is determined, and it exceeds the bounds of the human "world."[26] What something is, or "kamay," is gleaned from the altering cosmos rather than being anchored in intrinsic stable characteristics, including an outward appearance or "form."[27] For this reason, everything has the potential to become something else, as if a plurality of contexts of signification were always at play. Another way of articulating this is that "animacy" in Andean ontologies implies a radical perspectivism, a multiplicity of modes of engaging the cosmos through which the significance of things appears differently, impeding any kind of objectifying and instrumental comprehensive view of it. For this reason, the field of human interests, interactions, and projects does not become absolute within *pacha*.[28]

Insofar as "elemental poetics" (as the aesthetic described by Cummins and Manheim) entails ranges and modulations of significance, it is attuned to *pacha* in its unpredictable variance, specifically in its supportive or cataclysmic effect on human "worlds." This cosmic, poetic dimension eludes accounts of production (including "artistic" production) that imply a subject acting on a material to yield an object. It attests instead to an affective and imaginative joining with the cosmos in its metamorphic potency. This is a sort of cosmic intimacy that transpires across physical (affective, perceptual, embodied) registers that are repressed by subject-centered reflective processes and by approaches to the earth as if it were only a background of human history. In this sense, "elemental poetics" leads to a retrieval of physicality as a retreat into a cosmic sphere irreducible to the worldly significance of praxical aims, instrumental reasoning, and history. A "cosmological aesthetics" takes root in this sphere. It exposes radical, even cataclysmic, cosmic transitions with an insistence indifferent to human care, and provokes sensuous intimations of them. It attends to the way the elements poetize human "worlds." In this way "cosmological aesthetics" continuously traces the cosmos at a tipping point, in cusps of transformation. This is how I understand the "singing" of the world "such that the hard stones were experienced as turbulent rushing waters."[29]

I put forward the possibility of seeing "elements" as "elementals," something I find suggested in the text. Again, referring to those who "could not see," Cummins and Manheim state:

they could not see past . . . liquid or water; earth or sky; stone or mountain to understand and appreciate the dynamics of Andean expression, and especially Inka art, as something that was and still is so carefully attuned with the coursing of life and movement that it is impossible to distinguish between the natural and cultural, sacred and mundane. (2011: 6)

There is a way of sensing the elements that is unable to "see past them." This is an objectifying sensing, where the elements are taken as discriminate and available to be manipulated. Their statement refers primarily to Inka architecture and stonework, and to the tendency of recognizing in it an absence of craftmanship and technique. In this sense, the Inka appear "dull and lacking of any expression" (2011: 6). In particular, Inka built environments do not properly differentiate themselves from their surroundings, constituting what appears at first to be a confused mess of mountain, stone, and buildings; of light of sky, and enclosed spaces. They don't seem to abide by a proper sense of historical scenography.[30]

Yet, this approach to the elements distorts their peculiar ambivalence and phenomenality. Earth is never simply available but recedes into the mountain, for example. Light recedes into the sky. As John Sallis maintains, earth and sky, in their recession, open the space for the appearing of things but are not things themselves. This recession is a kind of movement that all elements share, both belonging and not belonging to a human "world." I would add water as well, in its ungraspable movement already rendered by Heraclitus. Elements recede from the senses in a way that opens, encompasses, and disseminates the sensuous. Another way of saying this is that the "elements" show a tendency to disappear, not necessarily to vanish, but to both enable and undermine the phenomenal articulations that support the appearing of things, including their objectification. This often relegates them to a marginal showing, like the changes of light that announce the passing of time as one sits by a window. When the elements are sensed in their dynamic recession, at the boundaries of sense, change, and time, I conceive of them as "elementals."[31]

Elementals, as I noted earlier, can be intimations of radical cosmic transitions that exceed the purview and control of human "worlds." I am referring to the lighting of the sky announcing heavy rain and coloring mountainous landscapes; or brown rivers as forces of destruction, carrying mud and stone; or hot, cracking earth exposed to an open sky in the absence of water. In all of these elemental phenomena there is a sensuous encompassing that renders bodies both enfolded into an attunement to cosmic transitions and exposed to possibilities of flourishing and destruction. This is a sensuous retreat into the elemental phenomenal margin that draws bodies in through modulations between light of sky, earth and water in which the elements become joined together, inciting in one another metamorphoses with a cosmic range.

Cummins and Manheim's text locates Inka art in this marginal realm, as it brings into relief elemental transitions that enact the "coursing of life." "Life," rather than belonging to organic nature, is here an elemental movement of the cosmos that transpires across and blurs organic/inorganic, nature/culture, sacred/mundane differentiations. The cosmic elemental dimension holds sway as a sensuous intensification that exceeds the frames within which these dualities are established. There is something immense, encompassing, indifferent, and living about it. Inka stonework has to be understood from this dimension as a "cosmological aesthetics."

Cummins and Manheim study a prayer to Wiraqucha to begin to draw out a cosmic sense of animacy or life: "The Sun and Moon, Day and Night, and the seasons of ripeness and freshness do not simply exist, but exist by virtue of an order among them" (2011: 6). The key to this prayer is the phrase "do not simply exist" (*manam yanqachu*). Simple existence would be "purposeless," a "useless action," or a "speech uttered without conviction" (2011: 6). In this respect, the sun and moon, then, are not simply "there," but are part of a cosmos or *pacha* from which they acquire sense. At the same time, sense acquired from placement within an ordered cosmos is not all that is at issue here, as if to exist in the cosmos were a matter of functionality, of properly fitting within it. To not simply exist is to join the "life" of the cosmos with conviction, taking a stand in the face of risk. Sun and moon do not simply settle within the cosmos, but also undergo its instability, loss of sense, and transformation—in the movement, for example, through which the moon replaces the sun, or night replaces day. Cummins and Manheim note that the couplets in the prayer "are relational, mutually defining in such a way that neither can exist without the other. And they are not merely static categories, but have kinetic existence" (2011: 7). The couplets are joined in a transitioning, reciprocal relationship in which they both sustain and destroy one another, establishing a precarious balance. They are in a kind of kinesis that is manifest as a gathering of motion at the brink of a transformative unfolding, like the motion in "the gears of a wristwatch, the workings of a political program, the sexual act, and the existence of mountain deities" (2011: 7).

In my view, "kinesis" is the central notion of the text: "*Kinesis*, meaning an energizing or dynamic rather than mechanical sense of movement, is a principle of Inka aesthetics that integrates rock, light, water, and air" (2011: 7). *Pacha* is kinetic insofar as it comes to pass in relationalities that are held in a fragile balance. It is obviously in movement: the movement of the sun and the moon, of the heavens, of rivers. But these are not "mechanical" movements, but "kinetic." The latter refers to the tensive relational orders in which the cosmos is held "energized" or "dynamic." Beyond Cummins's and Manheim's analysis, in my view the "dynamic" aspect of this balance entails the possibility of destruction or overturning of the cosmos (or *pachakuti*). Kinesis would name, then, a state of tension between order and destruction in the reciprocity and mutual determination across relational entities (such as sun and moon). This dynamism, in which forces of order and chaos are always latent, find expression through the elements as elementals, even in a cataclysmic aesthetics of "rock, light, water, and air."

2

An Approach to Andean Aesthetics

Standing before Inka stone walls in Sacsayhuaman, facing the perfectly seamed and gigantic stones that compose them, I notice that my gaze is overtaken by ways of looking at them that I have inherited, and that date back to early colonial times.[1] Back then, seeing these walls for the first time, Spanish priests noticed the size of the stones and their weight, and wondered about how hard it must have been to carry them across space.[2] The point of such walls, they surmised, was to show power over nature. Resisting this ingrained perception sends me on a difficult path. Instead of wondering about how Inka stones were carried across space, I ask: How do these Inka stone walls *space*? And, what kinds of spaces do they draw me into?

The spacing of these walls is uncanny. The sheer magnitude of their stones stops me from finding a common measure between us, and it is difficult to understand how I belong to their spacing. They turn me into a miniature.[3] In fact, the practical issues the Spanish priests focused on are an indication of this lack of common measure and miniaturization of human scale. Inka walls can have the dimensions of mountains, as if they were their rugged sides. This monstrous spatiality enhances the relentless obtrusiveness of Inka built environments. Moving through them requires difficult physical contortions, and their configuration of spaces is disorienting. Often one feels pushed out by walls and buildings. Sometimes it is easier to move through the mountainous un-built environments that surround them. I used to attribute this obtrusiveness to the sites being ruins, to them having collapsed. Then I realized many had not, they are as they were, as if meant for a different scale and form of dwelling. One frequently overhears visitors to the sites wondering if humans had made these sites. I think the more pressing question is whether they were made for humans.

The transhuman centeredness and insignificance of Inka built environments has to do with the way buildings not only conform to their elemental settings but also let them reign over habitable ones.[4] Stone buildings follow mountainous contours, letting mountains break into their spaces. They trace water paths and are oriented to capture the movements of the sun.[5] Such are the kinds of features that take priority over human habitability, and that I experience as obtruding. The elements (light, water, stone) are not brought forth so as to be contained in a habitable place. The orientation is the reverse: spaces of human dwelling are drawn toward them, and such places are transported and emplaced in an elemental and cosmological sphere. In my view, this transport toward the elemental is enforced by Inka stonework setting into play rhythms of light, stone, and water that reverberate across habitable spaces. In Inka terraces, for example, light and shade transport one toward the indifferent mountain sides where they sit.

The site of *Tambomachay* is emblematic: it allows water to echo in stone channels, and light to be reflected on water, in such a way that the building disappears into its "setting" and one is emplaced within the insignificance of natural streams.

These are examples that need to be set in a range of architectural obtrusiveness and incommensurability. Inka built environments open a spectrum between elemental spheres and those of human concerns. Maybe this stretch is their particular kind of spacing. There are elemental rhythms in Inka walls as well. Their seams appear with the play of light and shade to conjure an in-stilled,

Figure 2.1 *Tambomachay*, Omar Rivera, 2019.

undulating movement that transports one to the flow of rivers. This rhythmic draw can be strong. There are reports of people hearing gushing waters while walking by these walls. This hearing attests to Inka stonework as a "cosmological aesthetics."

In this chapter I analyze modes of sensuousness linked to what I interpret to be an Andean "cosmological aesthetics" (through architecture, stonework, and painting). On this basis, I articulate the possibility of physicalities that are not confined to human-centered dispositions and values. In particular, in the sensing of cataclysms as exemplary of a cosmological overturn or *pachakuti*, I explore visuality in relation to the elements and to a cosmic, rather than anthropocentric, time (*ñaupa pacha*).

Sensuousness of Rhythms

Rodolfo Kusch notes the prevalence of "rhythmic knowledge" in the Andes.[6] This knowledge is not based on sense perception as a subjective gathering of data from an object. It is drawn from a bodily, affective, and perceptual mode of being in and with the sensible that Kusch calls "estar."[7] Within a visible register, this rhythmic comportment "points to" the visible as if marking a beat, engaging its concrete eventuation without fixing it.[8] Rather than singling something out, this "pointing" brings forth the experience of a sensuous blurring. In my view, "estar" is attuned to visibility as permeated by the experience of transitions and slippage, rather than focus. That which is "pointed to" is, then, not a visible object but sensuous movements that configure things and disseminate them at the same time.[9] I find this movement in the effect of elements on things, like when light transforms mountains through variations of shade, coloring, and densities.[10]

In the case of Inka architecture such a rhythmic exposure lets massive stone buildings appear as if they, and the things they shelter, recede into modulations of their settings of light, earth, and water. In this respect, and beyond Kusch's analysis, I find in "estar" an Andean aesthetic eliciting a rhythmic, sensuous comportment joining compressions and distensions of visuality (and other sensible spheres) where things are suspended, hovering without settling with determinate significance. Instead, things are encompassed by elements, transfigured in Andean sensuous, cosmological dimensions of earth and sky, and marked by palpitations of an *así* or "sheer thusness" of a mutating and transiting cosmos. "Estar" refers to things in the filling and emptying of their manifestation, in their metamorphic being in a beat and cosmic pulse. In this way it refers to a "cosmological aesthetics."

I find Gadamer's analysis of rhythm helpful at this juncture. He states:

> If we produce a series of sounds or notes repeated at regular intervals, we find that the listener cannot help introducing rhythm into the series. But where precisely is this rhythm? . . . It is as true to say that we project the rhythm as it is to say that we perceive it there . . . we can only hear the rhythm that is immanent within a given form if we ourselves introduce the rhythm into it. (1998: 45)

Gadamer is interested in the location of rhythm, since it appears within a layer of sense that is not structured by an inside and outside. The rhythms of sounds and sights constitute this layer, configuring events in which sensing and sensed are inextricable rather than separated and objectified. Bringing Kusch to bear on this discussion, it would be a mistake to think that in beats of sensuous rhythms that which is "pointed to" is an object. It is, rather, an empty instant of indeterminacy between the gathering and release of sensuous appearances that does not let things congeal into a form. This instant is the "así" or "this is it" that for Kusch constitutes the fulfillment of the inextricability of sensing and sensed at the basis of "utcatha" or "estar" as a mode of being attuned to a cosmic pulse of generation, destruction, and creation.

As Gadamer notes, there is something necessary about rhythm.[11] In the case of sound, the in-between of the beat is a sensuous fringe through which silence envelops and carries sound both swallowing and rebirthing it. The beat is the opening of this in-between that defies patterns of sensuous presence attached to the definiteness of objects. Touch also seeks beats that turn surfaces into occasions for a play of presence and absence of the sensuous connected to rhythms of touching and being touched. All the senses are rhythmic in this respect, sheltering the possibility of being lost and disoriented, yet raptured, in a retreat into a sensuous sphere where differentiations between inside/outside and absence/presence are suspended. Bodies are organized rhythmically as well: heart and lungs are in rhythms and expose one to a zone of indeterminacy between life and death, to the facticity of living. Perhaps the necessity of rhythm is the pull toward immersion in this facticity beyond the articulation of significance. This pull joins a cosmic dimension indifferent to human concerns, and reveals the cosmos in its "this is it" or "así." Rhythmic sensuous experiences, then, do not belong to a subject anchored in a stable world, nor are they necessarily submitted to a demand for the articulation of worldly meaning.

This analysis resonates with Kusch's rendition of visibility:

> Behind the faculty of seeing things clearly and distinctly lies the background of darkness. The demonic margin that conditions the world is surely deposited in that background. The indigenous vision does not become concrete, then, in the simple tree, but in the numinous margin which surrounds the tree. The anti-object frame makes the existence relative to it. The faculty of seeing is made possible by absence, like the immersion of the existence in the non-existent, as if reality were viewed in the negative. (Kusch 2010: 79)

Rhythms can determine visibility. Sensuous attention to a visible thing does not attach to a definite phenomenal configuration. There is always a play between thing and background out of which it becomes visible. This play is rhythmic, leaping, discontinuous. Kusch's contribution to this phenomenological account is to note the background of a thing as the absencing of its distinct determinations, an absencing from which a thing appears and toward which it recedes. As he puts it, existence is "relative" to this pulsating movement. In this turn, I find that Kusch reveals the possibility to situate Andean aesthetics in relation to disseminations of things rather than to their configurations (the latter being prioritized in Western phenomenology).

This pulsation is also visible: there is a "numinous margin" that surrounds things and toward which visible sense can be directed. Kusch calls it the "anti-object." I think of it as a visible beating, a sensuous dissemination in the configurations of determinate things that transpires without objectification in a layer of the visible. Kusch himself does not make explicit this connection between rhythm and the sensible, but I find it implicit in his writings, and suggest it as an approach to Andean aesthetics, stonework in particular. He, instead, refers to rhythm in relation to ritual as a restoration of "estar" as a mode of being attuned to the manifestation of the cosmos as simultaneously destructing, generating, creating, that is, in its "sheer thusness" or "así." My view is that in Kusch's Andean cosmology there are resources to think of sensing as this kind of ritual enactment.

Elemental Seeing

Visible rhythms can blur the horizons that configure things within spatial and temporal relations with other things, curtailing the development of their significance.[12] Such is the effect of the visible "numinous margins" that Kusch thematizes. Within these margins, things are almost divested of meaning and appear as "merely being there" encompassed by the *así* of the cosmos. As I noted,

Kusch's reflections on Andean cosmologies and sensuous comportments leads him to posit an experience of visibility that sees things in "the negative." This dimension of visibility, apparent in the phenomenal pulsating of the interplay between things and their background, can be enhanced in particular settings. Landscapes, like those of the enormous mountains in the Andes or the ones painted by Pettoruti, can hold vision so as to suspend the possibility of configuring things as stable objects. Disruptions of scale, through showings of earth and sky for example, can be rhythmic in that they loosen the embeddedness of things within relational environments. This sheds light on the effect of the presence of gigantic Inka walls, their disorienting atmospheres, and their disruption of habitable orders.

Built environments can also elicit rhythms through sensuous schemas that modulate the senses away from objectifying dispositions. Such schemas expose rhythms and enhance sensuous openness to them. In my view, "estar" is a mode of being susceptible to these schematics and is given to sudden alignments and realignments with concrete sensuous pulsations. *Tambomachay*, for example, offers schemas in stone and water that allow buildings to recede into their background, loosening their significance within a throbbing mountain. In this site a series of fountains echo the streams that go through it and by it, and stone walls follow the contours of their rocky settings that thrust forth now and

Figure 2.2 *Echo Stones*, Omar Rivera, 2019.

again, rhythmically emplacing one into a concrete spatial configuration of an uninhabited natural spring.

Perhaps the most obvious schemas arise from "echo stones." They repeatedly bring forth the horizons of particular places by tracing mountainous skylines. Through them sight joins rhythms of the joints between sky and earth that delimit concrete landscapes and loses discernment of material manifestations of human orders of life. This flight of visibility occurs even as one strolls in the city.[13]

The mountainous skyline is not a "thing" but a gathering of vision that relieves sensing from focusing on definite contours and forms. In this respect, Machu Picchu's overwhelming visible presence can be understood as sudden sensuous rhythmic shifts. This is perhaps most apparent when one walks away from the site and looks at the expanse of the sacred city, attending to its upward and downward thrust that follows the orientation of the mountain on which it sits. The architecture of the city presents itself as a sheet laying on a mountain, with folds and crevices that bring the mountain into relief. The city is a complex and dynamic schema that is submitted to the mountain. The play of skylight on stone and earth, the throbbing movement of shades and coloring, are the medium in which a pulsating rhythm is manifest, robbing the city of its human relevance. Thus, the question, "was it made for humans?" This schematic play of light on earth and water on dynamic mountainsides is perhaps the culmination of an Andean "cosmological aesthetics." I gather that the Inkas marked with precision the remote places one has to walk to in order to see the distinct elemental rhythms of Machu Picchu, like the portal of the sun (Inti Punku).

This point brings me to the intimate relationship between rhythm as I have articulated it and elemental modes of appearing. John Sallis shows that the elements "have a bearing on the self-showing of things," yet they are not horizons (2012: 180).[14] He states: "elementals enclose differently from horizons, and thus their spacing is different. The spacing of the elementals is an encompassing; they encompass both the things that show themselves and those to whom these things show themselves." I understand the rhythmic dimension of elementals as linked to this drawing together of sensing and sensed, and to an envelopment of things within a non-horizonal modality of appearing that can dislodge them from their fixed relational settings. Like horizons, the elements enclose, yet they do not intimate a "beyond" since they do not have definite edges. Sallis mentions here the encompassing sway of storms, and of the "concurrence of earth and sky" (2012: 180). I would add throbbing mountainsides reflecting light.

These elemental scenes, then, in their phenomenal de-objectification of things, make instrumental and practical dispositions recede and lose relevance. Sallis states: "Coming before the elemental requires emptying our deliberate attentiveness into the elemental that lies before us, letting it solicit our vision and our other senses to open to it" (2012: 182). The lack of edges of elementals does not mean that they are not discernible or "jointed." In this respect, Sallis writes: "Wherever and whenever various elementals meet, there are joints, seams, articulations" (2012: 142). The issue for me is how in Inka architecture, as exemplary of a "cosmological aesthetics," these joints (the convergence of water, stone, and light in particular) can open non-human-centered spaces, or the "body of the earth" as I discussed it in Chapter 1. I explore this issue through an engagement with Gadamer's *Truth and Method*.

Displacing Architecture: Notes on Gadamer's Aesthetics from an Andean Perspective

My discussion so far intersects with hermeneutics, Gadamer's aesthetics in particular.[15] The foregoing analysis of rhythmic sensuousness can shed light on hermeneutic understanding as it relates to artworks.[16] At the same time, my approach de-centers self-reflection and subjective articulations of significance. I pay close attention to rhythmic sensuousness as an immersion in phenomenal processes in which things do not surface and settle in objective and intelligible spheres, and as enabling an embodied understanding that can become released from the tethering of things in relations of significance. In this sense, interpretation is not only horizonal, temporal, and situated, but disseminative and even metamorphic, prone to displacements, shifts, and interruptions.

In my view, the relationship between understanding and rhythm is at the center of Gadamer's hermeneutics. This relationship is apparent in pre-reflective understanding. Bodies constantly join rhythms that articulate experience. Bodily habits, for example, allow for understanding surroundings, for engaging them interpretively. I extend this point to state that sensuous rhythms in particular are essential for orientation (sounds, sights, smells for example) and for a feeling of engagement with everyday environments.

At first, it seems that rhythm is simply the presentation of order. Yet, if that were the case, there would not be a relationship between rhythm and understanding, since the latter is compelled precisely by the breakdown of an assumed order.[17] It is more accurate to say that rhythms, in their patterning of the most basic sensuous and corporeal levels of existence, are the means through which one becomes open to the unfamiliar and unprecedented. Habits, orientations, and senses of engagement occur with such openness. In fact, rhythms appear to be the sensuous prompting of interpretation as the working out of significance. In terms of my discussion earlier, rhythmic patterns are beats that initiate a double, interlaced process in which things pulsate in phenomenal gatherings and disseminations that displace them from their worldly anchoring. The draw of such pulsation is the condition for interpretive understanding as it emerges from sensuous spheres.

On the basis of rhythmic sensuousness, I find resonances between Gadamer's aesthetics, hermeneutic understanding, and Inka stonework as I have interpreted it, specifically in light of architecture.[18] My following discussion is rather narrow, focusing on functionality within Gadamer's account of architecture as a problematic from which to approach Inka stonework. At stake here is coming to terms with what I (drawing from Gadamer) call a building's "integrity," and with architecture making manifest this "integrity" as a singularity. Architecture is relevant in this respect because at first it seems to lack rhythm in the sense that it seems oriented toward settling things in places, preserving their relationalities and assuring order. At the same time, as the foregoing discussion shows, Inka stone architecture is profoundly rhythmic. Moreover, architecture plays a pivotal role in Gadamer's elucidation of hermeneutic understanding in *Truth and Method*.[19]

Gadamer shows that architecture, and artworks in general, do not serve purposes articulated through expanding relationalities within fields of projected aims. Instead, he finds artworks to be instantiations of recognition. He writes: "In recognition what we know emerges, as if illuminated, from all the contingent and variable circumstances that condition it. It is grasped in its essence. It is known as something" (2004: 113). In this illuminated emergence, what is known "as something" is not an abstraction. Yet it entails a release from the proliferation of aims that usually submits things to purposes and uses. In other words, understanding is the illumination of a thing appearing withdrawn from its familiar senses. This event of understanding is a challenge to interpret the world in light of a disruption of basic worldly orderings of significance and offers the possibility of tracing what something is with renewed sense.

According to Gadamer, this challenge constitutes the "hermeneutic identity" of an artwork, and through it works of art become, and render their world, singular. If works of art were overridden within larger contexts of purpose, they would not gather singularities, they would be flat, contingent, and subjective, and their "hermeneutic identities," their capacities to enable recognition and allow for differential interpretive understandings, would be subverted. Moreover, the sensuousness of artworks cannot be overlooked. Their "hermeneutic identity" arises from their appearing to sense. This, I suggest, relates to rhythm as the sensuous prompting of understanding within a sphere where things are displaced from their sedimented surroundings, so that their palpitation as they come forth from and recede into their background stirs interpretive dispositions toward renewed sense.

Yet, somewhat paradoxically, according to Gadamer, buildings are undermined as works of art when their purpose or functionality is disrupted. He states:

> In architecture... the thought regarding its purpose belongs to the very creation of the building. Where a building's relation to its purpose is quite unclear, this fact can be annoying: for example, the Porta Nigra in Trier, which has something eerie about it, like a gravesite; or when the Pergamon Altar in Berlin has steps that run right into the wall. (2004: 222)

Architecture does not allow for stairs, windows, and doors to nowhere. Even less marked disruptions of functionality, like awkward organizations of space or encumbrances to mobility, seem to not belong to this art form. This is evident in buildings "Where the original intention becomes completely unrecognizable or its unity is destroyed by too many subsequent alterations" (2004: 149). A difficult aspect of Gadamer's aesthetics is how to reconcile architecture as an art form with this requirement of functionality, which appears to make it contingent rather than singular. There seems to be, then, a tension in architecture between its "hermeneutic identity" and its adherence to functionality. In the following analysis I explore this tension in view of Inka stonework and its elemental rhythms.

Architecture, Hermeneutic Identity, and Functionality

I understand a hermeneutic account of architecture to emphasize that being in a building is first of all to be guided toward the accomplishment of particular tasks. With bodily competency (here understood as normalized and dominant bodily attunements to functionality), one takes for granted that the building is there.[20] The building does not present itself. Yet at times one gets distracted from tasks, competency becomes suspended, and one's body drifts, yet is still moved by the building. In this sensuous drifting, one can join the building's inner patterns that suddenly give themselves to a heightened awareness. I read Gadamer as suggesting that, through spatial rhythms that take root in wandering bodies, one is given to embodied meanings gathered by the distinctness of a building; that is, one is prompted to interpret it and its world.[21] He writes: "we have to go up to the building and wander around it, both inside and out. Only in this way can we acquire a sense of what the work holds in store for us and allow it to enhance our feeling of life" (2004: 149). Sensuous, spatial rhythms are, then, essential to architecture as an art form, to turning the simple moving through space into being corporeally open to the building in its "hermeneutic identity."

In this way, rhythms are triggered by spatial schemas making possible a hermeneutic identity that is revealed through a building's integrity and that interrupts one's embeddedness in functionality. Buildings, then, can be doubly present, which, Gadamer suggests, is characteristic of architecture as an art form. The rhythmic uniqueness of architecture lies in this doubling. While immersed in functionality, in a field of aims, it also has a "hermeneutic identity," allowing for the aesthetic disruption of the familiar sense of things to be most pronounced. Perhaps going beyond Gadamer's analysis, in my view the rhythms of built environments can present worlds and disseminate them at the same time, can both enfold the significance of things and let them take flight as in a daydream.

The relationship between buildings and the institutions they house sheds light on Gadamer's hermeneutic approach to architecture. Institutional buildings are sites of memory and renewal, of historical decisions. They are also bureaucratic entities. The administrative offices of a university, for example, can have an uncanny presence. In my case, I approach one of the oldest buildings of higher education in Texas with the intent to enter into dialogues that in my view could determine the direction of the institution. When I go up the stairs in this building it seems that a double framing of my experience is possible. The stairs can allow me to get to where I want to go, they are strictly functional. My intent gets reflected back at me flattened out in terms of administrative tasks to be accomplished. Or, the same stairs can present themselves within the building in a way that, as Gadamer puts it, "a context of meaning closes and completes itself in reality, such that no lines of meaning scatter in the void" (2004: 112). In the second framing, going up the stairs allows me to join a rhythm that lets my body inhabit distinct spatialities that reveal the building as a singular integrated whole. Something beyond sheer tasks is intimated through the building's integrity.

In the sensuous and dimensional experiences tied to architectural integrity, a strange "othering" is made possible. An aspect of rhythmically taking step after step in this particular stairway is a bodily awareness that others have done the same, probably without thinking, following the same built structures. The echoing rhythm of my steps, both tactile and sonorous, puts me at a kind of uncanny edge of the familiar, at the verge of encountering the world as a singularity through the building (something that sheer functionality does not allow for). In particular, the stairs as rhythmic schemas, and the integrity of the building, solicit in me a bodily awareness that others for whom life has ended have gone up those same stairs, others for whom those same stairs, and the building as a whole, were an episode toward their distinct fate.

The architectural presence of mortality makes the histories of the building, and of the institution it houses, seem definitive, unique, released from overriding and generalized sense; and, at the same time, up for interpretation, transformation, and resignification. Through architectural integrity, institutional buildings are in processes of destruction and renewal, processes manifest through sensuous rhythms arising with the sound of shoe soles. These rhythms are entailed in sensing the building's integrity as a "hermeneutic identity," not just its functionality—a distinction that comes forth sensuously and is perhaps the distinct experience of architecture as a hermeneutic, aesthetic form. The integrity of the building exposes me to the finitude of others and, through theirs, to my own. The building's capacity to gather and be gathered in rhythms, which is concretely expressed in the continuation of an original design, manifests the finitude and fate of historical existence.

In this way, in the administrative building I encounter others as others and myself as othered by them. That others and I have shared the same stairs does not mean that our differences have been erased. Rather, the building can open spaces for encounters and dialogues in finitude and difference. These encounters are sustained by a tacit bond between my rhythmic body and the building as an art form with a "hermeneutic identity." If I understand Gadamer correctly, in my example of the aesthetic being of an institutional building, the stairs have to go somewhere, that is, the building's original intended integrity has to be manifest and preserved. A dysfunctional building, like one that has been modified as to lose its original coherence, lacks integrity; it does not manifest itself in its possibility to be re-inhabited differentially, finitely, historically. At the same time, function is not the same as integrity because function on its own can be submitted to a dispersal of aims.

In this difference lies the secret of architecture as a hermeneutic, aesthetic form. This last point refers to a central statement in Gadamer's analysis of architecture:

> If a building is a work of art, then it is not only the artistic solution to a building problem posed by the contexts of purpose and life to which it originally belongs, but somehow preserves them, so that they are visibly present even though the building's present appearance is completely alienated from its original purpose. Something in it points back to the original. Where the original intention becomes unrecognizable or its unity destroyed by too many subsequent alterations, then the building itself becomes incomprehensible. (2004: 149)

My description also begins to shed light on the "hermeneutic identity" at stake in Gadamer's analysis of architecture. In particular, it shows the temporal dimension of architecture as an art form. Gadamer states that architecture

> poses the task of integrating past and present. Works of architecture do not stand motionless on the shore of the stream of history, but are borne along by it. Even if historically-minded ages try to reconstruct the architecture of an earlier age, they cannot turn back the wheel of history, but must mediate in a new and better way between the past and the present. (2004: 150)

The bond between architecture, integrity, and function shelters the possibility of the "integration of past and present." This is materially expressed in the retention of a building's original integrity (something fundamentally elusive), which exceeds the contingencies of contexts of aims.

The place-making thrust of architecture, its opening of concrete sites for the mediation of past and present as described earlier, relies on the sensuous emanations of architectural features (like stairs). Such features are schemas that rhythmically draw one to embodied awareness of built integrity through a pulsating of concrete gatherings and disseminations in sync with the passing of history. There is a delicate balance here between integrity and original intent: the original purpose of the building is manifest through the concrete, material, and schematic presence of the building; so, even if a building has been re-purposed, its original structural integrity and functionality must be apparent for it to be architecturally sound. This is why Gadamer puts buildings that have become "incomprehensible" outside of the purview of architecture, since they cease to be historical in the hermeneutic sense of this term.

This discussion brings to mind the Coricancha, a building that is a Spanish Catholic church and convent mounted on an Inka temple of the sun. Being there I realized that I was always trying to learn how to walk on that site. I was being solicited to move in accordance to two different organizations of space. The Coricancha is full of annoying features, as Gadamer understands them, like stairs going nowhere. This is because there are layers of different forms of habitability that find expression in that building. The Coricancha makes manifest to me Gadamer's insight into the connection between architecture, integrity, and functionality because I don't know how to be in it. This ignorance spreads from my body toward my sense of history. But, and I am not sure Gadamer would agree with me, this sensuous not knowing can be a particular kind of hermeneutic challenge that the building offers because of its contested history of colonialism. I have to move; the building is there, sharing space with me. Much is at stake, I think, in pursuing this spacing in the Coricancha. It would reveal something about the coloniality of architecture (rather than about colonial architecture). I continue this discussion in my analysis of the Church of Andahuaylillas in Chapter 6.

Inka Architecture as Cosmological Aesthetics: Elemental Reliance and Cataclysmic Potency

The Inka citadel of Machu Picchu, and other examples of Inka buildings, complicates the bond between functionality, integrity, and architecture. As I noted earlier, Inka architecture schematizes natural settings in order to bring forth elemental rhythms of stone, water, and light. In this way, elemental atmospheres disrupt and reign over functional, habitable buildings. I call one of such schemas "elemental reliance." It draws out the support of built environments provided by the elements, and it sensuously displaces things from their embeddedness in contexts of relationalities. *Tambomachay*, which I discussed earlier, is exemplary of "elemental reliance" in Inka architecture, rhythmically overriding the anchoring of things in sedimented worlds. Its stonework and architectural features, including functional ones, recede into its elemental setting, which bursts forth. It is as if the space for things and people had been forced out as the building was encrusted in the mountainside. *Tambomachay* allows water to reverberate through it in ordered sounds, and light be reflected on water, metamorphosing into a natural stream. The architecture thus reveals the harmonic elemental setting that supports it, even making possible human habitability, yet it is manifest in its own terms and detached from human concerns and histories.

I call "cataclysmic potency" an elemental rhythmic schema that manifests the instability of buildings in their specific settings. It effuses rhythms that join earthquakes (when earth opens itself up) and floods (where water exceeds all containment), for example. In Inka architecture, "cataclysmic potency" is manifest mostly through schemas that bring forth the movement and devastation of avalanches from mountain sides in a way that overwhelms functional, habitable spaces. *Machu Picchu* is exemplary in the presentation of cataclysmic potency and is composed of buildings that are reminiscent of those that Gadamer finds "annoying" because their purpose is not clear, as if they had collapsed. More evidently than in the case of *Tambomachay*, the non-human-centered spacing of cataclysmic potencies, in their disruption of functional, habitable places, seems excluded from Gadamer's aesthetics of architecture.

Rhythm, the sensuous pulsation of things as they gather and disseminate without settling into a relational or objective form, a pulsation that impedes their absorption into instrumental and functional orders, unlocks an architectural expanse that is perhaps larger than the one Gadamer focuses on. In Inka architecture it is the elements that are at play in setting this rhythm. Rhythm in my reading of Gadamer enables the "hermeneutic identity" of buildings, the ways in which their integrity exceeds their function so as to appear singular. As noted earlier, this "hermeneutic identity" prompts the understanding, the possibility of reweaving the sense of buildings and things sheltered by them, which is also the "integration of the past into the present." In this respect, architecture for Gadamer stands in an inextricable relation to a hermeneutic approach to history.

Yet, rhythm also releases things to an elemental sphere. In this case the prompt to understand unfolds differently. Rather than re-engaging the significance of things in their historical development, understanding becomes attunement to the "thusness" of the cosmos as the harmony between sky, earth, and the community. This harmony is manifest in the sensuous belonging of buildings within their elemental settings and is that toward which both schemas of "elemental reliance" and "cataclysmic potency" pull. The "así," as it determines the phenomenality of buildings and things, however, is not centered on worlds of human concerns nor does it have a history like that of institutional buildings. For this reason, Inka architecture is not solely a matter of "hermeneutic identities." Its rhythms manifest, rather, a "cosmological identity," within a cosmic time, perhaps.[22]

Gadamer and Inka Architecture

Nevertheless, my discussion of Gadamer sheds light on important aspects of Inka architecture. Specifically, the "integrity" of buildings remains an important architectural factor. In the Inka context, this integrity, if it is possible to even keep this term, is oriented more to the cosmos rather than to historical time. In terms of "elemental reliance," I would point to "echo stones" within buildings and citadels. As I mentioned earlier, they trace the contours of the mountainous horizon where earth and sky meet, the horizon that is their elemental background. Moving through Inka built spaces these stones set up sensuous rhythms from the earth supporting one toward a heavenly exposure, joining the elemental stability of the very spaces buildings are in. A gathering of meaning ensues, one that, beyond the reach of human, dispersed aims, encircles one's community in a cosmic embrace called *kay pacha* ("the space now over here").[23] The "cosmological identity" of echo stones manifests *kay pacha* in a non-human-centered strangeness that challenges one to understand worldly environments in terms of the "así" of elemental reliance. This is possible through a structural integrity, one that belongs to elemental orders and is not defined by tasks, which leads to an unprecedented architecture, at least to Western eyes.

In terms of the schemas of "cataclysmic potency," the integrity of buildings sets up rhythms in which the elements appear to disavow one another and encompass built spaces such that one's body becomes attuned to cosmic instabilities. Stone, light, and water are set against each other, undermining each other in syncopated rhythms. Inka walls, for example, bring forth light in its presence and absence by letting it irradiate from stone, usurping it from the sky. Disconnected from the sky as a source of light, this stonelight also evokes darkness, giving the effect of a lunar shine. Also, the seams of Inka walls appear as a joint between stone and water, despite the absence of water, as if they were rivers of flowing stone. A similar effect is apparent in instances of Inka stonework where rock is carved as if falling in a landslide, yet kept still.[24] Here the stillness of the stone shows water in its downward motion, and the absence of water with it. These monstrous appearances that bring together elemental presences and absences, transitions and transformations, rhythmically and physically open us to a sphere of *kay pacha* as connected to *pachakuti*, the overturning of the cosmos. A "cosmological identity" is at play here, and it prompts one to understand worlds in a fragile "mere givenness," in an "así," that is most distant from the field of human concerns.

In Andean cosmology, *kay pacha* is not overdetermined as strictly human-centered. Perhaps when architecture schematizes this dimension it exceeds the worldly and temporal/historical frames that Gadamer's aesthetics abides by. Yet this displacement of architecture could establish a dialogue across Andean and Western aesthetics that would be possible due to Gadamer's hermeneutic aesthetics. Along these lines, I take the discussion in this chapter up to this point as a preparation for an analysis of a dimension of sensing, and of the body more generally, that has remained implicit so far and that gives access to a "cosmological time."

Sensible Time

There is an embodied lineage of Andean aesthetics that retains the elemental character of Inka architecture, works of photography, and painting in particular. I explore this lineage in order to focus on an elemental *aísthesis*, which allows me to analyze Andean visuality oriented toward a sensible, cosmological time. This involves developing notions from my discussion so far. In particular, from architectural "cataclysmic potency" I draw out modalities of sensing attuned by earthquakes and articulated in relation to the spectralization of things (their release from their contexts of significance). Spectrality sheds further light on the disseminative force of rhythms as I have developed it in this chapter. It also allows me to delve into the visuality of an in-stilled movement or *purin*, accessible to *aísthetic* registers that are open to elemental transitional patterns, and into a creative cosmological force (*kamay*) detached from the confines of human orders. This particular analysis of *aísthesis* and cosmologies lets me reach toward the notion of a cosmic "visible past" that is different from the historical past operative in Gadamer's hermeneutics.

The following Quechua prayer (already cited in the previous chapter but now re-translated by me) not only evokes the rhythm of the days and seasons as generative and destructive. It also turns to the force of creation that moves them in a kind of cosmic stillness, and suggests the visibility of such a force. The prayer to *Wiracocha*, the mobilizer of *pacha* or cosmos, says:

> Sun
> Moon
> Day
> Night
> Season of ripeness
> Season of freshness
> In complementary destruction and generation
> Are not impotently in view, merely existing
> They are in a cosmic in-stilled movement infused with creative force[25]

How is the Andean cosmos or *pacha*, in its complementary generation and destruction, visible as an "in-stilled movement (*purin*) infused with creative force (*kamay*)"? In this respect, the prayer to *Wiracocha* evokes the visible registers of light and dark, and their coloring of the earth: registers like those of Andean mountainsides, where light, stone, and earth yield fickle luminous atmospheres as day and night blend and cascade. In fact, one of the common referents for *purin* or "in-stilled movement" is the kinesis of mountains apparent when skylight bathes them. Such visible registers are also suggested by the relational cosmology of *pacha* in terms of sky, earth, and the textured surfaces where they meet.[26]

In keeping with Andean aesthetic lineages, including Inka architecture and its elemental schemas ("cataclysmic potency" in particular), Julia Navarrete paints a play of illumination on mountains, which results in a spectral atmosphere: a metamorphic back and forth between, and generation and destruction of, light, stone, and water that enfolds sites of human dwelling. In, *Sín Título*, 1997, if one connects her painting to the Andean aesthetics I am exploring here, one sees vertical strips of different tonalities of light ranging from day to night, which allows mountains to move in a disarray of planes and dimensions. The unsteady earth even appears to swallow human-made structures, a process reminiscent of Inka stone architecture blurring onto the rocky rugged edges on which it is built. The painting in-stills these cataclysmic movements, especially as mountains appear to sit within a chamber and to be reflected by calm waters that turn them into a quivering reflection. Yet, in the painting sometimes water appears to recede, overtaken by stone.[27]

Figure 2.3 Julia Navarrete, *Sín Título*, 1997. Oil on natural linen. 180 x 200 cm. Private Collection.

Following Rodolfo Kusch's study of indigenous Andean cosmologies, I discern two layers of sensing. In one layer, things can be sensed in multifaceted but stable disclosures, configured so as to be set in a world, and embedded within dynamic and manageable spatio-temporal relationalities with other things.[28] In the other layer, sensing withdraws from things in their temporal unfolding and coherent manifestations, and is drawn toward and encompassed by appearances that are not articulated by sensible horizons, have no sides or dimensions, and do not abide by the temporal differentiations between past, present, and future. These are trans-worldly, kinetic yet in-stilled, elemental appearances involving sky and earth, day and night, and light, stone, and water.

The Andean conception of cosmos or *pacha*, as a generative-destructive creative force, is manifest in the latter layer, especially where and when sky and earth meet. When skylight shines on earth, for example, it forms and deforms things through coloring and shade, composing what I call a spectral atmosphere. Given this Andean topography of sensuousness, it is possible to detect differential phenomenal planes through shifting layers of sensing, where things become marginal, otherworldly, barely tethered to the substantiality endowed by worlds, out of focus, unfolded without a center, as if they were simultaneously becoming and passing and skipping a determinate coming into view. This visible, uncanny atmosphere is one exposure of *pacha* that the prayer to *Wiracocha* evokes.

Like Kusch, I am interested in the sensuous crossing toward the sphere of elemental appearances, and toward the manifestations of *pacha* within it. In this transition, I do not hone in on the way elemental appearances support the visibility of things, on how light, for example, makes it possible. I try, rather, to reach the cosmos in its silent distancing from the phenomena of things in the world and reveal ways "it" comes to be sensed. The sensible showing of the cosmos I trace is atmospheric, an expanding mist of light, stone, and water held by earth and sky in which things become specters. In my discussion "spectrality" refers to a manifestation of the cosmos in which things lose the phenomenal figurations (like sides, horizons, and densities) that lodge them into human worlds. I also show that spectrality is connected to visible temporalities that do not quite fit within the framework of past/present/future.

Cataclysmic Sense

In 1888, José Martí, the exiled Cuban poet, philosopher, and revolutionary, reports on a blizzard in New York City. He states:

the city found itself silent, deserted, shrouded, buried under the snow . . . the overpowered streetcar lay horseless beneath the storm . . . the suburban train, halted en route by the tempest or stalled by the drifting snow, higher than the engines, struggled in vain to reach its destination. . . . It was impossible to see the sidewalks. Intersections could no longer be distinguished, and one street looked like the next. On 23rd Street, one of the busiest thoroughfares, a thoughtful merchant put a sign on a corner-post: "This is 23rd Street." (2002: 57)

Throughout the text, Martí carefully exposes the way in which blizzards (one could add earthquakes, hurricanes, floods, and droughts) can modulate sensing and open it to unfamiliar phenomenal layers. He notes the silence after the storm, for example, that is detached from the sounds of things. It is, thus, different from and indifferent to the silence of the interval between cars driving down a busy street or the ticking of a clock. In these latter cases, silence stretches itself out in anticipation of expected sounds. The silence that Martí brings up, on the other hand, settles with things as they lose their functionality, purpose, and predictability (like snow covered streetcars, trains, and sidewalks), as they become specters, not quite of the world. Rather than the anticipation of sound, the silence after the blizzard is the absorption of sound, it has an encompassing and enveloping character, and it comes from nowhere.[29] The sounds within this silence appear as they vanish, like an echo or an ephemeral howling or whistling of wind. There are certain phenomenal planes that are hard to put into words, words such as "This is 23rd Street" after a blizzard. They shelter moments prior to the horizonal configuration of things and their settling into a world. In these planes things are enfolded not only by silence but also by light and earth, echoing, quivering out of focus, spectrally. Cataclysms can muddle and reorient sense toward them.

After a cataclysm there is also a modulation of visibility that brings forth spatio-temporalities that are not caught amid determinate things articulated in terms of relationalities of usefulness. They are receding spatio-temporalities that belong to elemental phenomenal layers. In 1886 Martí writes a report on an earthquake in Charleston that in many ways pre-figures his text on the blizzard. In particular, in this report the de-articulation and spectrality of things, their breakdown and collapse, also join a shift of the sensible. Trains stuck in bent or split rails and houses that fold as if they were made of straw are released from their surroundings, decontextualized, like toys that can be moved at whim, not quite belonging anywhere. The visuality of toys in particular can be revealing of cataclysmic sensing. There is a kind of spectrality in toys, a loss of substance, a tendency to be found in random places.[30] Toys are determined by miniaturization, by reduction in scale, by a sense of not occupying as much space as they should. This spatial impropriety is seen in and through a monstrous expansion of the visual field, as if the spectrality that miniaturizes things coincided with a stretch of the spectrum of the visible. Cataclysms can elicit this dilation of eyes perched in uncharted visual heights.

Reflecting perhaps on his own writing about the earthquake, Martí states:

> These sorrows that begin in the entrails of the earth, one has to see them from the heights of the heavens. . . . From there earthquakes, with all of their propelling of human suffering, are nothing more than an adjustment of the visible earth above its shrunk entrails, something indispensable for the equilibrium of creation. (2002: 62)

Earthquakes sweep sight toward the miniaturization of human lives and things; only through distancing can they be sensed. This sensing, however, does not focus on broken trains, on people running into the streets, or on barking dogs. In fact, earthquakes, and other cataclysms, cannot be brought into focus as world events, and always remain at the margins of worldly sense. Yet, as marginal events, they are sensuously liminal and elicit a spectral turn toward otherworldly silence and toward the sight of the earth as a turbulent ground that usually remains covered up by buildings and roads. "The heights of the heavens" means here an uncanny dimension of visuality. From such heights one senses in the stillness of earth tectonic movements of a magnitude and reach normally undetected.

In my view, Martí's "equilibrium of creation" is this stillness where movement and stasis, destruction and generation are held together in an exposure of the entrails of the earth to the sky. This movement sustains a cataclysmic, elemental sensing. I relate this sensing to Kusch's notion of "estar" as a translation of "utcatha" in Aymara (being). In his terms, it is a sensing of the "así" or "this is it" of the cosmos, of the simultaneity of its destruction, generation, and creation.

I further suggest that the sensing of the "así" is attuned by a temporality of "pastness." Cataclysms can only be in the past, since they are not encompassed by the present and undermine futural projections. At the same time, they cannot be "no longer present." This is because cataclysms reveal the ongoing cosmic destruction-generation-creation that always already is happening, a "past" that can unpredictably re-weave worldly presents and override worldly futures, as if coming from a different temporal plane. Since this cosmic past is not a "no longer," it does not belong to the plane of linear memory and forgetfulness, or of history. If anything, the creation and recreation of the cosmos, the work of the god *Wiracocha*, is a constant, indeterminate "whence" that can be manifest in its "this is it" or "así," rendering a spectral domain. It is also a sensible layer that enfolds the present.[31]

Ñawpa Pacha or Seeing the Past

The past is visible. This does not simply mean that it is present. The present, after all, allows the past to be in it in several ways: in the affects of memory and nostalgia, in habits and cultural practices, in monuments that represent the past and in books that record it in writing. In fact, the presence of the past in the present is the condition for developing a historical consciousness without which there would be no understanding, no sense of self and no communal identity.[32] The visibility of the cosmic past is different because of its persistence in a sensuous field. As a constant and dynamic "whence" rather than "no longer," the past within an elemental sphere of the sensible is seen through a turn of and in sensing.

When one looks at the stars, for example, one's sight is absorbed in a modality of seeing what has been there all along, for longer than everything else. This is not an imaginative projection, but a phenomenal layer of the present. Yet staring at the stars is not quite sensing the fullness of the cosmos, since it sees only the sky, and leaves out the earth. Cataclysmic sensing, on the other hand, sees the exposure of earth to sky as having been there all along, which is perhaps most apparent in earthquakes.

Cataclysmic sensing is also attuned to phenomenal events when sky and earth touch, events that at first do not seem to involve cataclysms. Mountains, like the Andes for example, sustain the touch of earth and sky as they shelter light on their rugged sides, offering a moving, rhythmic even, spread of light, shade, and color, a movement of mountains in stillness. There is a cataclysmic force in this appearing, something suggestive of an earthquake, a rhythmic passing of mountains in a stillness of generation, destruction, and creation. Sometimes when light and stone touch, stone becomes water and shines like a moving river. This in-stilled destruction of stone and generation of water reveals sky and earth as cataclysmic forces, as forces of creation, as configuring a visible "whence" that has always been there. Such kinetic sights, of mountain, light, water, and stone, are enveloped in a cosmic, elemental pastness. They are and have always been there, effusing spectral atmospheres.

Cataclysmic sensing, as I noted earlier, is connected to a turn in the visible that miniaturizes people and things, as if the field of visibility were expanded immensely. Sight is absorbed into larger, cosmic spheres where the relations between things are stretched out too thin, or broken, impeding the unfolding of comprehensive sense. As the world metamorphoses into a playroom with toys scattered around, the visible field becomes so vast that nothing can be held in focus; and earth and sky as creative forces in a past that is not of historical memory come forth in elemental appearances. This relationship between an expanded visibility and the past brings me to reflect on the temporalities of the pre-Columbian Andes. In an essay on Inka temporality, "The Past as Kin," Darryl Wilkinson and Terence D'Altroy remark that in Quechua

> the term *ñawpa* refers both to the past and the space in front of the speaker. It is also closely related to the term *ñawi* ("eye" or "vision"), and so a phrase such as *ñawpa pacha* ("olden times") can be given a literal gloss as "time of the eye" or "time in the eye." (2018: 113–4)

In Andean contexts, the visibility of the past is a defining determination of time. The cosmic past is a time of or in the eye. Yet this translation does not address the nuances of the word "pacha" in the phrase "*ñawpa pacha*."[33] I would add, then, to their translation: "the past of or in the eye is the cosmos," or "the past fills the eye as the visible cosmos," or "the past is the cosmos coming into view in the fullness of the field of the visible."

The previous quote hints at another aspect of the sensing of the cosmos which has remained implicit so far: the relationship between space, time, and the visibility of the past. As they put it, "the past is the space in front of the speaker," which implies that the past is a modality of space, or a spatialization of time. In Andean temporalities, Wilkinson and D'Altroy note:

> Tellingly, Rafael Núñez and Eve Sweetser's studies of gestures produced by Aymara communities indicate that the recent past is associated with the space immediately before the speaker, while references to the distant past, are accompanied by gestures to the far-off horizon in front of the speaker. (2018: 113–4)

It is tempting to interpret this too simply, as meaning that the past is far away and the present is near. I suggest, instead, to read the spatialization of time suggested here in its Andean context, where the horizon is the moment of touch between sky and earth at mountain peaks.

The gesture toward the distant horizon extends the field of vision toward *ñawpa pacha*, the cosmic visible past, toward the immensity of the mountains that dwarfs the world, toward mountain sides where light, shade, and color rhythmically spread and play, as if always anticipating the fall of earth due to earthquakes and landslides, and toward peaks where storms gather and hard ice turns into water. In this sense, the events right in front of us have an illusory stability and come to focus by a reduction of the field of visibility. They appear, even if as specters, in and from the cosmic past once our eyes dilate, and they are then submitted to forces of generation, destruction, and creation.

This interpretation of Andean cosmic time resonates with Quechua and Aymara ontologies, where things come to be ephemerally constituted through their relations with other things.[34] This constitution does not give them an "essence," however. What makes them what they are is *kamay*, a vital, whimsical, creative force that places and displaces them (forming them and deforming them) in networks of relations that also crumble, tossing them around like toys. In a paradoxical sense, things "are" this tossing movement that generates and destroys them and their relationalities, a movement of *pacha* that does not let them settle in a "form." Such is the effect of the visible past as the showing of the cosmos.

One of the possible, fragile relationalities between things that *kamay* tears down is the temporal distinction between past/present/future as a sequential order. To manipulate and predict, to sense the "past" as absent, recalled and represented, reduces things to their utility. Yet the sequential temporality of this comportment is fleeting, non-totalizable and localized; it does not ultimately ground the world. In this respect, Tamara Bray, in an attempt to convey Andean time to a more familiar modern Western perspective, states:

> Andean peoples were highly cognizant of the fact that persons, places and things existed within multiple temporal frameworks. For them, the multitemporal nature of the world was undoubtedly evident—in the enduring profiles of the snow-capped peaks, the daily ebb and flow of the ocean tides, the cycles of the moon, the seasonal variability of rivers and streams. (2018: 269)

This statement resonates with my analysis so far: the world is de-articulated, rendered spectral, even in terms of temporal relations. This dissemination and multiplication of temporalities comes forth by attending to elemental appearances of a generative and destructive cosmic creation. I find in the "enduring profiles" evoked by Bray (of snow peaks and flowing water) a sensing of stillness in movement, like the cataclysmic sensing of rhythmically moving mountains. As I have noted, the Quechua word for this in-stilled movement of *pacha* is *purin*. This word, together with *kamay*, plays an important role in the prayer to *Wiracocha*, the mobilizer god, I cited earlier. In it the cosmos is said to not be simply there, but to be in *kamachisqam purin*; which I translate as "in an in-stilled movement infused with a creative force." The cosmic past is not simply there, yet it is in the depths of the visible as elemental forces that are both germinative and adrift.

Sensing *Pacha*

I am approaching lineages of Andean cosmological aesthetics where visibility senses the cosmos or *pacha*. In this regard I return to Tom Cummins and Bruce Manheim:

> to appreciate and understand the dynamics of Andean expression, and especially Inka art, that was and still is so carefully attuned with the coursing of life and movement.... it is an aesthetic that takes light and liquid, hardness and softness as sources of expression and casts them in various guises across skies and landscapes, buildings and bodies. (2011: 6)

For modern, Western eyes, Andean aesthetics is a shock that widens them, extending their field of vision and the modalities and scope of visibility. It throws them into cataclysmic sensing.

Pre-colonial wakas or sacred places are emblematic of this aesthetics. Kenko looks like enormous rocks that dropped from the sky, after a landslide perhaps. At the same time, the rocks are carefully placed and carved. Moreover, their upper surface is carved as a miniaturized world: streets, terraces, rivers, plazas, stairs carved into stone. Yet they are collapsed into one another, their spatial relations do not make sense. It is a world of toys, architecturally nonsensical,

Figure 2.4 *Kenko*, Omar Rivera, 2019.

An Approach to Andean Aesthetics 87

Figure 2.5 *Kenko Altar*, staged photograph by Omar Rivera, Edwin Quispecuro Nina, Richard Peralta, 2019.

Figure 2.6 Julia Navarrete, from the Interstices series, *Sín Título*. Oil on natural linen. 180 x 200 cm. Private Collection.

with stairs going nowhere.[35] The aesthetic effect of these architectonic and sculptural features is the sense that rocks have fallen down on vulnerable worlds. At the same time, the sacred chamber inside the waka opens a cosmic space that makes the eyes float in the sky at night, sunset, or dawn. On the altar one sees a play of stone and light that turns stone into water and day into night. These metamorphoses are enhanced by a proliferation of planes that distribute light disparately, which stirs an indeterminate movement in stillness, or *purin*.

In this Andean "cosmological aesthetics," the proliferation of planes that disseminate light and shade can evoke the cosmos as a crumpling sheet of paper with unworldly, spectral textures and dimensions. This effect is exposed in paintings by Julia Navarrete. In them light, sky, and earth on mountainous planes compress and expand at the same time, making visible a crumpling of the cosmos with a rhythmic kinesis akin to that of a choppy sea. Elements turning against and into one another unfold a realm where a visuality attached to things becomes impossible. Prior to the visible arrival of things there is a phenomenal layer of fleeting elemental appearances that comes to pass in oceanic, immense spatio-temporalities that find no worldly articulation. In Navarrete's paintings the excess of folding dimensions, of cosmic wrinkles, is monstrous. In them, even the sky is a mere window, a portal to further irreducible spatialities that not only make the world tiny but incoherent, insubstantial, as if after an earthquake or a blizzard.

Part II

Embodiments of Resistance

3

Visions of Resistance

The turn to Andean "cosmological aesthetics" in the last chapter shows that, when one is drawn into the vastness of the sensuous and of its different phenomenal layers, it is possible for the cosmos (as a visible past or *ñaupa pacha*, manifest elementally and kinetically) to yield spectral atmospheres that release things from worldly logics, including temporal ones. The expanse of the sensuous, then, enables multitemporal determinations in which there is no overriding sequence, no event that is prior to another, absent in the present. Sequential temporalities, and even cyclical ones, are only effective in localized and specific situations. Such would be situations when there is need, for example, to draw out an agricultural calendar. The visible past of the cosmos belongs to a different temporal plane than the one of human interests and predictions, and flattens out the relevance and priorities enforced by sequential or phased temporal structures and hierarchies. I note here that there is no prevalent historical time in the ancient Andes, no comprehensive records or representations of the pre-Columbian past, no sequential lineage of kings or Inkas, who were taken to always hang around, continuing to rule in unruly political parallelisms.[1] And, without representation, there are no bodies in a past that is no longer, no bodies absolutely fixed in their appearance. Rather, human bodies turn into mummies, stones, mountains, and other material presences of a cosmic past.

Colonialism in the Andes is a temporal catastrophe. Sequential time is imposed as a justification of it. Suddenly the Inka were in a past that is no longer, and a Spanish world replaces them in the present and projects toward the future. This is the theme of colonial didactic paintings that depict a linear sequence of Inka and Spanish kings.[2] These paintings are emblematic in that they show the convergence between the imposition of linear time, colonial power, and the visual construction of indigenous bodies. Here the colonial origins and context of the modern, perceptual construction of race in the Andes are exposed: race as the artificial fixity of bodily appearance, so that the colonized and racialized are trapped in an irrecuperable, static past, excluded from the present. Yet this temporal colonization did not quite gel in colonial Andean visual registers.

One of the first vistas of colonial Cuzco, the former capital of the Inka empire, seen from above, is a painting of the earthquake that destroyed the city in 1650. This painting adheres to colonial sequential time but also, according to a cosmological aesthetic interpretation, conveys multiple temporalities. Patrick Hajovsky, in his essay "Shifting Panoramas: Contested Visions of Cuzco's 1650 Earthquake," offers a detailed analysis of the irreducible visions and multi-temporalities in the painting.[3] He shows that the earthquake exposes temporal parallelisms and localities, it reveals the Inka world very much present and alive alongside Catholic rituals. Hajovsky's analysis of the visible disarticulations of the colonial world is extensive. Here I note only one aspect of his discussion. Prominent in the painting is a sculpture of Christ on the cross surrounded by priests and other townspeople. This procession is happening as the earthquake makes the city crumble. A double, irreconcilable meaning of the cross becomes relevant. In Andean pre-Columbian religions the cross is a *chakana*, a bridge or site of cosmic transitions.[4] Hajovsky connects this bridge to *Wiracocha*, the god that mobilizes and recreates *pacha*, rather than creating it from nothing and having the power to fully destroy it. Earthquakes are cataclysmic cosmic transitions, elemental events that reveal the power of *Wiracocha* (more so than that of the Christian god). Hajovsky writes about *pacha* in this colonial context: "Spanish magistrates failed to fully recognize this Andean cosmic paradigm, in which disorder is part of the process that moves toward harmonious beginnings rather than being a sign of divine judgment" (2018: 39). The sculpture of Christ carried in the earthquake, then, becomes disarticulated, spectrally released from its colonial Catholic world and claimed by the cosmic forces of *pacha* and by Wiracocha. Infused by the in-stilled movement of the re-creation of the cosmos in a turbulence of earth, Christ is called *Tayta* Temblores, "father earthquake," a name that still refers to the sculpture guarded within the cathedral of the modern Inka city.

I am interested in the repercussions of the Andean cosmological aesthetics exemplified in this painting as a colonial rendition of *ñaupa pacha*, or cosmic time, and its temporal disseminations. Specifically, I turn to the disruption of the structure of the visibility of race articulated within a sequential temporality, to the different aesthetic processes evoked by the earthquake painting and by the portrayal of the series of Inka and Spanish kings.[5] As I have noted, colonial visual registers, with their orientation toward the production of social visibilities, racialization in particular, entail a narrowing of vision. They visualize the fixity of bodily appearance, and involve a sensing of paralysis, which is also a paralysis of sensing, in which non-white bodies are in a "no longer," stunted by the present and unable to form futural projections. Latin American aesthetics, through trends such as "costumbrismo," "indigenismo," and what Silvia Rivera Cusicanqui calls "miserabilismo," has developed an elaborate visuality to convey and reinforce the temporal determinants of race and the reduction of the visible they imply, perhaps beginning with the serial painting I just discussed.

At the same time, this aesthetic tradition also shows a multiplicity of registers that constantly undermine the temporal determinations of the visual construction of race, setting into play other kinds of seeing, and other kinds of time, through cosmic temporalizations like *ñaupa pacha*, that do not fit within the structure of past/present/future. In the Andes, in my view, this involves a showing of a visible cosmic past as a spectral rendition that unsettles the fixity of racist presentations. The photographs of Martín Chambi in the 1920s and 1930s, for example, are of light and its play on earthy surfaces, bringing forth the elemental appearance of *pacha* and the cosmic atmospheres of Inka architecture.[6]

Sponsored by Peruvian, lettered and colonialist classes, he practically invented the photographic rendition of indigenous Andean bodies, and his

Figure 3.1 *Wiñay Wayna, Cusco 1941* (belongs to the archaeological park of Machupicchu), Martín Chambi Jiménez. Chambi Family Collection.

Figure 3.2 *Queromarca Woman with Child in the Study, Cusco approximately 1925*, Martín Chambi Jiménez. Chambi Family Collection.

work in this regard still is an unavoidable referent for racial visual constructions of indigeneity. Yet, perhaps unseen by the dominant classes, he infuses these pictures with light in a way that contests such constructions, and even with elemental force in a cosmic in-stilled movement that reveals indigenous Andeans as belonging to a cataclysmic creation older than a past that is no longer.[7]

The visual presentations of race belong to colonial sensuous identifications that discern the difference between the human and the non-human. This involves the perception not only of skin color but also of physical manifestations of bodies stuck within a sequential ordering of time. What is seen in this way can be extensive: facial expressions, bodily posture, clothing, and emotional states (like nostalgia, anger, and frustration); as well as constellations of these, configuring layered appearances like those of being educated, assimilated, and even rebellious and resistant.

In this chapter I study a modern/colonial construction of the perception of anticolonial resistant agents, and the corresponding dehumanization of the oppressed who do not fit within this sensuous projection. I focus on this construction as it is perniciously operative in the formation of movements of liberation. At the end of the chapter, I return to "cosmological aesthetics" as a way of articulating an alternative mode of perceiving resistant bodies. I argue that the cosmic temporality of *ñaupa pacha*, as operative in Inka architecture and the earthquake painting, arises here again, but in contemporary artworks depicting oppressed, racialized bodies.

Perceptions and presentations of the bodies of the oppressed as stuck in the past, passive, violent, and in need of redemption influence the development of anticolonial movements (ranging from revolutionary guerrillas to social justice organizations). In this respect, I focus on the bodily aesthetics of the social formation of resistance in terms of racial and colonialist visual registers in order to shed light on what I call the "social closure of the political." By this term I mean the ways in which perceptions of those deemed non-human enforce exclusions from both dominant oppressive systems and liberatory sociopolitical movements that are supposed to represent the oppressed. I emphasize how perceptual patterns act as gatekeepers not only for dominant institutions of the state and the economy but also for belonging into groups identifiable as "resistant," "liberatory," or "decolonial." In other words, I recognize in the socialization of resistance a locus of oppression articulated aesthetically.[8]

My discussion brings together perceptual registers of resistant bodies operative in different geo-historical sites: the spectacle of violence during the Shining Path rebellion in Peru from the perspective of Mariátegui's "indigenista" aesthetics, and forms of exclusion of undocumented immigrant women by movements of "women's empowerment" in the United States. These two cases bring to the fore the "social closure of the political," a closure that is rooted in the sphere of colonial modes of sensuousness. In response to this, I propose a "cosmological aesthetics of resistance" through an analysis of María Lugones's decolonial feminism and Laura Aguilar's photography.

Optics of Resistance and Liberation: Whose Bodies Are in the Mass Graves?

One's body, its color, features, its movement, and the culture expressed in its movement and clothes, all up for mistrust and inspection. One's voice, the accent of one's voice, the culture in one's speech, deeds, ways inspected, over and over by those one would call one's own, or—alternatively conceived—those one has reason to think might be one's own people. (Lugones, 2003: 33)

In the 1980s and 1990s, during and after the "time of fright" or *Manchaytimpu*, it was common to find empty towns in the Andes with adjacent mass graves containing the corpses of their indigenous inhabitants. Bodies were dumped in such graves as the result of what the Peruvian "Commission of Truth and Reconciliation" describes as "the insanity of the Shining Path and the brutal repression of the military and the police forces" (*Commission for Truth and Reconciliation* 2003: 67). In these killings, it is unclear whether the perpetrator was the state or the Shining Path. Both the state and revolutionaries deemed indigenous lives dispensable. Often indigenous people or "campesinos" had opted to not participate in the war, to not take sides, a decision that cost them their lives at the hands of other natives and mestizos. These senseless massacres manifest the drive to annihilate those who are not one's enemies in anticolonial revolutionary contexts. I underscore the Shining Path's practice of murdering non-committed indigenous peoples, especially in view of its revolutionary goal to disarm the economic, political, and social structures that oppress them. And I am interested in the colonialist aesthetics and perceptual forms of this perplexing violence waged by the oppressed upon the oppressed for the sake of their liberation.

Peruvians in the 1980s and 1990s were constantly exposed to the spectacle of this specific violence. In particular, an image of the "revolutionary Indian" was propagated by the Shining Path meant to overcome entrenched, colonialist representations of the "Indian" as passive, complicit with their exploitation. Yet, this image only made sense in its contrast to images of "Indians" as lacking in revolutionary discipline, courage, and character. So, the Shining Path aesthetic drew from images of "Indians" as passive, reflecting bodies that had to be transfigured or eliminated for the sake of the revolution. The possibility of the aesthetic transfiguration of "Indian" bodies legitimized the guerrilla movement. That is, the aesthetics and violence of the Shining Path continued to depend on the colonial legacies of the construction of indigenous bodies (including their manifestation of affect, temperament, and character), even if as something to be overcome. This perceptual contraption of anticolonial resistance fuels a bloody colonialist mechanism through which the inspection of oppressed bodies is implicated in revolutionary violence. Can there be an anticolonial resistance that does not entail violence suffered at the hands (and eyes) of "one's own people"?[9]

Mariátegui's Image of the "Revolutionary Indian" and the Limits of Theory

> I think it is impossible to apprehend in one theory the entire panorama of the contemporary world. That it is impossible above all, to fix its movement in one theory. We have to explore it episode by episode, facet by facet. Our judgment and imagination will always feel to be lagging behind the totality of the phenomenon. (Mariátegui, 1998: 48)

Mariátegui's classic text *Seven Essays for the Interpretation of the Peruvian Reality* has defined the Peruvian social consciousness for almost a century. It in many ways inaugurates anticolonial social critique in Latin America, and it is also written with revolutionary intent. However, the book's guiding assumption is that social critiques should not control movements of resistance, since their study of oppression is reductive with respect to the conditions of resistance.[10] Although contextually effective in theorizing structural oppression, theoretical social logics and identities nevertheless afix social relations that are otherwise fluid, and raise limited and ineffective forms of resistant social consciousness. When theory overdetermines resistance movements, absolutist and exclusionary social forms (like social identities, for example) can claim to be the vehicles of "revolution." Mariátegui fears that this overdetermination will fall prey to a social determinism, projecting abstract oppositional social logics (like class or racial conflicts) as the path to "liberation," and resulting instead in authoritarianism. In this sense, the *Seven Essays* does not strive to be a coherent text, since theory and resistance are to be kept in tension.

In terms of anticolonial social theory, the well-known essay "The Problem of the Indian" attacks ingrained colonialist tendencies to socially redeem the "Indian." Redemption is a common solution to the much discussed "problem": namely, the existence of a subhuman group that cannot participate in or contribute to modern civilization. Mariátegui critiques legal, pedagogical, and humanitarian redemptive mechanisms meant to assimilate the "Indians" into the modern, Peruvian nation. He does not believe that assimilation into the state and its social orders undoes the dehumanization of indigenous peoples, because dehumanization is tied to the entanglement of race and capitalism as a global structure. In other words, in his view the liberation of the colonized cannot be a process of socialization into modernity (an insight that anticipates Lugones's decolonial feminism, as discussed later). In this sense, the theoretical contribution of the *Seven Essays* is to reveal the persistent colonial structures that define the social and political constitution of modern Peru in a global context, and the inefficacy of socialization as the redemption of the oppressed, indigenous peoples in particular.[11]

The other, less studied aspect of the *Seven Essays* is concerned with the possibility of resistance, and is intended to galvanize the indigenous populations as revolutionary agents rather than socialize or assimilate them into a modern nation.[12] For many other Marxists at the time, there appeared to be a social and historical logic accessible theoretically that could give the proletariat a sense of identity and revolutionary purpose. While affirming the revolutionary power of the oppressed, Mariátegui observed, however, that the postcolonial character of Peruvian reality does not enable "revolutionary Indians" to arise out of a theoretical reflection about their own material conditions. In this respect, Mariátegui shows that the Peruvian colonial social and historical structures do not abide by coherent and systemic socialities because they are defined by temporal simultaneity (a palimpsest of economies and historical phases) rather than by a developmental and progressive temporal logic mobilizing a single "human" civilizational process (the latter being a modern/colonialist illusion based on the invisibility of the colonized). Mariátegui invents the "revolutionary Indian" as he gives up on the possibility of a socialized resistant consciousness, one that is understood, and understands itself, theoretically within a modern/colonial social order, that is opposed to a system, and that can insert itself in a revolutionary and progressive historical trajectory.[13]

Especially in the Latin American postcolonial juncture, then, the formation of a critical consciousness through theory and social critique, and the socializations they envision, falls short as a condition for anticolonial resistance. In view of this, Mariátegui invents (rather than theorizes), poetizes even, a "revolutionary Indian" driven by a "myth" or religious faith in order to awaken a combative spirit without ultimate social intelligibility or theoretical backing, and with the intent to overturn the system in power with no definite end in view.[14] His particular "myth" envisions the recovery of suppressed pre-Columbian social and economic forms in a backward movement of revolutionary, not assimilationist, redemption of the "Indian." This myth does not reveal a social and historical logic. By giving protagonism to the "revolutionary Indian" through myth, Mariátegui intends, rather, to push the social and economic tensions of Peru to a boiling point, to an indeterminate revolutionary event.[15]

At this juncture, Mariátegui's religious proclivities become problematically apparent:

The religious spirit is not tightened except by combat and struggle. . . . The passivity with which the Indians allowed themselves to be catechized, without comprehending the catechism, spiritually weakened Catholicism in Peru. (2012: 181)

Here he implies that "Indians" have no capacity to have faith, they don't have a combative spirit, they are, as colonialism has always stated, passive, static creatures—a defining characteristic of their inferior race that was, as I noted, visually constructed in the colonial era. The socialist, redemptive myth, then, entails a transfiguration of the "Indian" spirit, a necessary initiation into resistance that complements theory. "Indians" (a pervasive colonial racial construction in the first place) are turned into socialist revolutionaries, and the latter liberate "Indians." This is a self-reinforcing circle of redemption that claims to circumvent the socialization that other modern projects for redeeming "Indians" imply. Yet, this is a difficult and dangerous claim. This is evident retroactively, since Mariátegui's myth anticipates the Shining Path.

Myth and theory together configure a revolutionary consciousness in such a way that a transfigurative initiation into resistance appears necessary. But isn't this initiation, mediated by the invented figure of the "revolutionary Indian," its own form of socialization? That is, an imposition of how such a figure should appear, both socially and sensuously, so that it fits into the revolutionary movement? In this context, indigenous bodies continue to be inspected, and a "social closure of the political" is instantiated in an inevitable double, perceptual exclusion of the oppressed: from the system of oppression and from movements of liberation. Does this mean, continuing colonial visual practices, that "Indians" inevitably must be inspected, mistrusted, tested in their revolutionary stamina? Is this Mariátegui's intent when he stated "Marxism-Leninism will open the *shining path* to the revolution"? A long path to the "time of fright," *manchaytimpu*, such as the massacre of one's own people? And doesn't this socialization imply colonialist perceptual registers for the discernment of resistant bodies?

I interpret Mariátegui as attentive to the aesthetic dimension of anticolonial revolt (literary and imagistic art in particular) as a site where the initiation of the oppressed into resistance is at stake. Revolutionary aesthetics begins where theory reaches its limits: that is, in the unearthing of the conditions for resistance.[16] In my view, however, this aesthetics can have a colonial and racist legacy that emphasizes the inspection of markings in the body as revelatory of the spiritual and moral characteristics of the oppressed. As I noted earlier, in the sixteenth century the Spanish colonial visible rendition of indigenous bodies was decided: these bodies were to be represented as static, as if carved out of stone, and impenetrable. This visuality reflected indigenous peoples as passive, stuck in the past, unable to join the progressive movement of history, always behind the Spanish, needing to be redeemed. It also provided an affective perceptual register connected to petrification: impotence, sadness, nostalgia, frustration. This aesthetic of colonized bodies is the background for Mariátegui's search for an image of the revolutionary "Indian," both in literature and in paintings, like Sabogal's "India del Collao" I discussed in the first chapter.[17] I suggest that for Mariátegui this kind of image can elicit a process of inspection of the "Indian" soul through her body.

The inspection looks for the capacity for a pure combative spirit with no need for socialization into resistance (not only socially unmediated, but also disruptive of linear logics of history) in the path toward a revolutionary event. This is Mariátegui's unique approach to "indigenismo." In the *Seven Essays*, in the sections concerned with the determination of a literary image of the "Indian" in particular, he searches for an affective and aesthetic transformation of the "Indian" from being paralyzed by nostalgia for an irretrievable past to invigorated by a nostalgia that disseminates the present. This could be applied to the "India" in Sabogal's painting. The person in the image seems to be static like a mountain, glassy eyed and evasive in her stare. But is she passive or waiting to launch? Is she weighed down by nostalgia or is her nostalgia an existential protest? Is her solidity potency or impotency? How does one understand her stillness?[18]

Mariátegui's "Indigenismo" becomes a fiction without any relation to a fixed reality; and it is ambivalent, as I noted in Chapter 1. In his aesthetics, instead of offering a view that fixes the "indio" to a so-called passivity, Mariátegui opens an infinite approach to the possibility of sighting a pure transformational and revolutionary potency in indigenous bodies. That is, a potency to transform and overcome a modern/colonial world. I should add, although in passing, that in Mariátegui's ambivalent resistive aesthetics this potency is ultimately nothing identifiable, it is something like pure motion, a cosmic leap, perhaps. And, I suspect that, for him, this "nothing" allows the "contemporary world" to always outpace theory. In his aesthetics, reaching toward pure potency, Mariátegui cannot be reconciled with the Shining Path. The latter wanted to see something definite, a social embodiment of resistance, positive evidence of a specific revolution in the bodies of the oppressed. Yet here, Mariátegui's aesthetics can be developed further in between the limits of theory and the elusive movement of the world, as he broaches a "cosmological aesthetics" I expanded on in Chapter 1 in the search for a sighting of resistance.[19]

Manchaytimpu and the Social Closure of the Political

I understand *manchaytimpu* (the time of fright) as also the time of racialized border crossers whose lives are dispensable, and who are not just oppressed by the law and state. In this respect, immigrant women, *indocumentadas*, can be drawn to organizations that procure jobs for them as "domésticas." Often, they are supported if they commit to attend "self-esteem workshops," such as for "women's empowerment," and submit to inspection "through a point system that incentivized their participation in marches, protests, civil disobedience, etc" (E. Grajeda 2016). That is, if they join a specific spectacle of resistance. Latinx activists running such organizations, oriented by intersectional analyses of oppression, can be committed to "change the minds" of immigrant women from south of the US border in order to "challenge gendered hierarchies in the family, particularly with respect to their husbands" (E. Grajeda 2016).

This story, narrated by Adela, sheds light on this dynamic:

> she asked me why I had missed a meeting, and I told her that my husband had gotten home later than usual and so I had to prepare dinner for him. She responded sarcastically, "so, when you leave the home you also take the refrigerator with you?" . . . She can run her household any way she wants but she shouldn't expect us to do the same. What we do in our homes and with our husbands is none of her business, and it shouldn't be even talked about at meetings or events. Those things are private. (E. Grajeda 2016)

Adela's missing a meeting was a betrayal that warranted inspection of her intersectional understanding and embodiment of her oppression as a woman of color, and of her commitment to her own empowerment.[20] The sarcastic remark demeaned both her and her husband, and assumed an abusive power differential between them. Adela's response is revealing. She does not disagree with the critical analyses of her systemic oppression or with the goal of "women's empowerment." She does not even deny that there might be oppression in her marriage. Her critique is, rather, directed at the demand that she be transparent to the gaze of the activist, and at the expectation that her private and intimate relations be exposed and turned into a prop for a redemptive liberation.

Adela appears to see herself as doubly oppressed: not only disenfranchised and erased by dominant economic, political, and social structures, but also excluded from "proper" liberatory socialities attached to an image of the empowered woman she has crashed into at the north side of the border. One oppression is justified by the preservation of the system in place, the other by the possibility of liberation.

For her, dominant and resistive social formations not only intersect but also complement and blend with each other as a complex mechanism of oppression.[21] This mechanism is evident when one notes that "women's empowerment" is used as yet another gatekeeping measure to exclude immigrant women from the workforce. Yet it is invisible from critical perspectives that do not understand that resistance can be a violent form of socialization; that is, perspectives from which resistance and oppression are clearly delineated and oppositional.

In fact, it seems that Adela's understanding of the social manifestation of the power that oppresses her is more accurate and nuanced than the mistrusting activist's, since she senses the enmeshment of oppression and resistance, especially as manifest in the instantiations and application of liberatory theory. From her perspective, staying at home, and her defense of privacy, are to be read differently. It is not a resignation to being oppressed, or remaining in a space without oppression. It is a stance reflecting awareness that her double oppression can be faced through enactments of the quotidian. In these enactments, resistance germinates in the intricate, embodied, and affective textures of both cultural traditions (that are not validated by or formed through theoretical stances) and histories of displacement. In the introduction I analyzed this form of resistance in terms of "propitiation." This is a resistance that does not depend on inspections resulting in social initiations or exclusions, as I will show in my discussion of Lugones later.

Adela is oppressed both by the state and by the liberatory institutionalization of theories of "women's empowerment" on the basis of her race, gender, class, national origin, ethnic background, among other socialities. Preserving the difference between these two foci of oppression is important in order to underscore that the dehumanization of Adela entails the denial of both belonging to and resisting the system that oppresses her. This complex process is aesthetic, has colonial roots, and deems lives dispensable through dehumanizing forms of perception that complicate the meaning of strict racial markings. Language, accents, affective constitution, posture, demeanor, fashion, or, markings of ignorance, ethnicity, lack of education, atavism, rurality are some of the elements that modulate the demarcation of the human and non-human in oppressed bodies in such a way that the oppression of the oppressed by the oppressed (even those sharing the same "race") is enabled for the sake of liberation.[22]

This involves a keen inspecting gaze judging the oppressed not-brown-enough, not-black-enough, not-from-the-right-barrio, not-of-the-right-gender, not-queer-enough, not-from-the-north-side-of-the-border (as in Adela's case) to stand against the system. This gaze configures socializations by exclusions that easily become habitual and trivialized in the organization of "social movements." Yet, in order to destabilize this gaze, one can always ask, for example: How is this gaze socially mediated? How was Adela turned into an image of the undocumented immigrant? How is liberation as a process of socialization of immigrant women dependent on that image?

Latina immigrants, haunted by the label "illegals," are difficult to imagine in their homes without seeing them through the lens of the difference between the human and non-human. In fact immigrant "homes," as a possible space of intimacy, the transmission of culture, and the initiation into and exploration of socialities, is most invisible to gazes that require immigrants to be socialized in terms of assimilation into the state and dominant culture, or of initiation into resistance. I surmise that Adela experienced this invisibility as a dehumanizing form of oppression.

In my view, this invisibility also draws the Mexican painter Aliza Nisenbaum to enter into latinx immigrant homes and, collaboratively, paint their quotidian lives. In *La Talaverita, Sunday Morning NY Times*, 2016, she paints an impossible image, or at least an image that strains the visible registers that have come to determine our sight, making it leap, lapse, become disoriented. The painting is domestic and quotidian, but at the same time deeply unsettling. The scene it reveals is propitiatory, resistant. Perhaps the way the body of a brown latina woman spreads on a couch on a Sunday morning, completely relaxed, is too much to take in, especially given that our eyes are used to settling on images of such bodies at work, cleaning, rather than carelessly enjoying a living room. For me, the image of the latina immigrant as a *doméstica* is evoked in this painting implicitly so as to be dispelled, which makes one uneasy.

This dispelling is intensified when one recognizes that the socially dominant image of the *doméstica* also confines brown women's bodies to house chores, even when not at work and at home, so that there should be no leisure, no possibility of relaxation for them. This image also fixes the view of brown women as helplessly subjected to men, of working for men. The painting is unsettling in this respect as well: the man in the painting, a husband or partner maybe, occupies less space in the couch, and his body is more tense and more proper. The contrast between his body and the woman's body adds to the tension in the painting, it challenges the expectations of gender roles that were projected on Adela, for example.

Yet, the painter draws attention to another aspect of the painting: the sprawled woman is reading *The New York Times* (it is unclear whether her partner is as well) on a Sunday morning. The paper, an emblem of progressive and liberal

Figure 3.3 *La Talaverita, Sunday Morning NY Times*, 2016, Oil on linen, 88 x 68 inches (223.5 x 172.7 cm). © Aliza Nisenbaum. Image courtesy of the artist and Anton Kern Gallery, N.Y.

intellectualism, is the focus of the work. Does it fit in the brown woman's hands? Does she have the education, the liberal social and cultural capital to hold it? In this moment the gap between the latinx woman, including the visual codes that are usually projected on her, and the possibility of understanding both her oppression and proper resistant demands is most marked. This gap is where Adela felt her oppression coming from the need for socialization into resistance. The image of the immigrant *doméstica*, or of brown woman in general, does not include reading *The New York Times*, especially not like in the painting: with easiness, as part of the quotidian, as if reading what is already obvious and expected. The newspaper is gleaned and falls on the ground as if it had nothing left to say.

The painting is a visual challenge: blindspots become apparent, dominant modes of visual social identification are fractured, one leaps from brown bodies, to *The New York Times*, to the implicit image of the *doméstica*, without gathering a coherent view. In this disorientation, it seems to me, the easygoing, relaxed body of the woman becomes most distressing to colonizing gazes as an embodiment not only of resilience but also of a kind of uncanny resistance that emerges atmospherically from the confusion and dissemination of visual registers of oppression and socialized resistance.

The woman's body, in fact, appears to be floating, only halfway on the couch. In the background wall, the image of la Virgen de Guadalupe is also floating turned toward the woman as if they shared an otherworldly connection. The icon of Guadalupe, as Anzaldúa writes, is also a knot of disparate histories, colonizing, and resistant appropriations that cannot be parsed within strict social intelligibilities and clean separations between oppression and resistance. The propitiatory resistance that emerges from this knotting is perhaps the one that latinx immigrant women come to embody, from a past that is heterogeneous, without overriding sense, that resists logics of opposition and linear temporality—a cosmic past perhaps? The painting arises from the mosaic-like, Mexican-inspired colorful and busy wall behind the couch, where the virgin is painted. The wall is reminiscent of the style of pottery called talavera, a colonial artform that emerges in the violent convergence of Spanish and indigenous hands and clay.

The cases of Adela and the Andean indigenous peoples targeted by the Shining Path show that anticolonial resistance not only seeks to dismantle social and political structures of oppression rooted in colonialism and its modern legacies. It is also an aesthetically mediated process of forced and marginalizing socialization to be critiqued in its own right through decolonizing lenses. I call the denial of the possibility for the oppressed to articulate experiences, senses of self, and critical stances through both dominant and resistive social logics, "the social closure of the political." In this "closure," those who are doubly oppressed like Adela are excluded from participating in processes of establishment, enforcement, and transformation of political power due to the multifocal burgeoning of dehumanizing social logics read from oppressed bodies. This aesthetic problem cannot be studied by critical approaches focused only on dominant/systematic oppression coming from the racial state while bracketing the socialization inherent in the formation of social movements. It demands, rather, an aesthetic turn, one in which the visuality of oppressed bodies is at stake.

What Does a Cosmological Aesthetics Have to Do with Resistance? An Interpretation of Lugones's "Decolonial Feminism"[23]

I suggest that the tension between theory and resistance at the center of Mariátegui's *Seven Essays* is key to Lugones's text "Toward a Decolonial Feminism." This is manifest in Lugones's following distinction: "I call the *analysis* of racialized, capitalist, gender oppression 'coloniality of gender.' I call the *possibility* of overcoming the coloniality of gender 'decolonial feminism'" (2010: 747, italics mine). This section is a schematic exegesis of this statement aimed to understand how decolonial feminism figures the possibility of resistance, a possibility that in my view has joint aesthetic and cosmological aspects.

The "Coloniality of Gender" as Theoretical, Critical Analysis.[24]

Aníbal Quijano theorizes race as a variable and visible colonial construction that demarcates the difference between the human and non-human contextually, and in accordance with dynamic global labor relations within capitalism.[25] Lugones agrees with this, but goes further in making explicit that in the context of modernity/coloniality the "human" coincides with the social, and that the colonized or "non-human" are not seen as embodying or participating in the social organization of life. Quijano also retains a universalist, biologistic attachment to sexual dimorphism and reproduction as the basis of various gendered social forms, including those of women and men of color. In this respect, Lugones critically points out that Quijano leaves gender unaffected by race, and lets gender remain uncritically *within* the demarcated social/human category.

The result of this is a dimorphic register of gender that remains as a matrix to understand multifarious gender formations, while leaving undertheorized whether "non-humans" are gendered. From this perspective, even LGBTQ and intersectional social formations can come to be theorized, inhabited, and made socially intelligible on the basis of a colonialist category of human sexual dimorphism.[26] Yet, by stating "No women are colonized; no colonized females are women" (2010: 745) Lugones studies the impact of race as a colonial category on gender. As a result, she proposes that colonized females do not have gender, since they are not involved in the socialities or reproduction of "humans." They do not rest within a socially intelligible category. They are to be used, abused, dispensed with. In this way the "coloniality of gender" reveals lives that are socially and biologically worthless and unintelligible.[27]

Beyond Quijano's "coloniality of power," the "coloniality of gender," then, is a mode of theorizing that traces a legacy of colonialism where the "human" coincides with the "social," which excludes the colonized from humanity, gender, and other aspects of what Lugones calls the "modern social" within a racist/capitalist global order.[28] In this sense, this theoretical approach understands gender as a colonial imposition and as applicable only to "humans." At the same time, the demarcation of the "human" from the "non-human" is fluid, contextual, in need to be obsessively marked and re-marked. This has at least two implications.

First, echoing Mariátegui, and referring to Lugones's own struggles with white feminism and feminist intersectional theory, anticolonialism should not turn into a project of socialization. It should not become a movement of subject formation and consciousness raising, even if for liberatory purposes, because this risks concealing the character of colonialist oppression, especially in view of the difference between the "human" and "non-human" and the "social closure of the political." Socialization is not liberatory insofar as it assumes a continuum between the positionality of colonized lives and the possibility of social recognition, thus remaining blind to the efficacy of the distinction between the "human" and the "non-human." This blindness is part of the reason why social movements of resistance can turn into colonialist institutions. Here I follow Lugones insofar as anticolonial critique demands a reconsideration of social identities in modern and capitalist orders, including the kind of power exercised by and among them; as well as a reenvisioning of the social from the cosmological as a different modality of relations between social positionalities.

Liberatory socialization, as Lugones stresses, can never turn the non-human into human. Without both attending to oppression outside of the register of the human/social convergence, and making "non-humans" salient in their social unintelligibility, anticolonial movements become oppressive mechanisms. Like in Adela's case: her socialization into resistance is plagued by the operation of the distinction between the human and the non-human; the activist treats her as if her culture and experience were worthless, effectively erasing her past, at the same time that she "empowers" her. She is not only "liminal" but must turn her liminality into a social, liberatory stance. A way of expressing this, in my terms and keeping Adela's case in mind, is that the "coloniality of gender" brings to focus the "social closure of the political."

Second, the "coloniality of gender" runs into the same aporia as Mariátegui's indigenous socialism. Lugones states: "the coloniality of gender hides the resister as fully informed as a native of communities under cataclysmic attack" (2010: 749). How is resistance possible when both systemic and liberatory socialities are complementary and oppressive, when the illusion of an initiation into liberatory socialities conceals the persistence of dehumanization, when the social support and social consciousness provided by anticolonial theories end up participating in colonialist mechanisms? How can one resist in the indeterminacy of both oppressive and oppressed socialities that interpenetrate, and when the demarcation of the human undergoes variances and intensifications? Or, in Mariátegui's terms, when theory always lags behind the movement of the contemporary world? It is not enough to suggest to continue doing theory with more awareness of its limitations and shortcomings. What is needed, in Lugones's view, is to assume the "coloniality of gender" as a portal to distinct form of resistance, and as having to be overcome.

Decolonial Feminism and the Cosmos/*Pacha*

The "coloniality of gender" critiques theories that use gender when analyzing colonial forms of interlocking and intermeshed social oppressions, engages the "modern" modality of the social as coinciding with the "human" and as a colonial construction, and reveals a level of oppression of those deemed "non-human" that cannot be overturned through projects of social integration and recognition. I interpret the "coloniality of gender" as showing that projects of resistance invested in such social integrations and recognitions, even if the socialities at play are those of resistant movements, fall apart and become oppressive given that their emphasis on socialization cannot heal the divide between the "human" and "non-human."

In my terms, the "coloniality of gender" shows the "non-human" within the conditions of the "social closure of the political" in which resistance appears impossible because it seems tangled up with a colonialist and modern process of socialization. The "coloniality of gender," then, reaches a limit that perhaps can be articulated through a question that points toward "decolonial feminism": Is there a mode of anticolonial resistance emerging from those at the mercy of the arbitrary imposition of the "non-human" determination that does not involve socialization, does not seek intelligibility within "modern" determinations of social orders, and ultimately exceeds the colonial framings of the difference between the "human" and "non-human"?

"Decolonial feminism" overcomes the "coloniality of gender" both as a theoretical stance and as concealing the possibility of non-socializing resistance. It is an interruption of a mode of anticolonial critical *analysis* and is not contained within theoretical trends or academic institutions. Decolonial feminists see the oppressed as resistant, regardless of the support of the socializations implied by critical consciousness-raising and initiations. Instead, they see oppressing-resisting as an active relation in everyday practices of the oppressed without the intent and will to socialize, a relation that lets possibilities of resistance surface.[29]

Decolonial feminism releases the "social" from the "modern," racist convergence of the social and the "human." It, rather, reads "the social from the cosmologies that inform it" and, thus, finds different modalities of inhabiting social categories and the power relations between them. Lugones elucidates this in view of the untranslatability of the Quechua term *chachawarmi*, which could be mistranslated as *manwoman* (even though *chacha* is usually translated as "man" and *warmi* as "woman"). *Chachawarmi*, however, is not understandable in relation to gender because it does not refer to individual social characteristics. It, rather, refers to a mode of communal being where incarnations of social positionalities are constituted by shifting reciprocal relations that are interwoven within the generation, destruction, and creation of the cosmos or *pacha*. The same individual can sometimes be *chacha* and sometimes be *warmi*, since the communal expectations tied to these terms need to be fulfilled not as an individual identity or agency but as participation in *ayni*, a dynamic cosmic principle that oversees the balance of reciprocal social formations. Following Silvia Rivera Cusicanqui's notion of *ch'ixi* in order to express *ayni*, an individual is woman and not woman, man and not man, and neither, because only the dynamic community embedded in the cosmos can lay claim to these, and all other, socialities in their reciprocity. Since *ch'ixi* does not involve processes of persistent selves in social formation, Lugones lets go of the "self" as the site of an identity in order to reenvision participation in community. At the same time, the cosmos as a web of reciprocities escapes the colonial differentiation of the "human" and "non-human" as the basis for the articulation of socialities.

In the draw toward community, one leaps across socialities in supportive relations to one another. In weaving community, *not* being is as important as being "man" or "woman"—or any particular social incarnation. *Ayni* allows for the "(k)not" of being and not being that binds social relations and communities together.[30] It is the power of the community, a force of transformation and renewal as much as it is of balance. *Ayni* does not belong to "theory" or an indigenous "myth." It is the unintelligible movement of the world that beats theorization. Even our imagination lags behind it. In *ayni* socialities are not absolutely hierarchically ordered, fixed, nor do they become colonially dehumanizing. If one attempts to claim socialities and turn them into mechanisms of exclusion as in colonialism/modernity, one would stop individuals from participating in *ayni* and become a *misti*, a colonialist oppressor. If *ayni* is preserved, then the community remains embedded in the cosmos or *pacha*: (not) night/ (not) day, (not) earth/ (not) sky, (not) water/ (not) stone, none of them and all of them, (k)notted, at once. *Ayni* is perceptually manifest in the elemental, when stone is and is not light, for example, and accessible through a "cosmological aesthetics."

I suggest that decolonial feminism reveals resistance by assuming a social/cosmological, rather than social/modern, basis. There are two irreducible, simultaneous social orderings, the "modern" social and the social/cosmological. In the former identities are formed along oppositional power dynamics, in binary logics of oppression and resistance, even if recognized as intersectional. In the latter (k)notting becomes an ordering social principle through which spaces of reciprocities and conflict emerge reciprocally without binary oppositions that entrap individuals in delimitations of identity, enabling social formations along non-dominant differences (or as anti-structures, in Lugones's terms)[31]. Resistance is the difference between these two modalities of socialities and subjective configurations:

> Resistance is the tension between subjectification (the forming/informing of the subject) and active subjectivity, that minimal sense of agency required for the oppressing/resisting relation being an active one, without appeal to the maximal sense of agency of the Modern subject. (2015: 367)

Active subjectivity is an enactment in a reciprocal field that leaps across social positionalities, without constituting a self, abiding by social hierarchies and weaponizing social categories as tools for oppression and inspection.[32] Its force comes from the community, *ayni*, and ultimately the cosmos, rather than from an agential self. In terms of the introduction to this book, it yields a propitiatory resistance. *Subjectification* is the way the colonial/capitalist/racist state enforces the social constitution of subjects on the basis of the difference between the "human" and "non-human," reducing the oppressed to the "social closure of the political" as studied by "coloniality of gender." The *colonial difference* is the irreducible spacing between active subjectivity and subjectification, where they come together and apart, sometimes blurring their difference.

Anticolonial, cosmological resistance, bringing Lugones's decolonial feminism together with the elucidation of resistance in this book, is the force that opens and keeps open this spacing between *active subjectivity* and *subjectification*. Resistance, in this sense, is not willed but propitiatory; it is not someone's mission. It is what happens when one participates in *ayni*, in community, while under siege by the "social closure of the political," when the cosmos breaks through as a (k)notting force of a social order other than the modern social and its investment in demarcations of the human.

Lugones states about those whose lives are aligned with the (k)notting of the cosmos "the movement of these bodies and relations does not repeat itself. It does not become static or ossified. Everything and everyone continues to respond to power and responds much of the time resistantly" (2015: 369). Thus, she finds resistance in the "colonial difference" between the violent subjectifications that theory elucidates and the lived participation in a cosmos that, through reciprocity, supports community while allowing people to be and not be their social identities (as in *chachawarmi*). Returning to the first part of this book, I call this cosmological/communal force of generation, destruction, and creation a "(k)notting": that is, the emptiness of intertwining.[33]

Decolonial Feminism as Cosmological Aesthetics

In my discussion of the Shining Path, of Mariátegui's "image of the revolutionary Indian," and of the perception of the undocumented immigrant, the "social closure of the political" appears grounded in aesthetic practices, in perceptions and presentations of the bodies of the oppressed, and in the possibility of perceiving the oppressed as resistant. Here I interpret Lugones's "decolonial feminism" not as theory but as an aesthetic intervention that makes visible *ayni* and the *cosmos*, and thus the "colonial difference" and anticolonial, propitiatory, cosmological resistance. This is an intervention in the perception of socialities, visibility in particular, in order to disrupt an "inspective gaze" informed by colonialism and racialization, and driven by suspicion about the humanity of the oppressed.[34] I am interested in this gaze as it is oriented toward the oppressed from the perspective of those who are oppressed but belong within socialities deemed resistant, inspecting whether the oppressed can be socially initiated into resistance.

Lugones explains this inspection as a search for "solidity,"[35] as an aesthetic phenomenon. To see someone as solid is to perceive them as supported by a social structure, which comes through in skin tone, gender, posture, tone of voice, among other sensible markings. Solidity seems at first to be a matter of individual presence and self-positioning, but it is actually the result of the way others look at someone. The appearance of "solidity" is rooted in the perception of a coherent identity. In the case of those supported by systemic power, "solidity" means competency in dominant socialities.

The "solid" oppressed is sensibly different, but is also discerned through inspections (like the one Adela failed). As in the case of the transformation of nostalgia in Mariátegui, the body of the solid-oppressed appears in its overcoming of markers of non-humanity. This is a way of carrying and re-signifying one's marginalized race, ethnicity, class, gender. The solidity of the oppressed, then, involves what appears to be a metamorphosis of the body that engages a non-dominant, yet supportive, resistant social logic. I include here fashion, body art, bodily movement, and so on. Liberatory activists and scholars can cultivate "solidity," including assuming theoretical language and critical competencies as markers of self-overcoming that are socially supported within resistant movements. Yet, both kinds of solidities involve logics of exclusion, and together enforce the "social closure of the political." Lugones calls the solid-oppressed, for example, "barrio raised." There are, however, "non-solid" oppressed, as she reminds us. Undocumented immigrants like Adela, discussed earlier, can find themselves in this grouping.

The appearance and perception of oppressed solidity can be a site for a decolonial feminist aesthetic intervention that displaces the supportive social registers of such solidity in perceivable ways. This entails revealing the solidly marked oppressed body as vulnerable, as if the body that had to be hidden in order to become solid and re-signify markers of racial, ethnic, gender, and class inferiority could be simultaneously seen. The effect of this is to make apparent the dynamic of both inhabiting and not inhabiting socially mediated solid and "non-solid" bodies, human and non-human bodies, at the same time. This is a manifestation of the power of *ayni* as (k)notting linked to the social/cosmological; a power that interrupts the "modern" convergence of the "human" with the social. In this respect, this aesthetic intervention is not a socialization because of its logic of simultaneously being and not being at either side of the colonialist demarcation of the difference between the "human" and "non-human." Rather than a social continuum, at issue here are cosmic leaps and lapses: that is, not temporal development or cultivation, but a cosmic time like the one I explored in Chapter 2.

I bring Andean aesthetics to bear on the work of the latinx photographer Laura Aguilar, who dedicated much of her work to undo oppressed solidity, to reveal vulnerability and the "(k)not" I find in *ayni* as a communal glue.[36] In *Clothed/Unclothed #16* Aguilar shows the metamorphosis through fashion of latinx bodies into oppressed solidity and back. The inspecting gaze looking for solidity is deactivated in the leap between the photographs. Through a double, *ch'ixi*, gaze one finds different inhabitations of gender and ethnicity without a subtending self in formation. The artwork makes evident that the socially mediated images are still, while the oppressed leaps in and out of them. And this movement is not willed, it is physical and responds to communal reciprocities that let leaps happen in the first place.

Figure 3.4 Laura Aguilar (1959-2018), American, *Clothed/Unclothed #16*, 1992, Two Gelatin Silver prints, 20 x 16 inches each. © Laura Aguilar Trust of 2016.

Figure 3.5 Laura Aguilar (1959–2018) American, *Center #73*, 2000, Gelatin Silver print, 11 x 14 inches. © Laura Aguilar Trust of 2016.

The community is, then, lived not as a rigid social order but through the force that knots socialities. In Aguilar's photographs, vulnerability expresses this force, not in the clothed and unclothed bodies, but in the leap between them. In this reading of Aguilar through Lugones and Andean philosophy, this (k)notted vulnerability is the cosmos itself, something that cannot be fixed to an identity or socialized, nor used as a prop for liberation, yet it joins a communal *ayni*. In her later photographs, she shows the vulnerability of the cosmos by setting her body by the earth, allowing her flesh to take on the stillness of stone and vice versa.

In some of her photographs there is a stonelight reminiscent of Andean stonework, as she reveals transitions in which forms are undergoing generation, destruction, and creation at the same time. It is as if her body became a mirror of the cosmos and her photographs belonged to a "cosmological aesthetics." Human, stone, neither, Aguilar's oppressed Chicana, lesbian, disabled body becomes the site of a cosmic, vulnerable, atmospheric, and propitiatory resistance that no one can claim or deny.

4

After-Bodies

While in the last chapter I discussed the possibility of perceiving resistant bodies, through visuality in particular, now I turn to another mode of sensing that transpires through our bodies rather than through the senses.[1] This physical sentience, or *aísthesis* as discussed in the introduction, can happen in a different layer than that of sight, even sensing the metamorphic potency of bodies embedded in *ayni*, and in the "seminality" and (k)notting of the cosmos.[2] In this chapter I focus on sentient physicalities that both belong and do not belong to "our" bodies, to bodies defined as human, competent, gendered; and to bodies that provide the basis for recognition through modern/colonial social structures. I call these unsociable bodies "after-bodies." They are bodies that are not exhausted by the individuations enforced by social categories, by the organization and management of socialities for the interests of globalization and capitalism, and by the demand to abide by linear, developmental, and progressive temporalities (that is, they are not competent or able bodies).[3]

The nails, hair, and bones of mummies, like those of the Inkas who were displayed in rituals and festivities exerting social and political power, constitute presences of the kinds of physicalities I am interested in. So are processes like breathing and beating hearts, aligned with rhythms that are insistently indifferent to us but give us life. There is a physical awareness in these processes that can become an in-stilled sentience of transitions, turns, and renewals of relations with transhuman and non-objectifiable cosmic events, a sentience that even connects one to animals and trees, to sky and earth.

Aguilar's photography (as discussed in the last chapter) conjures after-bodies. Here I pursue further the sentience elicited by the photograph of her still body as stone. I sense "her" body through mine, and through an awareness of the possibility of transhuman, cosmic extension. In this chapter, I pursue this sentience mainly in terms of memory and in-stilled posture (bridging mind and body) arising from physicalities that are not simply "ours."

Traveling Bodies

At the border between Western and Amerindian philosophical frames, the Brazilian anthropologist Eduardo Viveiros de Castro explains the body as:

> affects, dispositions or capacities ... an assemblage of affects or ways of being that constitute a habitus. Between the formal subjectivity of souls and the substantial materiality of organisms there is an intermediary plane which is occupied by the body as a bundle of affects and capacities and which is the origin of perspectives. (1988: 478)

What does it mean that the body is an "assemblage of affects or ways of being"? Assemblages are without overriding sense, put together without necessary order or coherence, and are subject to re-orderings and transformations. "Ways of being" are ways of making sense of environments, of rendering their meanings, including their social meanings. They occur in bodily, affective, registers ranging from postures, gestures, and habits to values and epistemic bearings (processes that are not centered around reflection and universalist, disembodied subjectivities).

Bodies are volatile, heterogeneous, multivocal in their entanglements with the emergence of orders of meaning (ontologically, socially, politically). A gesture, a posture, a movement, a disability, an accent, or a form of racial embodiment, among other physicalities, can threaten the dominant socialities that define and make intelligible habits and values within institutional settings, for example. This can charge a resistant atmosphere and catch off guard even those that embody dominant socialities most deeply, and thus engage a form of propitiatory resistance. These "threats" that can come from marginalized bodies are not necessarily deliberate, but can re-situate oneself and others within institutionalized spaces. In this respect, I find that Viveiros de Castro's work can draw attention to a field of the physicality of shifting, embodied meaning making, and to ripples within this field that may destabilize the inhabitation of dominant social structures through a proliferation of corporeal gestures and perspectives.[4]

Viveiros de Castro's notions of "multinaturalism" and "perspectivism" are helpful at this juncture. He proposes:

> the expression, "multinaturalism," to designate one of the contrastive features of Amerindian thought in relation to Western 'multiculturalist' cosmologies. Where the latter are founded on the mutual implication of the unity of nature

and the plurality of cultures . . . the Amerindian conception would suppose a spiritual unity and a *corporeal* diversity. (1988: 470)

According to Amerindian "multinaturalism," beings (humans, animals, and, especially in Andean contexts, things) share the same valuative and metaphysical orders.[5] This sharing does not eliminate the possibility of difference, since differences arise from a physical and *aísthetic* (in my terms) sphere that gives basic orientations and situates conscious, epistemic, and agential enactments in social contexts.[6] Differences and conflicts do not happen at the level of abstract conceptual orders detached from space and time, the level of what Gloria Anzaldúa refers to as a "rational, consensual reality," but across mutable bodily registers, such as posture, affectivities, inclinations, and physical senses of connection to culture and identity. Agreement would be, then, not a matter of being of the same mind but of the same body. In this way, agreement becomes connected to physical violence, or the reduction of one body to another. This is the core insight of Viveiros de Castro's notion of "perspectivism," referring to the incommensurability of physical standpoints through which meaning is rendered, and I would add, even within one "body."[7]

Bodies assemble sticky, unpredictable, fickle physicalities that not only render meanings but also develop attachments to them in the form of affects, habits, identities, and other social investments, and corresponding epistemic dispositions, anchoring interpretive "perspectives." Yet they also lose these attachments in processes of physical realignment. Racial embodiment can be understood on this basis. The internalization of the colonizing gaze, enforced by representations of racialized bodies, yields physicalities that embody a "perspective" displaced from the present, trapped in the past, attached to a rendition of social meanings temporalized by a linear, episodic temporality.[8] As a result, even the colonized, as Fanon describes, can remain invested in the present as a closed stage that excludes her. She is alienated from her own body by the presence of competent or able bodies that seem to fit seamlessly within the present.[9] In this way, an assemblage of "affects and ways of being" configure a "perspective" that persists in a dependency on social structures of coloniality and cannot shake off an internalized colonizing gaze.

Other accounts of racial embodiment are more sensitive to the physical realignments, leeway, pluriversality and heterogeneity that characterizes Viveiros de Castro's notion of "body." María Lugones's account of "traveling," for example, reveals bodies in transformation, crossing social orders with which they are aligned and dis-aligned, including social orders with a variety of racist projections. She does not emphasize or normalize bodies with a sense of belonging to or alienation from one dominant sociality. Instead, she reveals physicalities within social limina, sentient physicalities riddled by conflict and indeterminacy, yet where "perspectives" proliferate (using Viveiros de Castro's language). In "world traveling" Lugones also finds a physical sentience of liminal bodies in a deep affective stillness (she calls it "germinative stasis") that accompanies with awareness radical corporeal transformations.[10] However, from the perspective invested in bodily competency, this stillness may appear as a form of incompetency, and perhaps as indistinguishable from racialized physicalities stuck in the past, always "late," as Fanon says.

In-stilled Bodies of *Pacha* (Attachment/Detachment)

This stillness is a mode of awareness that arises from and with acute violent conflicts within bodies, transformative struggles between "perspectives," including the coming and passing of physical renditions of, and attachments to, social orders. In the Andes, elaborating from Kusch's notion of "estar," this in-stilled volatility can be seen as a dimension of the cosmos or *pacha* that is sensed in primarily affective registers.[11] In this respect, there is something terrifying about the physicality of Andean cosmology, especially when seen through modern, Western philosophical lenses. A deep layer of cosmic conflicts (including social, political, and environmental ones) takes place and elicits responses beyond the purview of instrumental rationality, consciousness, or agential phenomena. This field does not fully submit to our wishes and controlling projections. There is an aspect of physical violence, fragmentation, and transformation of selves, and communities, that we can't control. There is no transcendental opening of justice that rises at the horizon of such conflicts. No coming resolution. No transcendental self either. It seems that in this dimension of *pacha* there is no competency, nothing we can do but remain still.[12]

Here it is helpful to note that indigenous Andean notions of embodiment de-emphasize the perception of things. Kusch captures this in his inquiry into Quechua and Aymara: "what does it mean that in one language movement, events, the process of becoming are registered before things?" (2010: 32) The power of language is usually understood as the rendition of meaning: that is, as the attainment of conceptual clarity based on a fixation of things in the world with names. Quechua and Aymara, strikingly, seem oriented toward evoking the transitional character of the way things acquire significance, so as to hone in on their generative/destructive/creative eventuation rather than their conceptual containment. It is as if what we expect to be at the background of language (processes, change) suddenly appears foregrounded. In this reversal, the cosmos comes to be "registered before things."

This linguistic difference points to a physical attunement that is not anchored in epistemic or practical objectifying dispositions, that is not fulfilled by *doing* something, one that joins (rather than conceptualizes or instrumentalizes) *pacha*.[13] This is the core insight behind Kusch's notion of "estar" (a translation of the Aymara "utcatha" or "being"). "Estar" senses in *pacha* the coming and passing of configurations and disintegrations of habitual and embodied attachments to a range of meanings, including social ones, and of concomitant corporeal transformations (including affects, involuntary memory, and posture). This deep physical sentience shows detachment from specific physical modes of inhabitation of social orders, but it is drawn to their turns and modulations with the cosmos. It transpires as an affective stillness that can pass for passivity or for being displaced from the present.

I see in stillness both attachment and detachment. Detachment implies the possibility of release from pre-articulated dominant intelligibilities and forms of inhabitation. Attachment is the draw toward the transformative processes that this detachment reveals. This oscillation between attachment and detachment allows one to be in-stilled within a colonially informed social order *and* disposed toward it in its passing. Stillness is not a transcendent passivity, but a form of remaining with the concrete instantiation of social orders. Yet it is also not a mode of agency. In this respect, stillness is a form of physical sentience that does not seek to transcend the present, yet can discern in it the possibilities of radical re-orientations of, and departures from, socially dominant projections. Stillness does not *do* anything, but it is not passivity either.[14] It propitiates and resists.

Stillness is the beginning of resistance drawn by a physical sentience that opens a borderland between the turns and overturns of the cosmos or *pacha*, and the orderings of bodies and communities enforced by colonialism and modernity (here I am re-visiting my discussion of Lugones in the previous chapter). As I discuss later, "art" can offer leeway for stillness, but only when understood from the perspective of "invoked art" and "cosmological aesthetics," that is, outside of museums and galleries, emplaced in the spacing of the everyday, in homes where dead ancestors sit down for dinner.

Philosophical Convergences on Stillness

It should not be surprising that Kusch's interpretation of Andean indigenous philosophies is a referent in Lugones's work. "Estar" can be understood as a modality of in-stilled exposure to the limen between worlds of social meaning, where they infuse, transform, and displace each other, and manifest "traveling" physical re-alignments. "Estar," then, echoes Lugones's "germinative stasis." Viveiros de Castro's and Gloria Anzaldúa's elucidation of shamanism are also illuminating at this juncture.[15] The shaman joins conflicts in bodily spheres by becoming attuned to different emerging "perspectives" without reducing them to one another, by assuming multiple bodies and being drawn by their respective attachments to their worlds.[16] Yet this connectivity happens with a sense of detachment from any given meaning or world. Connected detachment, then, can allow for inhabiting a liminal or border position where the shaman is detached from orders of social meanings but drawn to their volatile and transformative happenings.[17] This in-stilled gravitation attends to the emergence of different bodies. In this respect, Viveiros de Castro states that Amerindian knowledges show "an emphasis on the methods for the continuous fabrication of bodies" (1988: 480). And the shaman can "activate the powers of a different body" (1988: 481).

At the border, shamanic detachment and desire are simultaneous, oscillating, in-stilled, and without transcendence. Bodies that arise at the border, in Nepantla, Anzaldúa would say, do not necessarily promise resolution to conflicts.[18] Yet, in their emergence, the specific valence of the attachments to socialities that entrench us in conflicts recede. Emerging bodies are not "better," but can bring an uncanny in-stilled awareness of transformations, contingencies, and insignificance in the instantiation of crises. Anzaldúa writes about this kind of physicality, one in which an in-stilled body joins the cosmos:

> The shamanic balance is not achieved by synthesis; it is not a static condition achieved by resolving opposition, a tension that exists when two forces encounter each other headlong and are not reconciled but teeter on the edge of chaos. The balance is not that of the highest good as the golden mean. (2015: 31)

And she writes about the transformative body of the shaman as:

> the dreaming body, a mode of consciousness that's emotionally complex, diverse, dense, deep, violent, and rich, one with a love of physicality and the ability to switch bodies and their expressive codes instantly. You invoke this sentience to help you, not transcend but to more passionately embrace the physical. (2015: 105)

Stillness is a form of *aísthesis*, a sentience that arises from a physical embeddedness in the cosmos. It is a sentience that does not belong to "us" as individuals. It is nowhere to be found if we probe our interiority and self-consciousness. The shamanic body does not unfold in a time that returns to a self, so it does not undergo development or cultivation, and it is given instead to a time that cannot be measured (2015: 105).

An Embodiment of the Cosmic Past

I approach time in view of in-stilled shamanic detachment from and connection to the transformative happenings of the cosmos or *pacha*. Physically transitioning between bodily configurations (affects, perceptions, memories), one senses no anchor that would ground them and their conflicts. The weak cosmic threads that weave and unweave bodies into wholes are even thinner from a shamanic standpoint, so that bodily configurations come and pass in one constant movement. Embodied inter-relationality and multivalency are most apparent to the sentience of the shaman. Bodies dragged in multiple directions, as when one is caught in terror by an earthquake and becomes disoriented, are border spaces in a cosmic plane that is indifferent to human constructions: a plane where transformative processes come to pass, where bodies are configured and disintegrated, and rebirthed. These processes are more like lapses and leaps because they do not settle within determinate occasions, and cannot be counted. And, insofar as there is no counting, time, in its most dominant, episodic meaning, becomes impossible.

When sensing the cosmos or *pacha*, even emerging social orders and the bodily attachments to them are always already undergoing transfigurations, that is, they are "passing." In this respect, an uncountable temporality of "passing" is picked up in Andean ontologies, socialities, affects, and languages. In particular, a physical, in-stilled, modality of sensing *pacha* is to feel that one is persistently "after" the passing social orders and inhabitations. This "after" is not only without transcendence but also beyond episodic time. It is an awareness that emerges with the time of *pacha* rather than "things," and faces an indeterminate horizon "toward the past." In this respect, however, "past" cannot be understood within countable time, and therefore cannot be differentiated from the present and the future.

One feels the draw of the cosmic past when one, for example, lets a friend, a lover, a family member, walk away after a moment of betrayal, a moment in which who they are, what they have done, and why they have done it, seems patently clear. One watches them walk forward yet effectively toward (what will be) the past, to spheres beyond one's life. The lost love eventually becomes faded, enfolded, disseminated to the point that the betrayal becomes insignificant or unexpectedly acquires new significations. The threads tethering together the "who," "what," and "why" loosen up, so that the definiteness and the weight of the betrayal drift away; revealing that one is no longer the one having been betrayed.

Yet there is no undoing of the loved one passing, of their becoming part of a past that ceases to be one's own. There is no forgiveness, no reconciliation; just passing, loss of density, fading. This is not about nostalgia, guilt, or resentment, or their overcoming, even if all these affectivities are at play. It is the cosmos sweeping one into the sentience of the "así" and emptiness of its holding sway. This affectivity helps me understand the temporality of a shamanic sentience that not only senses the evanescence of others, but the vanishing of one's own affects, senses of self and normalcy, moral bearings, as well as identities and feelings of righteousness and indignation. In these cases, in passing, other bodies surface, other volitions and vulnerabilities. This sentience can see, with other eyes, the planes where these transformative enactments come to pass, a plane that is the cosmos or *pacha* "itself."

With this last point I am trying to convey, now more speculatively, the difficult, yet prevalent, Andean temporal sensibility of *ñaupa pacha* that I discussed in Chapter 2. I suggest that incomprehensible, disseminative physicalities, bodily multiplicities, are submitted to the movements of *pacha*, appearing from a passing-past that is in front of one's eyes, and momentarily lingering in it, gathered in-stilled in a bodily awareness: as when memory brings something forth with the sense that it is passing (memories of the dead, of lost friendships, of places one has been exiled from). This is an *aísthesis* that generates affects, desires, porous senses of identity. The memory of the lost friendship brings to presence the friend, and you with them, though the "you" the memory conjures is detached from the "you" now. At the same time, the memory draws you toward the friendship. There is a stillness here that modulates our bodies not only in terms of what one feels but of how one comes to feel.[19]

This temporalization of an "after," of a passing-past, resonates with an ancient Andean form of memory that, as Terence d' Altroy notes, "[treats] the past as if it were cumulative, since the beings and places of the constantly expanding past were always accessible for interaction" (2015: 137). "Interaction" evokes here volatility and transient responsiveness. This memory sheds light on the notion of *ñaupa pacha* denoting a visible past and an embodied sensibility in which one senses events moving forward, past one and into an enfolding yet disseminative temporality. In this sentience one is always "after" the cosmos in the sense that the cosmos both has always already passed and draws one's body toward it, as in a chase.

This is an oscillating, shamanic physicality of an "after" that implies detachment and attachment at the same time, becoming in-stilled. In this temporalization, the passing-past is not sensed as heavy, weighed down by episodic and sequential definiteness, as if closed, frozen. It is, rather, light, volatile, porous, and mutable. From it, the present is rendered heterogeneous and indeterminate, moved by a passing-pastness rather than by a promise of futural progress. D' Altroy posits: "the past and the present as a unified entity, separate from the future."[20] This evokes *ñaupa pacha* again, a cosmic past where "the" future is behind our backs, inaccessible and mute (2015: 143).

The in-stilled physical sensing of the passing-past is shamanic: it is "after," yet without transcendence, or fixity. This physicality is passing as well, unable to disengage the movement of *pacha* that it joins. It can find a mode of affectivity that Andean notions of body bring forth (as described by Kusch in terms of "estar," for example): namely, attunement to the cosmic happening of *pacha* and an affective affirmation of its passing configurations, which is also an awareness of its constant withdrawal. This connected detachment is a sensibility of passing-in-stillness that has a corresponding bodily posture and comportment, those of what I call "after-bodies," evoking the presence of mummies. I connect these bodies to Anzaldúa's shamanic enactments:

> When I encounter la víbora, my guardian spirit, a deep stillness comes over me. I'm aware of my breath and heartbeat, but nothing else. Time collapses. My body shifts gears. Mi cuerpo becomes part of, merges with, "disappears" into my surroundings. I feel my body's intense focus on an awareness of the snake. (2015: 27)

After-bodies[21]

Perhaps memorial sensibilities are most revealing of "after-bodies" temporalized by a passing-past. I find helpful at this juncture to read Charles Scott in between Western and Andean frames when he writes:

> I invite you to imagine the time of your dying, a time when the importance of your past accomplishments fades and the events of your life appear past with little or no future prospect . . . a time in which the loss of presence that comes

with the presence of memory is especially pronounced and poignant. (2007: 453)

This is an account of a memorial, embodied affectivity in which events in our life evanesce toward their sheer happenings, loosening and mutating in significance. In it the sway of memory lets drift away a self attached to pre-articulated linguistic, moral, social, political meanings that configure a definitive and familiar present. In this memorial enactment, in the indeterminate moment of our dying perhaps, we are always "after," or posterior to, events (including physicalities that are of others and one's own), thrown into a sentience of, in my view, a passing-past that is detached from the weight of the coming and passing of such events.

Perhaps in the moment of our death everything, including ourselves, walks away from us as if after a betrayal, losing significance and density. I also find here disengagement and indifference toward the future. Its valence has shrunk considerably. In this respect, Scott sheds light on the in-stillness that after-bodies are submitted to when they are caught in the drift of the passing cosmos. The "presence of memory" seems to name here this in-stillness and this draw, which is also the draw of forgetting, or a "loss of presence." I understand this as a mode of being "after" *pacha*.

It is noteworthy that Scott encounters a form of desire at this juncture:

What happens in memory happens with the force not only of loss and letting go but also of a draw toward the remembered. Withdrawals, letting go, and being drawn, all at once.[22]

This is a desire that, in pastness, always "after" (both in the sense of posteriority and of chasing), can be drawn toward the passing of the cosmos. He states that this desire "wants the world in its difference from our systems of grammar, meaning, and sense, wants the world living dying, wants the edge where silence, utter silence, happens, where sound and movement begin always to pass" (2007: 7). I suggest that this complex memorial affectivity and desire belong to after-bodies, to their embodied, affective repose in the loss of worldly sense and in the draw of the cosmos. One can imagine that, in the evanescence of people that we love(d) walking past us, toward dissemination and reconstitution without return, there can be a desire oriented to their irrecuperable passing as revealing a dimension of living that remains, deathless in its cosmic transfigurations, and that is simply "así" or "thusly," as Kusch would say.

This account of memory resonates with Kusch's notion of "estar" (of dwelling in *pacha*), which carries with it a sense of stillness that he encounters in Andean ritual practices. "Estar" names bodily repose that in rituals brings bodies to a simultaneous loving and releasing that transpires "without time" (2010: 12). He connects *utcatha* or "estar," to the Aymara word "*amucatha*," denoting both memory and flowering. Kusch, then, gives an account of ritual that resonates with the passing-in-stillness of bodies captivated in a memory with a budding release of sense, including the social underpinnings of senses of self. Scott and Kusch bring to mind after-bodies as enfolded bodies withdrawn from social expectations and competencies, in the sway of what I earlier called the (k) notting of a cosmic sociality: "livingdying" I think Scott would say. He writes: "Boundless repose enfolds-in-stills-movement," evoking for me a loving stillness with which after-bodies sustain shamanic transformations in the borders of physical transformations, and with attention to the emergence of other bodies in them (2015: 2).

Affects and Resistances of After-bodies

For Kusch, Andean notions of body include a physical, specifically affective, disposition oriented toward solving crises as external. It seeks a feeling of safety in response to cosmic instability through the reliance on instrumental knowledge, the objectification of all entities, and in the capability of controlling one's environment, including socially. This physicality constitutes the *aísthetic* configuration that supports investments in a self-certain subjectivity, in an autonomous, agential subject, in doing and accomplishing projects "outside." This is a physicality that is ecstatic, always out pacing itself. It is also the one that modernity/colonialism nurtures in order to facilitate the administration of global capitalism and its supportive institutions (that modern state, universities, museums, among others), and it aligns with the modern socialities in which the social coincides with the human.

Yet there is another physicality connected with "estar," and to the stillness of after-bodies, I suggest, that does not find safety in crises being externally resolvable but, rather, in the heart or *chuyma*. *Chuyma* physically discerns whether an event is "auspicious" or "inauspicious." These two affective registers are not "externalizing," and are both oriented to the feeling of safety given by the ultimate in-stilled sensing of the cosmos in its "así," emptiness, or "seminality" (its generating, destructing, creating). In the first part of this book, I attended to the manifestation of this physicality through the notion of a "cosmological aesthetics," in Andean stonework in particular.

"Auspiciousness" senses that a crisis is manifest within a community and embedded in the cosmos in such a way that the community could weave the crisis into ways of being and knowing that are conducive to a transhuman collective renewal.[23] This weaving happens, however, with indifference to predictable and manipulatable outcomes. Here one finds safety as a manifestation of the "así" in the form of cosmic (rather than instrumental) reliance. "Inauspiciousness" senses that a crisis signals the overturning of the cosmos, bringing the community to a breaking point, a *pachakuti*, that forecloses any instrumental projections. Here the "así" is predominantly disclosed as emptiness, and with the detachments from ways of being emptiness enables. "Inauspiciousness" senses the possibility of finding generation/creation in processes of destruction. In this sense, "auspiciousness" and "inauspiciousness" come to correspond to "elemental reliance" and "cataclysmic potency" in the register of a "cosmological aesthetics."

Both auspiciousness and inauspiciousness are non-objectifying affects, since what they sense is the possibility of safety in events that exceed the predictable power of people and communities, events that do not let themselves to be grasped in terms of the future; events like earthquakes, for example. They rely on a memory that unweaves and re-weaves the present in view of a coming and passing crisis, and they allow for enduring it through a feeling of safety belonging to the in-stilled *aísthesis* of after-bodies facing cosmic overturns, one that, in my view, is manifest in Inka stone architecture.

Kusch's well-known example of the rejection of a water pump by an Andean indigenous man facing a drought is illuminating here. From externalizing and instrumental dispositions, this rejection seems irrational (as one of Kusch's students concluded). Through the affectivity of *chuyma*, however, the colonialist dependencies connected to the acceptance of the water pump may appear to be incompatible with the cosmic unfolding of the community formed by ancestral cosmic reciprocal relations or *ayni*. It is important to note that the rejection of the pump does not mean that the drought was sensed as "inauspicious." It had to do with the expectation that a community accept an instrumentalist disposition, one that effectively suppresses, shuts down, and mocks "estar" as a way of being, as well as the sensing of the "así" of the cosmos that allows for developing individual and communal senses of safety in non-externalizable crises.[24]

In short, the colonial imposition of the water pump brings with it the dismantling of the physicalities that discern between "auspiciousness" and "inauspiciousness," threatening to make absolute a way of existing that can only be understood on the basis of modern/colonialist epistemologies and forms of subjectivity. This reduction of living in and with the cosmos is what is ultimately rejected by the indigenous man. In this respect, he enacted a mode of cosmological, anticolonial resistance that was invisible to the modernized and Westernized academics.

The rejection of the pump is the manifestation of a sentience that resists from *chuyma* and arises from the "colonial difference"; it is a non-agential (in terms of modern senses of agency) and propitiatory resistance that makes no sense from within the socialities and instrumental reasoning of modern, capitalist orders. Kusch helps us see the affective register that informs this resistance: *manchariska*, the fear of losing the endurance that finds safety in the "seminality" and "así" of the cosmos, in its turns and upturns as non-objectifiable. In the colonial situation, *manchariska* can arise as an affective response to the enforcement of modern socialities, epistemologies, and economies that seek to make the human world absolute (in terms of the first chapter), an enforcement that not only saps cosmic endurance but also seeks to bury "estar," and the physical and communal forms that correspond to it, as primitivism, spirituality, or cultural curiosity.[25]

I suggest extending Kusch's analyses more explicitly toward the physical and modern/colonial oppression. To this end, I note two orders of physicality, an instrumental one and a cosmological one that involves after-bodies. Modernity/colonialism enforces the former together with global economic interests, and ableist, patriarchal, and racist institutions. It marginalizes the latter as a responsiveness to the seminal and non-objectifiable cosmos. This tension is affectively experienced, registered, and parsed both individually and communally. In this sense, it is appropriate to see bodies as sites for both colonial violence and resistances to it, processes that can become enmeshed. Colonialism severs the body and turns dimensions of it against one another. Yet it also re-weaves it beyond oppositional and binary logics. *Manchariska* is the affect that emerges in this process, and it is a mode of fright that resists the colonial disciplining of bodies; it is part of an affective and physical anticolonial struggle of after-bodies drawn to and detached from *pacha*. I find in *manchariska*, then, the suggestion of the *aísthesis* of after-bodies that yields a form of resistance from within the delimitations and borderings of modern socialities that differentiate between the "human" and "non-human"; this propitiatory resistance yields charged atmospheres emanating from bodies rather than praxical projects, atmospheres that in my view are linked to those of the elements encompassing instilled ancient stone buildings in the Andes.

5

Resistant Gestures

In view of my analysis in the previous chapter, I suggest that Anzaldúa's notion of imagination is a physical sentience of and within bodies undergoing simultaneous generations and de-configurations, transient bodies across socialities under the sway of cosmic (k)nottings. It shamanically senses the arrival of unprecedented bodies, including their inhabitation of social forms of colonialism/modernity and resistances to them. In this chapter I pursue Anzaldúan imagination in order to further understand the social and resistant manifestations of what I call "after-bodies." Turning to artworks and performances allows me to focus on the relationship between this modality of physical sentience of the cosmos and resistance.

The core of my discussion is composed of interpretations of the work of two artists: Mario Moreno Cantinflas and the painter Liliana Wilson. The interpretations include critical reflections not only on Anzaldúa's work and its reception but also on Lugones's "decolonial feminism," which I discussed in Chapter 3.[1] I do not intend these interpretations to fit neatly with or build on one another. They constitute decolonizing aesthetic interventions that reveal colonized and oppressed bodies resisting through a transhuman, cosmic sentience that witnesses the colonial and racist violence inflicted on them without turning this witnessing into social capital.[2]

Anzaldúa's Corporeal Imagination

Bodies are expanses of the imagination. In "Creativity and Switching Modes of Consciousness" Anzaldúa states:

> Whatever occurs back in the external world first occurs in the imagination. We use the imagination to rehearse what we are going to say to our friend, to our

teacher, what we want five years from now.... We constantly act these scenarios in our minds, playing them over and over again. (2009: 106)

Imagination is for her a corporeal, pre-reflective capacity to anticipate and rehearse experiences mediated by social positionalities. In the previous quote, Anzaldúa mentions the re-enactment of "scenarios in our minds," yet she does not distinguish between mind and body. Instead she evokes an imaginative or "dreaming" sentience that eludes this distinction. This is the sentience of bodies shamanically cast when, while day-dreaming, one is able to fly, become an animal, or feel and look differently; of bodies in which we get lost and carried away as in a dream with a cosmic range. In terms of her examples, through a rehearsing that invokes and shapes it, the dreaming body shelters the shamanic capacity to become another self, what one could be in specific social contexts that challenge one's sedimented habits and responses. Such a metamorphosis is not a mental projection, but a corporeal sentience and potency.

Facial gesturing expresses this kind of corporeal imagination. The face is, perhaps, the zone where dreaming as rehearsing comes through the most. There are gestures in our faces that we can't catch up with, that surprise us. Through facial gestures the dreaming body can sense and deliver us to another body, one that appears to have rehearsed, without us knowing it, the precise situation we are in. For the oppressed, angry expressions of indignation, for example, can arise from the sentience of a dreaming body. Self-reflection may not register what triggered the expression, but this does not make it irrational. Such unexpected, involuntary gestures can manifest insight into discrimination or abuse that self-reflection (having internalized social oppressive logics) remains confused about. They can conjure a body and self that are out of character, and out of time, especially within hierarchical social contexts. In this case, gestures are portals to bodies that have anticipated and prepared for involvements with pre-articulated social structures and roles, bodies that do not abide by normalcy and oppression, or by the managerial forms that modern socialities take on. The dreaming, gestural body resists.[3]

The dreaming body is, in my view, a cosmic, sentient physicality akin to "after-bodies." It involves a corporeal, anticipatory, imaginal disengagement from entrenched socialities, and an engagement with a volatile multiplicity of bodies in simultaneity. The memorial sense of after-bodies, where there is detachment from specific physicalities and a draw toward their disseminative and transformative eventuations, where there is a physical oscillation across bodies, now appears as a release from socialities informed by colonization and administered for the accumulation of capital. In Anzaldúa's terms, the dreaming body puts the oppressed in border positions—and in a sort of stillness.

In particular, she calls in-stilled facial gestures "making faces" or "haciendo caras." Through them, self-reflection can be blindsided by the metamorphic sentience of the gestural body, a sentience that is indifferent to the bounds of a colonially constructed social normalcy, ability, and competency, including those imposed by a linear temporality. This sentience ushers a border existence and contributes to disorientation in "nepantla" by facilitating processes of physical transformation (through the Coyolxauhqui imperative) in which the social roles of the oppressed are shed, leading to the loss of the intelligibility that social assimilation, redemptive liberatory politics, and internalized oppressions can offer.

In this respect, the dreaming and gestural body of the oppressed and dehumanized, leaping away from their managed socialized identities, oscillates between the fear/love of loss of self (of the self oppressed within social norms) to the fear/love of self-as-other (a resistant self simultaneously within and without dominant social norms). Yet, this oscillation is already resistant, manifest in physicalities undergirding the configuration of selves. Thus, for the oppressed, catching up with corporeal gestures can be a process mediated by leaps of fear/love that overcomes attachments to internalized, oppressive senses of what counts as social and human that are encoded in bodies. As such a body in the limen, the gestural, dreaming body does not fit within modern, capitalist social arrangements in their rootedness in the difference between the human and non-human.[4]

The Social, the Human, the Non-Human

As Lugones notes, lineages of colonialism, like those of racial hierarchies, enforce the difference between the human and non-human. Socialities and their transgressions (behaviors that are understood as a deviation from what is acceptable, like criminality, social taboos) can all be read as within the sphere of the human. On the other hand, the *pelados*, the racially oppressed and colonized, immigrants who cross borders in hiding, are not deviants or criminals. They are deemed non-human. In this sense, the behaviors and lives that lie outside of social norms are not coextensive with non-humanity. One can be deviant and "human," but not colonized and "human." I am drawing from "Toward a Decolonial Feminism," where, as I discussed earlier, María Lugones analyzes gender and its deviations (in terms of the distinction man/woman) as socialities that cannot be assigned to the colonized. To recall a statement quoted earlier, she states: "There are no colonized women," because the "colonized" are not "human."[5]

I am bringing up here the convergence of the human with the modern social, and the limits of attempts to socialize the colonized discussed in Chapter 3. The social framings attached to the category "women," and the deviations, oppressions, and norms at issue in such a categorization, tend to be determined from within the bounds of the human. White women experience the social dominance of white men, but that does not necessarily mean that they are oppressed as non-human. The colonized, on the other hand, are deemed non-human, and their oppression is not due to their lack of fitting and recognition within social norms and identities. The violence and exclusions that affect them respond to their ontological dispensability, to their inability to challenge or contribute to the development of social formations and renewals. A re-integration into the social, through the creation of more inclusive social identities that are given recognition, for example, is not an option. As Lugones puts it, that would amount to a transformation of the nature of the colonized.

There are embodied, aesthetic forms that approach the delimitations of the social, testing them, exploring transgressions, seeking to re-determine its norms, even seeking the social liberation of the oppressed and excluded. The contingency and historicity of social roles, the confines of normalcy and perversions, the uncontrollable and transgressive force of the erotic, the recovery of cultural forms erased by modern colonial capitalism, become themes in the exploration of the possibilities of transformation of the social. In these cases, behaviors, desires, and lives that are deemed beyond social norms challenge these norms, but only so as to give them a more distinct shape. Art can deepen one's awareness of social expectations or modulate their purview by instantiating new senses of propriety. Art can invoke the outside of social norms (call it the unconscious, the taboo, the perverted, the criminal, the liberatory) but ultimately can remain involved in an *aletheic* or truth-making movement of the social. In this movement the social is made to appear familiar, ordered, and intelligible. While this movement can be subversive, it is fundamentally socially conservative, because it "reveals" the outside of the social only to re-inscribe it. So, the exclusion of the non-human is still operative in such cases, no matter how extensive the mystery of art appears to be. My discussion of mime later, as reaching for the convergence of intimacy and transgression, where one feels at home even while appearing to be transgressing social norms, fits within this *aletheic* aesthetic delimitation.

Yet, how can one conceive the aesthetic forms that arise from the unsocializable borders of the human/social? Do they also participate in an *aletheic* function of the social? Or do they call for another aesthetic approach?

Cantinflas: Border Miming

Corporeal imaginative processes can make involvements in dominant socialities teeter between the seemly and the whimsical. This can come across in mime, an art of gesture that emanates from fanciful rehearsed bodies and faces. Imagination draws one into the body of the mime, into a bodily capacity to linger in a state of dream and déjà vu, when a situation feels as if it had been rehearsed, letting a wise body playfully test sedimented social framings. In this way, mime imagines and embodies the world anew. With uncanny slowness, the body caresses the edges of the socially proper (emotionally, gesturally) with the abandonment of a dream. For this reason, in mime there are no tired situations. Moreover, its dreamy atmosphere renders words unnecessary. Social categories and norms having been spelled out, communication is distilled into a function of immediate and exploratory gestural dynamics between affects and bodies. The silence of mime is a corporeal poetry that reaches toward an ideal convergence of intimacy and transgression. In this way, the body becomes the vehicle of social harmony. Such miming, however, is not a form of the corporeal imagination Anzaldúa envisions.

Alternatively, Cantinflas's classic comedic and mimic rendition of the Mexican *pelados* sheds light on border, resistant dreaming bodies. The Mexican philosopher Samuel Ramos's description of the *pelados* reads:

> The *pelado* belongs to the lowest of social categories, and represents the human detritus of the big city. Economically he is less than the proletarian, intellectually he is a primitive. His anger is mainly verbal and is usually aimed at self-affirmation through crude and aggressive language. His anger is an animal performance aimed at frightening others and making-believe that he is the strongest and most resolute. (quoted by Monsiváis 2000: 99)

This account of the *pelados*, whom Cantinflas impersonates, is significant due to its slippage: it starts at the bottom of social and economic categories, continues into detecting primitive and underdeveloped mental and emotional capacities, and ends in animality. The humanity of the *pelado* slips. At best, he is an imitation of the human.[6]

The Mexican philosopher and social theorist Carlos Monsiváis focuses on Cantinflas's body and mime in order to show the singularity of his artform. This approach is unique. It is Cantinflas's language that has received most attention: his meaningless verbiage, his incomprehensible word formations, his ability to always say nothing. Monsiváis, instead, understands this kind of language as a derivative of mime. He sees in mime "a double language of that which seeks to be expressed and that which does not feel like being thought."[7] He suggests that this language is organized by corporeal gestures.[8] The body of mime here oscillates with respect to social meanings; it broaches the social but in such a way that is also detached from it in a kind of expressionless state. It is attuned to the configuration and de-configuration of social norms through gestures and rhythms that emerge physically, without investments in the preservation of dominant, intelligible senses of value or even humanity. In this sense it is akin to an after-body. There is something cosmic about Cantinflas's body.

In its oscillation, Cantinflas's mime-body splits language between expression and understanding. In this split, incentives to become socialized (educated, absolved of a crime, wealthy) lose traction. When Cantinflas faces authorities that could either condemn him or redeem him, he flouts both—creating a social vacuum where physicalities come to pass transformatively, and multiple bodies arise that do not fit within the bounds of the social.

There is no illumination of socialities from this liminal opening, no *aletheic* function, no convergence of intimacy and transgression. Specifically, gesture seeks to express and, at the same time, muddles meaning. This double language, I suggest, is a way of re-inhabiting the dehumanization of the *pelado*.[9] His language can't help but double, attesting to a border zone between the human and non-human, where mutterings, murmurs, accents, and words that, as Anzaldúa states, move through the body, can be heard but not thought.[10]

Cantinflas's physical, double language both is directed to and leaves out those on the dominant side of the difference between human and non-human: politicians, the wealthy, intellectuals. In colonialism and its legacies, rationality, understanding, and language are weaponized to enforce this difference.[11] Cantinflas's language "does not feel like being thought" because it does not seek to participate in this enforcement. In fact, he shows the impossibility of this enforcement, its baselessness. His nonsensical verbiage is not due to the confusion of the *pelado*. His barbaric sounds are not the reflection of a primitive mind. They are the systematic dismantling of the language of the oppressors, of the entanglement between the piety of reason and the identification of non-humans. Cantinflas's bodily non-sense mirrors the nonsense of the rationality that oppresses him. The *pelado*, in Cantinflas's physical rendition, thus, refuses to be categorized through the dichotomy of human/non-human. Cantinflas is neither. This is also a refusal to be assimilated or transform the social, to be its outcast, its unconscious, its redeemer; a refusal to even be the mystery necessary to trigger an *aletheic* social transfiguration.

What is it, then, that the *pelado* seeks to express through his corporeal imagination, by invoking an other body that is not of the human/social? Monsiváis is clear about this: "the message is in the body," a message spoken from the indeterminate border of sociality. Cantinflas, he states, expresses "what has not happened to him." He expresses what has not happened to "him" as framed within the social, when the social is meant to coincide with the human. His is a silence that is not theorized or socially curated.

Anzaldúa's rehearsing, dreaming, shamanically sentient body is at work in this miming. As Monsiváis states, Cantinflas's body is "sped up," anticipating, "translating," oppressive situations for other *pelados*. In fact, Cantinflas is the corporeal imagination of the *pelados*, it anticipates and rehearses situations for them. Cantinflas's body shows that their corporeal imagination allows for a silence that does not let politicians and intellectuals in, the silence that fragments words and empties out phrases as they rush to catch up with a passing, disseminative body. No language, insofar as it is framed by social intelligibility, can articulate what Cantinflas's body expresses.

The gestural body of Cantinflas has a message for the *pelados* that needs no words: they are neither human nor non-human. Double language, a corporeal language, is their expression. Their bodies may not say much that could be socially relevant, but are able to be in-stilled in an oscillation at the borders of the human, bearing witness to oppression without being swayed by the human/non-human dichotomy. That is, they are able to witness without sublimating the violence against the non-human into social capital, without turning their oppressed lives into an unconscious other that holds secrets to be integrated by dominant socialities. This resonates with what Anzaldúa states about women of color: they are not perverts or putas. But they are not socially acceptable either.

The message of bearing witness does not need to be theorized, it does not need to be made socially intelligible. It is something for the *pelados* to hold on to in order to outpace the physical and psychic disintegration inflicted by colonial oppression. Bearing witness, here, is a kind of memory of oppression that detaches from the purview and social logics of the oppressor, and even from the fragmentation that these social logics wield on the oppressed; a memory carried in bodies as a mode of sentience, in rehearsed, shamanic, dreaming bodies specifically, as in the angry gestures of the oppressed that catch him by surprise.[12] Through this corporeal imagination, Cantinflas's lesson can be learned (as

Monsiváis understands it). The oppressed, angry and surprised by her dreaming body, in the liminal tension between expression and thought, learns *to not be taken advantage of*, which is a wisdom that cannot be shared with the oppressor. Mario Moreno, the actor who plays Cantinflas, describes the witnessing face of this *pelado*: "Cantinflas age is always the same, because Cantinflas has no age. He has a round face with a nose that is too small for the mouth—which is too big! Over the upper lip, two strands of moustache fall like a pair of out-of-place eyebrows" (2000: 94). Displaced eyebrows that make his big mouth an organ for seeing, for witnessing, as it casts nonsensical words.[13]

The Face of the Border Witness

Re-reading *Borderlands/La Frontera* after Lugones's "Toward a Decolonial Feminism" leaves me wary of interpreting Anzaldúa's being in "Nepantla" as being in-between identities, in a border located in a crossing of social categories. In particular, I am concerned about reducing the purview of her writings within the bounds of the human, and the "self," turning her texts into a social analysis of the exclusions, perversions, and transgressions of social identities. "Nepantla," in this sense, would be an *aletheic*, or even "therapeutic," place for the generation of new, more inclusive socialities.[14] Such a reading puts emphasis on socialization, self-discovery, cultural mixing, truth. Even though I find that sometimes Anzaldúa's own words point in this direction, I also find that the border that is definitive in her thinking, the one that puts her in the space of "Nepantla," is that between the human and non-human that colonialism continuously enacts and enforces. As I have noted, this dichotomy does not correspond to that between the socially normative and the perverted, abnormal, or criminal.

As I have discussed, Lugones thinks of a "modern" construction of the social as one based on the operation of the dichotomy human/non-human, where the social coincides with the human. She is concerned with the mobilization of social identities as a project of political liberation on the basis of social recognition as well as with projects of social oppression, and with how these two projects remain within the bounds of the "human" category. She points to, for example, the formation of "solid" oppressed identities which seek participation in social intelligibility as if it were a form of liberation, and the way this feeds an oppositional project that reinforces the colonial dichotomy human/non-human.[15] For her, then, the decolonial task is not social in its "modern" instantiation since this task involves the possibility of community not defined by this dichotomy. She turns instead to "non-modern," cosmological socialities that are organized, inhabited, and interrelated by "(k)notting," for example (as I discussed in Chapter 3). She shows that when liberatory projects work on the assumption of the human/social convergence, they erase socialities that may draw from non-modern communal forms. In this respect, she notes the impossibility of understanding the Andean notion of *chachawarmi* (man/woman) from Western socialities because, as colonial impositions, they bury the cosmological, non-anthropocentric world *chachawarmi* belongs to.

Approaching Anzaldúa from a "decolonial" feminist perspective (as Lugones calls it) means that the multiplicity of the oppressed selves is not only due to overlapping and marginal positionings within social identities but also because, being deemed non-human by colonialism and its legacies, there is an irredeemable void of social sense at the core of the lives of the oppressed. This void is not simply being in-between identities. It is being in-between identities without hope for social support in the past, present, and future, beyond social integration and redemption. The void of social sense, however, can be inhabited resistantly in a way that is incomprehensible in terms of the dichotomy human/non-human. The possibility of this inhabitation is sheltered, for Lugones, in the cosmological socialities that persist in the Andes, among other postcolonial sites.

Anzaldúa theorizes sensing this void of modern social intelligibility through the "shadow beast," the physical impulse to reject and destroy any imposition of identities and social roles, even those that are self-imposed and "good," redemptive, and liberatory. It is a drive beyond normalcy and perversion.[16] The shadow beast is the reason, for example, why the anger of the oppressed cannot be translated into the language and affective registers of dominant socialities, and why social identities do not stick to the oppressed. Instead, the shadow beast instigates physical processes of self-overcoming that are ultimately indifferent to accomplishing the social coherence (including self-coherence) made possible by the dichotomy human/non-human. In my view, the shadow beast emerges with the ability to witness the violations inflicted on those deemed "non-human" from beyond this dichotomy, and with the refusal of turning this witnessing into a socializing project of liberation. The shadow beast is the sense of unsociable bodies.

The faces of the ones deemed non-human by colonialism do not simply grimace, frown, laugh, and express other feelings. For them, according to Anzaldúa, to "make faces" can also be subversive, especially when gesturing so as to not be taken advantage of (as in Cantinflas's mime): when gestures signal "get out of my face," for example.[17] Anzaldúa notes:

> "Face" is the surface of the body that is the most noticeably inscribed by social structures, marked with instructions on how to be mujer, macho, working class, Chicana. As mestizas—biologically and/or culturally mixed—we have different surfaces for each aspect of identity, each inscribed by a particular subculture. (Anzaldúa 2009: 277)

She goes on to call the identities imprinted on oppressed faces by social structures "masks," that yield physical yearnings for social integration as well as self-hatred, disassociation, double consciousness. Between the masks (but not "under" them—there is no original face to be disclosed) are "interfaces" where the imprints of social identities intersect. Like after-bodies, interfaces show detachment from social sense and are drawn to both its decomposition and regeneration as passing processes. Interfaces are the corporeal surfaces where the shadow beast resides. These are the surfaces where the anger of the non-human becomes gesture. They are the material of Cantinflas's mime. Interfaces are the leeway in/of bodies, a surface of folds and layering of masks that allow for growth and metamorphosis across identities, and for the shaping of identities. Yet they are also a space of "struggle with *all* our identities."[18] The bodily struggle where, in one mime gesture, the shadow beast both refrains from social processes of identity formation and cracks all masks, even those that are self-imposed.

Anzaldúa also finds in the interfaces connective tissue that exceeds the bounds of the "human" body (the body of a socially mediated subject, the able body, the working body, the gendered body, the modern/colonial body). This tissue physically and affectively expands toward plants, animals, and landscapes. Interfaces embody a sentience across linkages with/of the cosmos and bear witness (witnessing within the body, through the heart or *chuyma*, through breathing lungs) to ways in which the cosmos destructs and reconstitutes, stopping one's breath. This sentience bears witness to suffering beyond the human/non-human distinction. As she states:

> It feels like the tree is teaching me how to perceive not only with the physical eyes but also with the whole body, and especially to *see* with the eyes of my other body. The Guadalupe tree reminds me of something I'd forgotten—that my body has always sensed trees' special relationship to humans, that we have a body awareness of trees and they of us. (2015: 24)

Building on Anzaldúa's analysis, I interpret interfaces as woven by the force of *kamay* in the Andes, the physical awareness of reciprocity and horizontality across all beings, and of their volatile overturning in a cosmic time.[19] I find in *kamay* the energy of the cosmos or *pacha* as an all-encompassing physical sentience of witnessing that sees nothing but (k)nots. This cosmic witnessing is not anthropocentric, and the colonialist evocation and demarcation of "humanity" is useless for it. For Anzaldúa, plants, animals, and mountains feel and witness non-human sorrow—or, more precisely, cosmic sorrow (since the term "non-human" is now rendered insignificant) and vulnerability (like in Aguilar's photography). And "human" physicalities can metamorphose into plants, animals, and mountains through the sentience of *kamay*, which is manifest in the tissue of interfacial gestures.

The gestures that I am concerned with do not appeal to the drive to uncover a hidden social or human truth. They can hold faces still and in a cosmic exposure, turning faces into grainy or rocky reflective surfaces elementally carved by the wind, sun, and water. They have an elemental shine. The facial folding of skin can yield a gesture that is beyond the colonial distinction between the human and the non-human. The contours of such gestures can be indistinguishable from those shaped by the dry heat and sun, mirroring the cosmos. The gestured face can be a creased cosmic fabric that extends across the borders between human bodies and natural settings: a materialization of the cosmos or *pacha*, with the intensity of a gesture of bearing witness. This is an in-stilled work of gestural imagination, a liminal work that, in Anzaldúa's terms, casts the "body of the earth."[20]

This earth-body is the body of an imagination that stretches out from the face, accumulating layers of sensorial patterns, postures, enjoyments, and expansive senses of both balance and imbalance that exceed the delimitations of human corporeality. In this respect, Anzaldúa writes, for example, of "images as animals," noting ways in which the imagination can elicit and rehearse animal physicalities within "human" bodies in a shamanic, cosmic realm.[21] There, "animal" images re-configure sensibilities, affects, and perceptions of "humans" beyond the strictures of humanity. In this realm the "human" body attains its form in relation to fish, bird, and river bodies. This animal imaging is a layer of the imagination that always informs the posture, movements, and dispositions of "human" bodies, although it remains mostly undetected. There are other similarly inconspicuous imaginative layers that also involve the "body of the earth" but in relation to vegetal and even inorganic presences. Anzaldúa's own path to her mestiza consciousness and *conocimiento* begins with the imaginative casting of the "body of the earth." She recalls early experiences of dissociation when feeling the pain of grass, trees, and insects. This is a dissociation from dominant socialities because she is exposed to a pain that appeals to a body that is neither human nor non-human. The "body of the earth," in its expansiveness, can witness cosmic pain.

In *Borderlands/La Frontera*, the "body of the earth" is at play in her notion of "invoked art," which I discussed in the first chapter. This kind of art is not defined by technique or intended to be placed in museums. She refers to totems and cave paintings as examples. The former enacts ageless transitions between the animal and the human, and the latter have accompanied "humans" from the beginning, as one of their first gestures. Both totems and cave paintings belong to an endurance that is seen and felt more than it is timed, and to a past when the delimitations and centrality of human worlds were not established apart from the formation, destruction, and regeneration of the cosmos: that is, from a cosmic past. "Invoked art," as a form of *Border Arte*, attunes us to the presence of the sentience of plants, animals, and mountains.

The cosmos is the rehearsal of this sentience, one manifest in the eyes of dogs, the gait of horses, the folds of desert sands, that can all be gathered up by a facial gesture. And in this rehearsal, the cosmos prepares to bear witness to the violence resulting from the breakage of cosmic reciprocity, from cosmic sorrow, as when deeming life dispensable, "non-human." In this sense, "invoked art" elicits a kind of cosmological sensing, "it dedicates itself to managing the universe and its energies" (2007: 89), and it "contains the presences of persons, that is, incarnations of gods or ancestors, or natural and cosmic powers" (2007: 89). The cosmos bears witness to the lives excluded from the "human," in a way that dispels the "human."

Liliana Wilson: Bearing Witness[22]

I read Anzaldúa's late and short essay "Bearing Witness: Their Eyes Anticipate the Healing" on the work of Liliana Wilson as tracing the expression of a cosmic witnessing. She finds in Wilson's characters a bodily stasis and solidity that gives them an "other-worldly presence" (2009: 277). Their postural stillness is gathered as both the tension and abandon of a kind of "seeing" or "witnessing."[23] I interpret this mode of bearing witness as a sentience that oscillates between detachment and being drawn, similar to the memory of after-bodies facing the turns and overturns of the cosmos. The sights are horrendous: the brutal murder of political prisoners in Chile by Pinochet's regime, the violence against immigrants and women of color in the US Mexican border, death and corpses in the desert. Wilson, a Chilean exile and Latina in the United States, renders her own experiences of oppression and that of others as embraced in a painted atmosphere of transhuman physical sentience that bears witness. Colonizing dichotomies (man and woman, human

Figure 5.1 *Bearing Witness* 2002 by Liliana Wilson. Private Collection.

and animal, human and cosmos) are blurred, (k)notted, and elicit a sight that sees through the expanse of the social and "the illusions of consensual reality" that dehumanize the oppressed (2009: 277).

Wilson's paintings of bearing witness depict almost blank faces with the subtlest of gestures, gestures that are almost inexpressible, unintelligible (like Cantinflas's mime). They embody the vulnerability of a seeing that not only sees tortured and disposed bodies but also bears their pain without turning it into a social project. Bearing witness is not the function of an objectifying gaze, but a physical sentience that does not abide by the violent reduction of bodies to the non-human. It senses resistance-in-oppression, and the embeddedness of oppressed bodies in cosmic processes of destruction and regeneration that elude the control and enforcement of the human/social.

In this way, the body of the oppressed is seen both as subjected to the negation of humanity and as given to rebirths and physical transformations attuned to a transhuman expanse in which this negation is not definitive or comprehensive in its dichotomous and oppositional logic. Bearing witness sees with "other eyes" an unbridgeable "colonial difference" between the violent subjectifications wielded by modernity/colonialism and bodies of the oppressed that join a cosmos in which both generation and destruction are part of a living movement. It sees resistance at the "colonial difference" and intimates the possibilities of cosmological socialities. Modernity/colonialism, instead, seeks to erase this difference, to see an absolute destruction of the oppressed, either by extermination or incorporation into the human/social, and foments investments in the illusion that there are events, such as psychic and corporeal forms of violence (ranging from everyday events, to quarrels with friends, to political unrest, to cataclysms) that have to be faced with the fear of a total exhaustion of life.

Bearing witness sees through this illusion from a cosmological perspective, in the awareness of physicalities that exceed the absolute framings of colonialism/modernity and are manifest in the sentience of mime-bodies, interfaces, after-bodies. The cosmic excess of modernity/coloniality, that is lived in enactments that both belong and do not belong to our bodies, is the "así" or "thusness" of the cosmos, to use Kusch's terms. It opens the "colonial difference" that can be inhabited by oppressed physicalities akin to after-bodies. In this excess, bodily transformations happen at unassimilable borders of colonially enforced physical regiments. Bearing witness sees at this border the resistant pain and vulnerability of bodies resisting the difference between the human and non-human (I am thinking of Laura Aguilar's body in the photograph in Chapter 3).

Wilson's art turns bearing witness away from the eyes that see things to another set of eyes that enjoin a physicality akin to breathing, an in-stilled oscillating of taking in and being taken by the cosmos. This turn enables resistance against "being taken advantage of": that is, being objectified and instrumentalized; a resistance that arises from the sentience of the cosmos rather than from "humans," as if the ultimate resistant gesture were a form of self-abandon into the cosmos. Resistance arises as a corporeal, cosmic sentience that prepares to bear witness and to "anticipate the healing," as Anzaldúa puts it, the healing of an other body seeing and seen through other eyes.

Yet this healing is not an integration into the social, a crossing from the "non-human" to the "human." It is also not assimilation, fetishization, occupying an "outside" of social norms as an externality that can be sublimated, or made conscious. Women of color, returning to Anzaldúa's phrase, are not putas or perverts, but they do not have social purchase either. She states about Wilson's painting:

> It teaches us to "see" through the roles and descriptions of reality that we ourselves, la gente, and our culture imposes on us. It makes holes in the assumptions and beliefs self/others/communities have about reality. El arte de la frontera is about resistance, rupture, and putting together the fragments. (2015: 32)

Like Cantinflas's mime, Wilson's characters do not want to illuminate the social, reveal its truth, and re-establish a sense of justice. There is no yearning for the redemption of the oppressed imprinted in their gestures. They are indifferent to such projects. They, rather, crack, fracture, explode the social realm and its outside with a cosmic force. The fragments that remain are to be put back together but only so as to reveal "interfaces" between them (that is, "the material between two pieces of fabric to provide support and stability") as sites of cosmic interconnectivity and disintegration. Maybe Wilson's paintings are "interfaces," not only in terms of the liminal faces they show, but in their lack of dimensions and absence of mystery, as if the unsociable bodies that compose the cosmos were in the same plane, and their bearing witness were without depth. Anzaldúa notes: "her textured, detailed architecture of vision makes the background y los espacios vacíos seem like subjects in their own right and as important as las imágenes y las figuras" (2015: 32). Maybe resistance is a gesture of abandon into a cosmic space that is ana-topic, or without set dimensions, and like a thin veil that conceals nothing.

Part III

In Company

6

Ana-topia (in Dialogue with María Lugones)

On the basis of my discussion of "after-bodies," I focus on physical spatialities that challenge notions and embodiments of space derivative from colonialism and modernity.[1] Decolonizing space entails a profound change in bodily and aesthetic experiences. It faces the inertia of bodies, especially those under the spatial influence and disciplining waged by categorial socializations, like the modern/colonial alignment of bodies with ability, intelligible (that is, properly "human") affects, and markers of race and gender. Decolonizing space is, effectively, a corporeal transformation, a modulation of physically finding one's bearings within spaces layered by colonial histories and socialities that determine one's perceptual and affective habits.[2] At this juncture, Lugones's phenomenology of space is helpful. As discussed earlier, it centers on the experience of "traveling," where bodies mutate depending on the localized, inhabitable social architectures they are in. Traveling is a pre-reflective, corporeal enactment that is common among the oppressed. It is not to pretend to be other people depending on context. It is effectively the emergence of another body within one's own body, an emergence that can be, as I explore here, spatially triggered by what I call "ana-topic space." In this chapter I also pursue a phenomenology of space inspired by Lugones in view of the colonial Church of Andahuaylillas in the Andes, and I bring forth spatial aspects of anticolonial resistance. At the end, I re-visit Lugones's concept of "world," and complement it with notions of space and memory from Silvia Rivera Cusicanqui's work.

Leeway

One's sense of space can be informed by modernity/colonialism so that a univocity of inhabitation is not only dominant but also assumed as natural. This assumption includes reliance on a normalized "competent body," the investment in a naturalized embodiment that inhabits places as if responding to the imperative that space be inhabited by everyone in the same way, as if it were neutral in its social bearings. The spatialization enforced by colonialism, in its single sense of inhabitation and emplacement, is uni-topic.[3] For Lugones, instead, there is no spatial neutrality; that is, in space one is always undergoing embodied negations and validations, which lead to transformations of one's bodies. One is always traveling through spaces that are different in the ways they physically enforce structures of oppression, possibilities of resistance, and expectations of capability. For her, there are no set dimensions, and there is always leeway to travel. This leeway is a determination of space as neither homogeneous nor universal; and it is a form of decolonizing spatiality that can modulate the structure of experience. In my terms, this leeway makes space ana-topic.

Lugones theorizes space as always undergoing localizations and contextualizations, becoming "worlds," that is, constellations of forms of embodied sensing and inhabitation, including heterogeneous dynamics of oppression. Lugones's "worlds" are sensed when traveling with leeway, and in registers of variant categories of difference like race, ethnicity, and gender.[4] Moreover, colonizing, racist, sexist, ableist gazes are dominant and internalized in the sensing of most "worlds," but not all.[5] When they are dominant, they can manifest differently across space. One's body schema and posture, for example, are not always disrupted by a colonizing gaze; but when they are these disruptions vary. The clean distinction between bodily competency and incompetency is, thus, not prioritized in Lugones's ana-topic phenomenology. I find in her indifference toward it. That leeway is characteristic of ana-topic space means that our bodies are multiply exposed, that dominant gazes lack a center, and that a normally functioning, competent body (including physicalities, affects, and mental states, as well as social determinations of race and gender) is a colonialist illusion.

In my view, Lugones's contributions to a phenomenology of space begin with the observation that "world traveling" means undergoing profound and involuntary bodily mutations. Physical dispositions, affects, habits, and modes of perceptual alertness that are absent in some spaces become dominant in others; one's bodies multiply. In this sense, ana-topia involves re-alignments of bodily awareness (including the embodiment of identities) manifest in postures, perceptual habits, dispositions, among other physicalities. Bodies that are ours await to be discovered across ana-topic spaces through transformative processes that cannot always be predicted or anticipated. These constitute experiences of traveling corporealities that configure and reconfigure our embodied identities evading self-reflection and the projections of a continuous and coherent "self."

The leeway of ana-topic space does not make it abstract. It concretely emanates through architectural features, and has a temporary and situated sway. Portals, for example, are sites of transition, of leeway, of a way in and out, and are incommensurable and disruptive, yet localized and contingent. This is clear in the function of portals in Inka architecture. They prepare one for a transition that could otherwise disorient one's physical bearings. When one is about to cross a portal one cannot anticipate how the space accessed through it will embrace and affect one's body. Portals mark indeterminate spatial transitions that make one vulnerable, and manifest a leeway exceeding homogenizing inhabitations of space, including social ones.

Ana-topic space allows for a decolonizing reversal: rather than assuming homogeneous space as primary, concrete spaces and transits become manifest from embodied experiences of "world traveling." Instead of prioritizing the white "granting" of space, one could theorize space from incommensurate enactments of leeway that occur in the irresolvable tension between simultaneous bodily emplacements and displacements. In this respect, it is important to note that in leeway the colonized body does not become competent. Gloria Anzaldúa puts it well: "to be disoriented in space is the 'normal' way of being for us mestizos . . . it is the sane way of coping with the accelerated pace of this complex, interdependent, and multicultural planet. To be disoriented in space is to be *en nepantla*, to experience bouts of dissociation of identity, identity breakdowns and buildups" (2007: 40).

Embodied Ana-topic Imagination

Lugones's analysis of "world traveling," and what I call ana-topic space, leads to bodies that hover in-between embodied spaces or "worlds." She deepens a decolonized spatiality by noting that one can inhabit more than one of these "worlds" at the same time.[6] This simultaneity is not a synthesis of different spatialities or modes of sensing and habitability, but a form of remaining in leeway as a heterogeneous, dynamic limen. There are bodily enactments that are manifest between spatial worlds and configurations of embodied identities that correspond to them. Perhaps it would be misleading to see these enactments as in a "body" because this may imply bodily coherence, and bury the proliferation of habitabilities that come to pass with leeway. Instead, in my view, at this juncture

Lugones points to a kind of *aísthesis* and corporeal imagination through which one is constantly imagining oneself in and from other bodies (here I am also referring to my discussion of imagination in Anzaldúa's work in the previous chapter).

From a colonialist/modern perspective that affirms uni-topic space, positing that space as leeway allows for the alignment and realignment of bodies with orders of social meaning ranging from postures, to perceptual practices, to affective registers, to cultural habits and senses of identity, may suggest abstraction from concrete places, as if these social factors were external to space. However, ana-topic imagination arises physically and does not revolve around abstract faculties contained within self-conscious processes. Ana-topic spatial imagination irradiates from our very posture, which sentiently exposes us to places in an open search for bearings that involves a wide range of physicalities. By joining limina and translations embedded in the concreteness of our surroundings, this postural imagination both facilitates and undermines senses of belonging to modes of habitability. In this respect, Lugones's "world traveling" can be elicited by concrete spatialities, such as portals, as constitutive of postural projections.

My suggestion of an embodied ana-topic imagination is intended to evoke a postural expansion that senses differential atmospheres emanating from specific material settings, draws out an irreducible multiplicity of socially mediated forms of habitability from them, and both explores and undertakes possibilities for traveling. Our bodies are not univocal in their motility and other spatial projections, nor do they necessarily blend naturally or habitually with comprehensive practical logics within environments. They are mutable, and can be unpredictable in their traveling, astounded by space. Ana-topic space is shocking and transformative, discontinuous, and engages a liminal imaginative power through which we inhabit and depart from our bodies, through which we dream ourselves as different bodies.[7]

The purview of this ana-topic spatial imagination comes across throughout Lugones's work. For example, she writes:

> For something to be a "world" in my sense, it has to be inhabited at present by some flesh and blood people. . . . It may also be inhabited by imaginary people. It may be inhabited by people who are dead or people that the inhabitants of this "world" met in some other world and now have in this "world" in imagination. (2003: 87)

Unpacking ana-topic imagination from this statement foregrounds that a primary bodily sensing of concrete spaces registers distinct modes of habitability.

In this respect, there is no anterior sensing of an "empty space." Instead, there are proliferating possibilities of physical dwelling that emanate from spatial and architectural features (portals, stairways, porches, kitchens, can be loci for such emanations) configuring atmospheres without overriding sense.

These atmospheres enfold and expose specific habitabilities and are intensified in the presence of persons, particularly of their bodies and their physical projections. Moreover, such atmospheres that carry present or imaginary inhabitants do not homogenize space, but diversify it through mixings, overlaps, and effusions across a range of permeable bodily presences encoded in the materiality of built environments. Thus, the sentience of the embodied imagination that blooms in our posture is also oriented toward sensing spaces as peopled, with the kind of alertness that characterizes strolling around crowded plazas or cemeteries. It has sufficient latitude to sense "imaginary people," like those whose presence seems to depart from the present immediacy of space, and those who have passed yet remain with an undeniable spatial presence. Through this imagination, space is revealed as sustaining a multiplicity of co-existing modes of habitability, triggering constant travel. Traveling bodies sense and become other bodies teased out from places by an ana-topic imagination.

Self-less Time (an Ana-topia of Colonial Architecture)

In the context of Andean colonialism, ana-topic imagination configures resistant bodies in buildings, spatially in between cosmologically based indigenous socialities and colonially enforced social subjectifications that configure the "human"—at the "colonial difference" in Lugones's interpretation.[8] This spatial/social in-between can happen in religious registers. Ana-topic space is inhabited resistantly so as to imagine in concrete religious sites forms of habitability that have been deemed "past" and irrecuperable, but that hold sway in the leeway suppressed by a colonialist uni-topic space. Catholic churches can, beyond their colonialist intent, effuse spatial atmospheres for such a corporeal imagination.

In this respect, I approach the process of converting Andean peoples to Christianity, and possibilities of indigenous resistances to it, on the basis of the architecture of the Church of Andahuaylillas. How is it possible for a religiosity that interacts with the sun and the earth, rivers and sky, mountains, and the cosmos in its formations and destructions, to be corporeally imagined within a colonial church? This problem is apparent when one compares the interiorized space of Western churches, its controlled heights and depths, with the spatiality of *huacas*. The latter emerge from mountains and streams, elementally, and complicate the distinctions between exterior and interior, built and unbuilt environments.

The priest Pérez Bocanegra designed the Church of Andahuaylillas, challenging attempts to forcefully impose a Christian faith onto the indigenous populations by indoctrinations and by denying and erasing native Andean rites and deities. He believed, instead, in translations between Inka and Catholic religiosities as necessary for conversion, perhaps enabling interpretations of colonial and modern Andean religion as "syncretic." Bocanegra was especially attentive to the differences between word and image, and more so, to the necessity of an aesthetic (figurative and architectural) translational approach that would draw indigenous peoples to Catholicism.[9] For this reason, the influential priest considered space as a vehicle for conversion. His conception of space was, however, uni-topic. He relied on the possibility of integrating Andean cosmological space into the interior spatialization of the Christian church. Architecturally, he projected the interiority of the church, where souls/bodies are shaped, tested, and saved, toward the outside. Uni-topic space, crossing in and out of the church, is then assumed as neutral, as just the background for the unfolding of the travails of human souls in temporal, internal, and self-centered processes of redemption.

As Sabine MacCormack notes, the inside of the Church of Andahuaylillas is carefully designed to emphasize the priority of such processes, to carry human souls through the stages of life, from birth to death—a transport for which the landscapes and skies outside are just a setting. The church, then, becomes a temporalizing condensation of space, a distillation of life to its purest elements and in a set, timed trajectory toward salvation. It does not allow for leeway. The church would be, then, the concretion of all space, since space (inside or outside) is ultimately just a staging for Christian lives. In this way, uni-topic space becomes ornamental and allegorical: not only the paintings and murals in the church, but also the mountains and skies outside are staged scenographies for the temporal unfolding of a human drama. Uni-topic space thus becomes theatrical.

The fresco of the Church of Andahuaylillas, however, as interpreted by MacCormak beyond Bocanegra's intent, can suggest a different kind of spatiality. It includes a skylight that not only stands for the resurrection of Christ in the painting but also opens to the sunrise given its orientation. The positioning of the skylight is ana-topic: opening limina for transitions between spatialities in which the concrete, constant destruction and rebirth of the cosmos is undergone, and spatialities articulated around a singular event of resurrection and the futural promise of a divine return and salvation. The skylight, like a portal, allows for a physical ana-topic leap.

One can corporeally travel, drawn by the particular cosmic orientation of the church and the skylight, and follow the transfiguration of the building into a *huaca* (an Andean sacred site) by an elemental exposure of light reflecting the movement of *pacha*. This transfiguration is concretely manifest in the way the skylight illuminates the interior space of the church, letting light move in it throughout the day as if it were a sundial or *intihuatana*. Moreover, the church has a striking feature, namely, that the words "the holy gate to heaven [*bendita puerta del cielo*]" are inscribed on the door within the church, leading to the outside. This inscription, together with the skylight, resonates in the Andes with a spatialization oriented toward elementals and the cosmos, which is still visible in Inka architecture. MacCormack's analysis shows that the compounded architectural effect in the church is a physical leaping in opposed directions within one sacred building. One faces toward the inside of the church, toward the altar where the priest preaches and forgives souls. The other faces toward the sky and landscape. This leaping reveals the leeway and ana-topic character of the Church of Andahuaylillas.[10]

Bocanegra was unaware of the ana-topic spatiality of the church he designed, of its tensional arrangement, of the simultaneity of its irreducible habitabilities. This lack of awareness is connected to colonialism, which is here expressed in the connection between the fixation on conversion and the assumption of uni-topic space. Belonging to a colonial endeavor, the priest operates within a narrow sense of architectural spatiality. On the other hand, Inka elemental and cosmological architecture, interwoven with Andean religiosities, allows for an approach to the spatiality of the church in which its ana-topic manifestation is palpable. In particular, the cosmological time of *ñaupa pacha* (discussed in Chapters 2 and 5) visibly irradiates from the sky and mountains, and elementally poetizes landscapes and stone buildings through light, which renders human significances contingent, mutable, disseminating—and allows for disintegrations, parallelisms, and juxtapositions of materially and bodily inscribed social and historical orders through a phenomenal force of earthquakes and other cataclysms. From this Andean perspective, the Church of Andahuaylillas appears as kinetic, in the cusp of transformations. In short, the Andean context provides a richer understanding of the church's spatiality than Bocanegra's.

Ana-topia can be seen in this context as the spatial dimension of *ñaupa pacha*, of a cosmic time, emphasizing corporeal traveling, leeway, and leaps between modes of habitability. Thus, prevalent modern, Western philosophical conceptions of time cannot be simply translated into the Andes, not only because of an emphasis on linearity and sequence, or the distinctions between past/present/future, but also because they return to a self (emphasizing an ensouled interiority) or to a self in action (to a "now" as a moment of decision). This modality of time is connected with moments of gathering of meaning, truth (even if temporalized), self-cultivation, and insight. It is precisely the self-centered time that one can glean from Bocanegra's architectural design, the time of conversion.

Ana-topic space can be understood, instead, as disseminative of modern, Western temporalities. It is not invested in returns to a self, it spreads emptiness or (k)nots within a cosmic realm in which Western time is not dominant, but one temporality among others, like those of lightning bolts, wind, ocean tides, earthquakes, breathing: that is, times emanating from the body of the earth. Ana-topic space is not timeless, but holds sway with a self-less time.

In terms of the Church of Andahuaylillas, it is possible to extend MacCormack's analysis of the opposite spatializations within the church, corresponding to Andean and Christian religiosities. This spatial tension, this ana-topic expansion, is itself a cosmological moment in terms of *pacha*, so that the oppositional architectural spatiality of the church can come to be interwoven, with leeway, in and through Andean bodies. This embeddedness is not a translation of Christianity into Andean religion, but a letting be of Christianity together and in tension with other modes of habitability, belonging to a spatiality that is neither "Andean" nor "Christian," but ana-topic, cosmic, and temporally self-less.[11]

Bocanegra could not see this possibility through a uni-topic sense of space and a self-centered temporality of redemption and salvation. This means that he also could not see resistance as architecture: that is, the physical tension between the spatial colonial subjectification he intended, and the cosmological, ana-topic spacing that submitted this subjectification to spatio-temporalities unintelligible within projects of conversion; the resistance in the church out of which unprecedented religiosities were born.[12]

Playfulness and Rhythm

Ana-topic imagination unearths sensibilities and other physicalities involved in possibilities of resistance that are not defined by dominant, modern Western determinations of time, both by the tripartite ordering of past/present/future and by the return to a developing "self." This point echoes my earlier discussion of Lugones. In Chapter 3, resistance appears in the tensional difference between colonial/modern modes of subjectification through socialities constructed as "human," over and against a "non-human" array of dispensable lives. These lives, invisible to colonial/modern gazes, in fact participate in cosmological embodiments of transhuman reciprocities, where entities both are and are not their relational polarities, especially in terms of social hierarchy (such as in *chachawarmi* or man/woman). This possibility of being and not being at the same time (which Rivera Cusicanqui relates to *ch'ixi*) is another way of articulating ana-topic space and self-less time.[13] It is also a resistance that is not anchored in a modern sense of agency. It propitiates charged bodily atmospheres that shelter possibilities of non-oppositional resistance already operative in the concreteness of space.

On this basis I turn to Lugones's early notion of playfulness emphasizing its spatial and resistant dimensions. She states:

> The playfulness of our activity does not presuppose . . . a particular form of playing with its own rules. Instead, the attitude that carries us through the activity, a playful attitude, turns the activity into play. . . . The playfulness that gives meaning to our activity includes uncertainty, but in this case the uncertainty is an openness to surprise. (2003: 95)

Lugones distinguishes between play, playfulness, and activity. The issue for her is: How does an activity become play? Play is the outcome of a process that transforms an activity. This emphasis on transformation shows that play cannot mean here simply a system of rules set in advance that frames and orients an activity. Lugones attends to play as it arises, as it becomes play. In this respect, she describes the activity of throwing stones so as to break them and see their insides. This is an activity that can be happenstance and unthought, and that can also turn repetitive. Through this repetition, it can also turn into play. In this process, it is impossible to pinpoint when the activity becomes play. Re-tracing one's steps, inspecting the stones or one's bodily movements would not help. Play does not arise in a locatable space/time.

Repetition offers a clue about the becoming of play. Yet, repetitive activities can be boring and predictable, like following rules. They tend to be the opposite of surprising. At this juncture Lugones reveals a paradox at the core of play: repetitive activities eliciting an "openness to surprise." One throws a stone and sees its inside after it breaks. One is surprised by how beautiful it is and then moves on. Play does not arise in this instance. However, if one were to continue to throw stones and repeat the activity in such a way that one is not only surprised each time but persistently open to being surprised over and over again, one would be playing. In other words, play arises "when" one is taken to inhabit conditions for the continuation of sameness and predictability as conditions for unprecedented transformations. I also understand play as a retreat from self-centered time to self-less time.[14]

Extending Lugones analysis, I approach this uncanny arising of play as "rhythmic." "Rhythm" does not belong to a thing, person, or moment, and it does not mark time linearly. It also constitutes an affective disposition that not only suspends the linkage between repetition and predictability but also shelters an openness to surprise in this suspension. I suggest that this rhythmic disposition that preserves an affect of openness to surprise in conditions otherwise ripe for certainty, controllability, and instrumentalization constitutes "playfulness," which "turns the activity into play." I emphasize "rhythm" in play because I think it conveys the physical, non-subjective, and pre-reflective enactment that moves playfulness as a disposition. Being playful is not something one does.

Playfulness assumes a central role in Lugones's analysis of the possibility of resistance in colonial and postcolonial contexts. It informs what she calls "active subjectivity." As I noted earlier, Lugones theorizes a modern, Western conception of agency that "presupposes" a "world" laid out in advance with sedimented meanings that guide actions. Instead, "active subjectivity" "has no such presuppositions, no ready-made sense within which our actions and intentions can be made congruent with our domination" (2005: 4). This is not to say that "active subjectivity" has no relation with the way socialities and values are laid out in advance in dominant worlds (including determinations of identities with their expected norms defined from above and below) as spatial habitations. Rather "active subjectivity" plays with such determinations, repeating them, rehearsing them and reprising them. More precisely perhaps, it finds their rhythms, turning them into something distinct and unexpected, releasing them from their sedimentation within imposed and overarching oppressive structures. Active subjectivity engages in play as a practice in the limen and leeway of worlds.

Insofar as socialities and values are spatial or even architectural (that is, shaping and enforcing modes of inhabitation), an ana-topic, corporeal imagination seems to be involved in their mutations, overcoming, and release from a social sphere configured on the basis of colonialism and for the sake of exploitative economic and political calculations. In this respect, I align ana-topic imagination with rhythm and with "active subjectivity." Drawing from the previous chapter, I find "active subjectivity" in borders, breeching the modern/colonial sphere of the human/social without joining its instrumental orientations and with indifference to investments in its preservation. In this respect, "active subjectivity" can be a mode of resistance. It rhythmically and imaginatively weaves, unweaves and re-weaves social and political fabrics in the depths of one's bodily transformations, including spatial bearings, with a sense of non-belonging and unsociability. It is important to note with Lugones that one cannot always play, that there are colonialist spaces that can construct one as unplayful.[15] I venture that the rhythms of weekly going in and out of the Church of Andahuaylillas could become play and stir a decolonizing, imaginative resistance of this sort.

Ana-topic Memory and Resistance

Lugones's "world traveling," which I understand spatially, is a form of "active subjectivity." Within a dominant "world," namely, a habitable space constitutive of social embodiments, the needs and bodily projections of the dehumanized oppressed do not conform to pre-articulated hierarchical social, economic, and political orders, and are, thus, rendered meaningless. Yet, the oppressed develop significant postures, dispositions, and intentions in the marginalized spaces of their homes, communities, cultures. These physical bearings cannot be actualized within dominant worlds. One's posture, for example, can feel obstructed and reconfigured upon entering an oppressive spatiality, significantly impacting the projections of desires and intentions.

However, the oppressed can remember being spatially supported even as they inhabit a dominant space.[16] This memory is a way of finding leeway; it is ana-topic. Through it the oppressed can find postural possibilities and unprecedented spatial bearings that arise unpredictably, rhythmically, playfully—even in the apparent fixity of the worlds that oppress them. This memory is a way of finding a corporeal rhythm within dominant inhabitations; it manifests playfulness or "active subjectivity," and makes possible "world traveling." In the everyday rhythms of the inhabitations of oppressive worlds, the active subjectivity of the oppressed lets marginalized bodies break through memorially by creating spaces of play, and searches for bearings, imaginatively: even *haciendo caras* or making faces (Anzaldúa would say) to the colonialist priest behind the altar.

According to Lugones, this playful, rhythmic memory is liminal because it does not rely on the pre-articulated inhabitations of either dominant or marginalized worlds. It is not in an actual in-between space, but it is a mode of inhabitation in which bodies become rhythmically exposed to temporal, spatial, and social layerings and simultaneities. From within dominant worlds oppressed cultures, socialities, and histories appear fragmented, unable to congeal with overarching sense. For example, silenced histories do not support valued senses of identity, suppressed cultures do not ensure the proper inhabitation of institutions, and marginalized languages do not participate in public discourse. And the resistant, ana-topic memory of "world traveling" does not bring assimilation into the sense of dominant worlds. At the same time, the oppressed who "world travels" does not simply remember the orders of social and cultural meaning of their excluded communities in order to become efficacious in dominant worlds. For this reason, I approach this memory spatially, ana-topically. The assimilationist hope, like Bocanegra's, reflects a dominant, modern, Western, self-centered temporality. It suppresses leeway and the transformative capacity of ana-topic memory, a memory that is not sustained by a self (in processes of self-reflection, self-cultivation, development, and socialization), one in which different bodies are manifest, shamanically.

I stress that, as when traveling through a portal, the ana-topic memory in "world traveling" does not remember or inhabit "worlds." For it, dominant inhabitations are not overarching and encompassing, and marginalized inhabitations do not provide sanctuaries or direct paths for action. Ana-topic memory is not within or of a "world," if by "world" one means embodied orderings of practical, social, and institutional meanings that guide actions and make possible agential formations of selves. Even though Lugones uses the notion of "world," I read her approach to resistance, "active subjectivity," and "world traveling" as emphasizing the porosity and leeway of "worlds." Thus, I bring to bear on her discussion "rhythm" as a modality of inhabitation that both insists within a spatial order but ends up inhabiting it transformatively, with leeway.

In my view, Lugones's notion of "world traveling," especially when approached spatially and ana-topically, shows both the relevance and limits of the notion of "world" for the analysis of anticolonial resistance. Maybe focusing on rhythm can provide a complementary way of understanding this form of resistance without falling prey to the modern/colonial enticements of the notion of "world," which includes, anchoring affectivity and spatio-temporal bearings in a "self," investments in clarity of purpose and of moments of decision, and demarcating between the socially valuable and the dispensable. I suggest that these enticements may cover up the sense of cosmological resistance I have been working through in this book.

Emphasizing rhythm rather than "world" may also guard against understanding "world traveling" as the activity of a mobile self. In particular, "world traveling" is not something that a self does, even if it can situate the self as a mode of physical awareness, and it is not a passing through delimited worlds as constellations of habitabilities. It is, rather, the experience (through spatio-temporal sensibilities that do not align with processes of progression, development, or cultivation) of the blurring and indeterminacy of inhabitations, of their porous enmeshment. Perhaps the notion of "world" is too clean, too integrative, to convey the physical/cosmological enactments I have been focusing on. I think Lugones becomes aware of this. Thus she can be read as making a cosmological turn in her theorizing resistance in relation to decolonial feminism, and, in this turn, the centrality of the notion of "world" in her lexicon appears to recede.[17]

Rivera Cusicanqui and the Rhythms of the San Pedro Market in Cusco

Lugones's account of the memory of "active subjectivity" and "world traveling" can be developed without fixating on and fixing the notion of "world." In particular, rhythm, which I link to playfulness, can configure a kind of memorial, playful insistence that involves physical exposures to the enmeshment of irreducible habitabilities in their conflicts and transitions, an insistence that enjoins inconclusive and surprising pulsating dynamics of dissemination and cohesion of social embodiments. In this regard I find it helpful to make more explicit the connection between Lugones's work and Andean philosophy.[18]

For Rivera Cusicanqui, the concept of *ñaupa pacha* or the "cosmic past" implies a memory that is in front of one's eyes, directly facing one. More precisely, through this remembering one advances toward the past in a movement that reveals the texture of the present. In this remembrance the present is not disrupted by the past, nor is it fused with the past. Yet the past is not clearly distinguishable from the present. The memorial experience of *ñaupa pacha* is more like approaching a receding fabric or textile, and glimpsing that what first appear as solid colors are, rather, a mesh of multicolored threads different from one another but bound up together, (k)notted, forming a complex, disseminative, multifocal fabric.

The memory of *ñaupa pacha*, or the cosmic past, senses the present as a fabric of socialities, historical formations, and even temporalities that are distinct yet enmeshed. It is attentive to rhythmic patterns and sightings in which the present pulsates. In particular, it lets the cosmic past bestow body, dimensions, dynamism, and texture to the present by entangling and disentangling it, and by dispersing it. This memory allows for ana-topic inhabitations of space as a living mesh or *ch'ixi* in Aymara, a notion that in my view complements and clarifies Lugones notion of "world."

In colonial and postcolonial contexts, this kind of memory is a resistant opening. In such contexts, colonized cultures, socialities, and religiosities are deemed to be non-human, and in an irretrievable, non-modern past, always behind, excluded from the present. Thus, the relationship between anticolonial movements and memory can appear to be the overcoming of this exclusion through redemption, historical disruption of the modern present, or the healing of trauma through the reconciliation with the past. Yet these possibilities are illusory; they are ultimately projects of socialization that do not recognize the perniciousness of the difference between the human and non-human that determines colonial/modern socialities.[19]

The *ch'ixi* memory, on the other hand, does not fall for such redemptive gestures and socializations. It, rather, traces the weave between past and present in its simultaneous differentiation and enmeshment, and reveals the tensional force of the *ch'ixi* fabric of the now that cannot be reduced to temporal orderings, including colonial ones. In this movement, the tensional force arises in between modern/colonial subjectifications and ana-topias stirred by a cosmic time: that is, as a resistance that is not assimilated into social projects, even liberatory ones.

For Cusicanqui, in my reading, markets can be ana-topic spaces where the rhythms of the quotidian are strongly felt as one inhabits blurs and divergences of social spatialities that do not settle in a worldly arrangement. The everyday is constituted by repetition and pulsations, by skips and leaps, and can be inhabited with an in-stilled disorientation, like when strolling through crowded plazas and markets.[20] The Mercado Central San Pedro in the historic center of Cusco, for example, more than a "world" is a rhythm that interweaves simultaneous economies that draw from pre-Columbian, colonial, and modern eras. Following Rivera Cusicanqui's analysis of marketplaces in the Andes, these economies, and their corresponding socialities, which both coexist and repel one another, cannot be subsumed under a single form.[21] Even if capitalism is dominant, other economies continue to be operative, both remaining non-assimilable to it, yet participating in it. This is evident in San Pedro, especially in the difficulty of the way value is determined, in the leeway for negotiation and in the importance of who is buying and what is their relationship with the seller. From a modern perspective, all this only appears as a badly run capitalist endeavor.

Rivera Cusicanqui, however, has a more thorough explanation of this in terms of the simultaneity of capitalist and pre-Columbian economies:

> in our case it was a matter of a play of values that were not always material, nor were they necessarily measurable in terms of an abstract and universal notion of labor. Prior to colonization, it seems that there was no word for "labor" as an abstract concept in the Aymara language . . . all the imaginable forms of work correspond to a specific word. (2018: 44–5)

In the market it is possible to find *ch'ixi* goods that simultaneously participate in at least two irreducible yet enmeshed kinds of economies. In one exchange values are mediated by abstract labor, and in the other labor is understood as work in terms of larger and more complex systems of specific reciprocities, including ritual and religious ones, that relate human and non-human worlds. While the former seeks the abstract accumulation of capital, the latter, like Anzaldúa's "invoked art" or "Border Arte," seeks social and cosmic validation. One could pretend to hold on to one economy or the other, but this would miss the texture of the simultaneity of economies, and overlook the social and political possibilities of resistance at stake in the ana-topic market.

A similar oversight would result from understanding capitalism as the economy toward which all others are tending. A *ch'ixi* physical memory, on the other hand, rhythmically remains in the everyday mesh, in one or the other economy and in neither at the same time, undergoing surprising bodily liminalities and transformations that elude fitting within a set inhabitable sphere. This memory challenges the claim to overarching dominance of a capitalist economic logic without "returning" to an "authentic" indigenous one. This challenge is a form of resistance; it playfully suspends the predictability of a seemingly sedimented system of oppression and shelters the possibility of finding the unexpected which arises from a *ch'ixi* fabric of economic forms emplaced in the market. This kind of resistance constitutes the atmosphere of marketplaces and cannot be registered through modern conceptions of liberal politics and agency.

Rivera Cusicanqui is thus both a theorist of resistance and a theorist of the quotidian in colonial and postcolonial contexts. I interpret her work as showing the conditions in which resistance emerges so that it is not the result of an ideological imposition, an intentional intervention carried out by avant-garde intellectuals or a subjective projection. These kinds of revolutionary politics tend to become oppositional to systems of domination, claiming some sort of pure externality to it, often essentializing and manipulating fabricated oppressed identities (indigenous identities, for example), and missing the decolonizing potential of ana-topic quotidian rhythms.

In the everyday return to the ana-topia of the market, there is the possibility of inhabiting it as a mesh, with *ch'ixi* memory, and the repetition can become rhythm guided by, in Lugones's terms, an openness for surprise. In this physical inhabitation, it becomes apparent that the market is not of or within a world, it is not even a convergence of a plurality of worlds, yet it is most concrete and quotidian. This is evident from a sentience that is intensified in the rhythms of markets, when anonymous bodies pass and run into each other, when voices blend and smells pull in unknown directions. Such markets cannot be assorted into orders of social, economic, or political meanings that enable overarching instantiations of power and univocal organizations of resistance. They are where communities are at ease, as if dancing to unprecedented familiar rhythms. They are also where people are working, busy, stressed, or bored.

I find resistance in the leeway, in the ana-topic spacing, in which this dance transpires as it embodies the rhythms of a cosmic fabric in which *ch'xi* holds sway: as (not) day and (not) night, (not) man and (not) woman, both and neither, all (k)notted together in the market. The market is, thus, manifest as a tensional fabric, as a cosmos even, and within its texture arise possibilities of quotidian unworldly praxis that make oppression less definitive, and that are not guided by the intention of a subject or by historical destiny. In the market, resistance is the enveloping ana-topically charged, propitiatory atmosphere of quotidian rhythms that sound from the cosmos rather than from "worlds."

Rivera Cusicanqui shows in detail the emergence of indigenous movements of anticolonial struggle, led by women, that arise in these resistant atmospheres through the enactment of what she calls "*ch'ixi* gazes," which, in my terms, would be an ana-topic imagination. She focuses, for example, on entrepreneurial indigenous women who are able to weave and (k)not networks of commercial exchange with ancestral practices of solidarity and organization of communal autonomy in relation to a state submitted to the interests of global capitalism. These are *ch'ixi* economies and social insurgencies that do not assume the exploitation of labor and the environment, and that have been able to transform the socio-political landscape of Bolivia. Rivera Cusicanqui is not shy to claim, perhaps playfully, a *ch'ixi* indigenous modernity in this respect, one perhaps unfathomable from within the modern/colonial "human" world. Such a modernity arises as an ana-topia, without being developmental or progressive.

7

Aísthesis (in Dialogue with Enrique Dussel)

I dedicate this last chapter to exploring the resonance between the themes of "cosmological aesthetics" and anticolonial resistance discussed in this book, and the aesthetic dimension of the philosophy of liberation.[1] Just as in the last chapter, I attempt to establish a dialogue that helps situate my analyses within larger philosophical discussions with more established critical frameworks emerging from Latin America and the U.S. borderlands. This is an attempt to show the philosophical relevance of *aísthetic* approaches to decolonizing conceptions of resistance, including related approaches to art and embodiment. In this respect, I am close to the recent work by Alejandro Vallega, whom I will discuss further in the conclusion in view of his relationship with the philosophy of liberation. This chapter is a critical interpretation of the role aesthetics plays in central moments of Enrique Dussel's work from the perspective of a "cosmological aesthetics."

I approach Enrique Dussel's aesthetics by bringing to his work an analytic distinction between the interrelated moments of resistance and liberation.[2] "Liberation" implies the transformation of systemic and oppressive social, political, and economic structures, including the ways they are internalized by the oppressed through senses of self and attachments to values that oppress them. A liberated "world" where the demands of the oppressed are addressed is not derivative, however, of such structures and their internalization; it is not their development nor does it emerge from their oppositional negation. In Dussel's terms, liberation is "analectic" rather than "dialectic," or, from "exteriority." It is not progress, or a continuous social project, but involves a leap, a lapse in historical trajectories.

By "resistance" I mean the force of this lapse manifest as a release from the insidious affective, cognitive, memorial, postural, and perceptual hold of oppressive systems. Resistance is the formation of dispositions (like those of unsociable bodies, including their affects, memory, and capacities to "bear witness") disinvested from the modern/colonial project to administer socialities constructed as "human." Resistance is non-socializable, non-progressive, and non-redemptive, and constitutes the *aísthetic* possibility of liberation as ana-lectical. It is also propitiatory: that is, incongruent with modern conceptions of agency and praxis. This germinative, resistant, physical moment is for Dussel a potency of the people from "exteriority." Corporealities and intimacies, "fiestas" and popular art, are resistant in ways that systemic studies of oppression find hard to theorize.[3] Effectively, there is no liberation without resistance. Theoretically, however, one can focus on liberation without seeing resistance. I emphasize the moment of resistance since it sheds light on the role of aesthetics in the "philosophy of liberation," and on its living instantiations.

Vallega's notion of "anachrony" as disclosive of resistance helps me introduce critical engagements with Dussel's work. "Anachrony" is akin to what I call self-less time and is a development of Dussel's "analectics." It is the dissemination of sequential temporalities that enforce the progressive episodic closure of historical stages or phases. It is the disempowerment of temporalities that do not allow for parallelisms and simultaneities, and that come to be gathered in a present as a moment of decision. Anachronies temporalize resistant sensibilities that are indifferent to—and destabilize—the modern/colonialist disposition to both assume a demarcated "human" world as controllable and predictable, and to valorize the historical protagonism of "humans." Instead, through "anachrony," resistant bodies are given to an affirmative disposition toward non-human lives, excluded from the human "world," lives that are rendered unintelligible within its progressive social order—lives in "exteriority," in Dussel's terms. Yet, Dussel continues to hold on to a notion of history, as when he envisions "exteriority bursting into history." Following Vallega's development of analectics as implying anachrony, it may be more appropriate to think of exteriority dispelling history, enveloping it and miniaturizing it, rendering history ephemeral like a temporary projection, or a ripple in the cosmos.

"Anachrony," then, does not only mean a rearrangement of past, present, and future, but also the absence of a "now" that would disclose a strictly human, historical order disconnected from cosmic reciprocities. In this absence, temporalities emerge that are not anthropocentric—cosmic temporalities like those of "after-bodies" or the "body of the earth," for example, in which the values of demarcated "human" interests recede. Formed by such cosmic temporalities, resistant bodies depend on a physical sphere that cannot be reduced to agential logics and, thus, is hard to elucidate. A large part of this book has been an attempt to offer such an elucidation on the basis of Andean aesthetics. Dussel, however, does not turn to the cosmos in this way, even though I think his notion of "exteriority" calls for this turn. He seems attached to a robust notion of the human that continues to center his ethics, something that, I suggest, curbs his anticolonial stance and makes his account of liberation appear as a form of socialization despite the central role of "exteriority" and "analectics" in his philosophy of liberation.[4]

Through my approach, based on the distinction between liberation and resistance, and on the notion of "anachrony" or of a self-less time as disclosive of resistance, I do not intend to offer a strict exegesis of Dussel's work. I enter into a critical dialog with him in view of the anthropocentrism and value of liberation as historical agency in his ethics. At the same time, I find his recent determination of *aísthesis* to resonate with the way I have rendered the relationships between aesthetics, resistance, and the cosmos or *pacha*.

The Inescapability of Oppression

There is a theorizing gaze enthralled by seeing the oppressed as oppressed, one that sees the exhaustive, negating character of structural oppression. It is driven to approach oppressive systems as if they also constituted the conditions for resistance. Consequently, it articulates liberation as if its possibility were given by the critique of social, economic, and cultural structures, thus reducing the resistant-oppressed to the way they are envisioned through the structures that oppress them. This is a search for the possibility of liberation that, even if necessary, perhaps unwittingly renders oppression "inescapable," as Lugones would say.[5] She gives Marx's analysis of capitalism and the alienation of workers as an example of this:

> Laborers sell their labor power to obtain the means of subsistence that under capitalism they cannot obtain except through the alienation of their productive activity. The exercises that end with their alienation are the only exercises of their praxis—their conscious productive activity—open to them and these only further their alienation. (2003: 54)

She concludes that it is difficult to see how "class struggle and the production of class consciousness" are possible under such a rendition of oppression (2003: 54). In this respect, the possibility of both resistance and liberation are buried. This effect can be extrapolated to similar analyses of the structures of patriarchy and racism, among others, especially bearing in mind not only their material implications but also their psychological impact on, and embodied and subjective configurations of, the oppressed.

One way to address this "inescapability of oppression" is to assume a resisting disembodied self that can access an universalist and objectivist standpoint from which to articulate liberatory projects (this self would be de-historized, a-cultural, de-gendered, trans-racial in its resisting enactments, suppressing the lived, embodied, oppressed positionalities that trigger its own critical stance). Such an abstract resistant self would elude the material, psychological, cultural, and social hold of oppressive structures, and its internalization, that otherwise appears inescapable. The result of this is a contradiction within liberatory theorizing between positing an embodied oppressed self and a—mostly unthematized yet decisive—disembodied resistant self.

Antonio Cornejo Polar's analysis of a resistant subject on the basis of Domitila Barrios de Chungara's testimony in *Let Me Speak!* sheds light on this. He writes:

> Barrios' is a classic testimony in which the original narrator represents an oppressed group and is thereby obliged to be a strong, stable subject who is both political (vindicating the mining proletariat) and redemptive (the suffering of the individual and the group will bear fruits of justice in the end). (2013: 155)

This relationship between representation, vindication, redemption, and a stable subjectivity reveals the consolidation of a so-called resisting self supported by dynamics of (self) recognition, one that stands for a group of oppressed peoples. This representative self both essentializes oppressed identities and ties the resolution of oppression to a comprehensive, retributive future event that appears as a task to be accomplished. In this way, a kind of resistant subjectivity is constructed, one that in its liberatory function abstracts from the embodied vulnerabilities of the oppressed, the enmeshment of their identities (cultural, ethnic, gendered, and racial identities, among others), their impure participations in dynamics of oppression and resistance, and the complexities of their geo-historical determinations. Cornejo Polar continues:

> the main agenda of *Let Me Speak!* Is to transform an individual subject (Barrios) into a broadly collective one, growing first from miners' wives to the mining proletariat, then to the working class, and finally to the socialist nation of the future ... through constant and overarching synecdoche, the part (the individual and her biography) becomes the whole (the people and their history). (2013: 156)

In this gradual expansion of the resistant subject, through which she loses specificity as she gains in representativity, a universalist and disembodied critical perspective emerges as allegedly the only vehicle for liberation, a critical perspective that is articulated through analytical categories such as race, gender, and class and their intersections. This abstract subject, however, not only represses the specificity of complex experiences of physical oppression/resistance that cannot be integrated into self-consciousness and abstract articulations but also excludes concrete oppressed peoples erased through its representative and redemptive function. In this way, colonial dynamics of oppression are reinforced under the guise of liberatory projects.

Another related attempt to tackle the problematic of the "inescapability of oppression" thematizes the difference between theory and praxis, and focuses on the role of the "intellectual" in relation to the oppressed masses. This prompts the development of critical, liberatory pedagogies as well as demarcations of the role of "organic" intellectuals embedded in popular culture, folk wisdom, and subaltern lineages (rather than assuming a representative, leading, avant-garde function). In this respect, the possibility of liberation is at stake in the success of a transformative subjective and communal path of critical education and in mobilizing excluded knowledges and other cultural resources of the oppressed— without betraying their authentic sense—in order to facilitate liberatory options. These processes appear to have the potential to overcome material, embodied, epistemic, and internalized oppressions, and to even redeem the oppressed through their liberation.

Difficulties that arise in these kinds of projects relate to whether liberatory pedagogies include disciplinary measures that continue to reinforce the view of the oppressed as passive, and to whether there is an emphasis on translating a politicized, cultural authenticity of the oppressed that dangerously essentializes their identities, rendering them manipulatable.[6] Certainly, these issues have been tackled in important texts by Antonio Gramsci, Paulo Freire, and Dussel (especially in his sections on Marx, Freire, and Rigoberta Menchu in *Ethics of Liberation*), among many others. Furthermore, intellectual leadership and pedagogical liberatory efforts may include investments in processes of socialization that prove illusory, especially given the differentiation between the human and non-human, the coincidence of the social with the human in modernity/colonialism, and that the oppressed cannot be humanized in colonial and postcolonial contexts. Not addressing the issue of socialization in movements of anticolonial resistance ends up perpetuating violence against the oppressed waged by other oppressed who "resist" (this is discussed in Chapter 3).

These two attempts to address the "inescapability of oppression" help explain the difficulty of a critical shift in focus from oppression to resistance. The latter cannot be understood from the articulation of the systemic character of the former. Oppression appears "inescapable" if this difference is not attended to. However, the shift toward elucidating the conditions of resistance is elusive due to the insidiousness of oppression, of colonialism and its legacies, even within liberatory projects. This is why it may be tempting to focus on liberation and let resistance fade into the background.

Structures of oppression operate on a far-reaching field of physicality ranging from bodily encodings (of race, gender, and other embodied social forms), to psychological/affective phenomena (like double consciousness, impostor syndrome, resentment, nostalgia, and guilt), to perceptual orders, to attachments to culture and identity (through experience, memory, and habitual participation, including ritual practices), to socialities and epistemologies. In theories of liberation, according to Lugones, emphasis is put on revealing the effects of oppression in all of these physical registers and on giving a rendition of oppressed selves encompassed and configured through them.[7] This, however, does not shed light on how these levels of exhaustive physical oppression can be sustained by an embodied, persisting oppressed-in-resistance. How can the oppressed, remaining with their embodied vulnerability within an oppressive world, live resistantly without transcending their physicality and being socialized? What are the physical conditions for the oppressed to be able to resist when they have internalized racist gazes, and their cultural referents have been colonized and denied in their coevalness and historical relevance?

These questions have driven this book and also frame my engagement with Dussel. They reveal why positing a disembodied, self-certain, agential, resisting self, as well as a process of education and political leadership that mobilize the cultures and socialities of the oppressed, appear as enticing approaches to uncovering the possibility of liberation. As I have noted, these options, however, can reinforce colonialist structures and turn into mechanisms of oppression. Yet there is an illuminating tension that becomes apparent when these options are seen in relation to one another.

The incentive to posit a disembodied self is that specific identity-based attachments (specifically in terms of the embodied, affective, and psychological instances of oppression they imply) seem to be obstacles rather than conditions for resistance. At the same time, critical pedagogies and an intellectual, "organic" leadership valorize experiential and identity-related facets of the oppressed as embodied resources from which to manifest their resistance both individually and collectively. In this way, the problematic of the "inescapability of oppression" seems to reside in the embodiment of oppression (including affective and perceptual enactments).[8] What physical potencies, then, do the oppressed draw from when living resistantly? In this book I have addressed this question via cosmological physicalities, including sense perception, as well as spatio-temporalities and engagements with artworks. In my view, the study of Dussel's aesthetics, and his notion of *aísthesis* in particular, can also speak to this question.

An *Aísthetic* Approach to Dussel's Epiphenomena

By resistance I do not mean the agency of subjects, but physical configurations that include interrelated affects and sentient enactments that are irreducible to colonially imposed subjective positions, and that transpire across dominant and oppressed social positionalities without investments in the systems they support. In particular, resistance involves sensing oppressed bodies (including one's own) that are not assimilated into the intelligibility tied to modern/colonialist socialities. This is reminiscent of Lugones's finding that resistance is in the colonial difference: that is, in between modern/colonialist subjectifications (disclosed through the analysis of oppression) and "active subjectivity" (as living, physical enactments of the oppressed that do not depend on the social orders that sustain their oppression). Dussel's phenomenological analysis of the "epiphany" of the oppressed from "exteriority" illuminates the possibility of this kind of resistance.[9]

For Dussel, "the oppressed" does not constitute an essentializing or pure characterization.[10] This term denotes the inhabitation of contextually determined and enmeshed positionalities, and the inability to articulate needs from them that are intelligible within dominant social, political, and economic systems. Dussel attends to the ways these excluded positionalities are embodied and appear to physical (specifically affective) registers that are not anchored in self-centered, unified, and abstract subjectivities.[11] Following him, I focus on a physical field in which the oppressed become manifest. This is a field irreducible to totalized "worlds," including oppressive ones, yet it is perceptually and affectively sensed. Conditions for the emergence of resistant physicalities are at stake in this sensing.[12]

Building on the phenomenological tradition, on Heidegger and Merleau-Ponty in particular, Dussel is attentive to the role of the body (through physicalities such as sense perception, and affects) in interpretive renditions of worldly meaning. He states, for example: "Concept and precept (sensible image) are given simultaneously because interpretation is an act of sentient intelligence and perception is an act of intelligent sensibility."[13] This points to a sentient, hermeneutic reasoning of a bodily oriented self within a practical field articulated as a significant totality or a "world."

In this context, Dussel mobilizes, and shows the limits of, the notion of "phenomenon": "One says 'phenomenon' in reference to the fact of appearing in the world, with respect to the significant totality" (1977: 37). This delimitation of "phenomenon" sheds light on a crucial moment in liberatory philosophy. It posits both the sensing of things and persons as they are meaningfully articulated within significant totalities, and the concomitant yet distinct physical sensing of the non-thematic and non-objectifiable manifestation of such totalities or "worlds." This suggests the possibility of worlds of significance not appearing as a "phenomenon," insofar as they are not within a "significant totality." This would be an "epiphenomenon," and it is given, in my view, to physical, pre-conceptual registers.

In connection with my earlier discussion of the social implications of the difference between the human and non-human in modernity/colonialism, Dussel helps me understand that there is an epiphenomenal field that exceeds the circumscription of significant totalities articulated in view of "human" interests and controlling dispositions, where the "human" is colonially constructed. For agencies rendered intelligible through socialities aligned with dominant political institutions and economies, these totalities appear to demarcate the sphere of the "human" as such, and render what is outside of it dispensable. Thus, I interpret Dussel's notion of "world" as a significant totality to coincide with the modern/colonial absolute human sphere that dehumanizes the oppressed.

Yet, it is also possible to attend to physical, sentient, and interpretive enactments as they develop from an epiphenomenal aperture, and sustain a sensing of and through the delimitations, emergence, and passing of "human," totalized worlds. Anticipating Dussel's recent notion of *aísthesis* I discuss later, I suggest that *aísthesis* not only senses entities within a significant totality but also senses "epiphenomena," which renders the significances in which entities are embedded contingent, ephemeral, and transient. In the earlier chapters I discuss such epiphenomena as elemental or cosmological, even as cataclysmic in their destruction of orders of sense. I suggest, going beyond Dussel's analysis, that *aísthesis* senses (both perceptually and through inner awareness) the "human" in the instability of its absolute modern/colonial construction.

The *Aísthesis* of the Ethical

Now broaching the ethical, *aísthesis* can sense mediations for decisions in terms of passing, temporary delimitations of practical options as well as of humanity (in terms of fluctuations of the social valuations of lives).[14] In its epiphenomenal aperture, embedded in the passing of worlds as totalities of significance, *aísthesis* senses moments of decision in the variance of paths of action and the contingency of social orders. Thus, "situated freedom," and the choice it implies, depends on *aísthesis* as a sensing of epiphenomena.

Thus, through *aísthesis*, institutional, social, and economic orders that promise the completion of human tasks and fulfillment of human lives appear contingent. This is the case because there is always a volatile epiphenomenal margin that challenges instrumental or controlling dispositions. Freedom, then, implies an *aísthesis* of articulations of worlds, but only as they arise out of a larger, dynamic, and incomprehensible background: a cosmic background I suggest, going beyond Dussel's analysis. This is why choice appears only in terms of "possibilities," unsettled in its grasp of practical options and their valuative frames.

In this way, freedom involves the epiphenomenal *aísthesis* of an indeterminate fate coming from an unassimilable border of the orders of significance within which one's choice acquires sense. I note here, then, an "*aísthesis* of freedom." Thus, I find *aísthesis* implicit in Dussel's description of freedom: "this openness to the duty of determining oneself for this or that possibility, this being sometimes disconcerted and not knowing which to choose, this power itself to choose and not to choose, this capacity or dominion over mediations has been called freedom" (1977: 38). Up to this point this is an account of the ethical that centers on the possibility for decision making and the subjective experience of freedom, one that can be traced back to Aristotle and is at the core of Heidegger's *Being and Time*.

Exteriority and the Epiphenomenon of "Distinctness"

Dussel's analysis of freedom entails a further aesthetic dimension that is the opening to another sense of the ethical (beyond decision making), one directly involved with the possibility of resistance. Dussel's notion of "exteriority" in particular expands the *aísthesis* involved in freedom and reveals the ethical moment the philosophy of liberation is concerned with. Exteriority "is meant to signify the ambit whence other persons, as free and not conditioned by one's own system and not as part of one's world, reveal themselves" (1977: 40). When the *aísthesis* of freedom senses the freedom of others as an epiphenomenon it comes to its liberatory instantiation: that is, when the epiphenomenal margin is not assumed to be populated by objectifiable entities, but by others as free, beyond managed social logics and instrumental calculations.

This *aísthetic*, physical enactment in, of, and from exteriority undermines exploitative social reductions of persons to worldly significant projections. This is the "epiphany" of the other. Exteriority shelters, then, a form of epiphantic *aísthesis*, and for this reason it is not an "outside" of the world, since being "outside" implies objectification. In exteriority, the physical and affective intertwinement of one and the other, of sensing and sensed (the sensing in freedom and the sensed freedom), is emplaced in the epiphenomenal ambit, in the marginal insignificance of "human" worlds. At this juncture I find a resonance between Dussel's "exteriority" and my development of the notion of the human insignificance of the cosmos.

"Exteriority" also implies an *aísthesis* of the epiphenomenon of an incarnated sensing/being sensed arising out of the limen between an oppressive, exclusionary "world" and a "world" where the freedom of the excluded can come to be realized. The sensing/being sensed of the oppressed in exteriority implies a turn toward a "world" in which her freedom is supported. I suggest that in this limen a kind of echoing of concrete yet irreducible worlds is also sensed in their passing emergence. This is an excessive, turning moment when projections of the "situated freedom" of a self are divested of the self-determination supported by social and practical orders, and self-certainty lapses through a proximity with others that is not contained within or around a subjective position. In this turn, processes of self-development, cultivation, and socialization are suspended, and a resistant turning toward liberation transpires liminally and in a self-less time.

Rather than denoting an "outside," "exteriority" constitutes a physical portal that enables the exposure to others and to oneself beyond the frames that circumscribe one's interests and social investments. In this way, the necessity for the systemic closure of social and political orders to assign value to people (their projects, biographies, and histories) recedes. Instead, through an open "epiphany,"[15] persons appear "distinct."[16] "Exteriority," then, also names the aesthetic realm in which one's sense of freedom becomes a sensing of the other (and of oneself as "other") in "distinctness." "Distinctness" is an ethical dimension that supersedes the moment of decision in a liberatory ethics.

The epiphenomenon of "distinctness" assumes a liberatory role in connection with the epiphany of the oppressed. Instrumentalized and denied in their humanity by the allotment of social functions within closed worlds, the projects and needs of the oppressed, and their "situated freedom," cannot be articulated within dominant totalities of significance. Their "distinctness," however, can aesthetically release the hold of such totalities and constitute an "interior transcendentality" that undermines the physical anchoring of oppressive systems from within and without.[17] With respect to "distinctness," then, "exteriority" is also the realm in which dominant, totalized worlds are given leeway to be aesthetically upturned.

Through the *aísthesis* of "distinctness" the systematic negation of lives is exceeded by an affirmation of possibilities of living for the oppressed. This aesthetic enactment entails an overcoming of resentment, guilt, nostalgia, and other affects that re-enforce oppressive systems. In this overcoming, the "distinctness" of the oppressed takes the form of "dignity,"[18] granting an epiphenomenal axis for the overturning of the physical, specifically affective, hold of oppression. The affective register of this granting is "respect." It senses the possibility of "dignity" and entails an excessive affirmation of living in vulnerability and non-belonging. The lives physically given through sensing and being sensed in "respect" are resistant since they embody the affirmation of an "other" world than the dominant one, yet they are not lived by abstract, disembodied, universalist selves, self-certain in their articulate and objectifying agencies. Also, in terms of my earlier discussion, they do not represent and redeem definite oppressed identities.

Faces

Without representational investments, Dussel understands the "dignity" of the oppressed as the aesthetic epiphenomenon of the "face" of the other.[19] Up to this point, the emergence of resistance from exteriority may have seemed to be a modulation of interior affectivity disconnected from culture, race, gender, and other socialities. The epiphany of the "face," instead, manifests "dignity" as a lived gathering of buried histories, biographies, social forms, and cultures of the oppressed without presenting them exhaustively and comprehensively.[20] It reveals the oppressed as a porous and dynamic people, rather than as a closed identity, and elicits a commitment to join them in liberatory struggle.

The "face" does not appeal to an abstract individuation nor does it acquire significance in terms of socializing potentials. It, rather, makes manifest that "dignity" and "respect" are concrete epiphenomenal enactments of resistant lives articulated through excluded cultural and social lineages, and it calls for a situated and physical form of *aísthesis*. In this sense, art can be the materialization of the "face." The art of the oppressed in particular can grant an opening, a portal, that sets into play excluded cultures and other socialities in "dignity" rather than through fetishization. This allows for an *aísthesis* of the overturning of oppression in the affirmation of lives irreducible to it.

Earlier, in connection to the "inescapability of oppression," I noted the difficulty of theorizing the conditions of resistance without abstracting from the embodied vulnerability of oppression. In this section and with Dussel, I posit the *aísthesis* of an epiphenomenal field in which oppressed lives are given to appear in "dignity" and sensed through "respect." This is an aesthetic movement (that happens within and across oppressed and dominant positionalities) of "exteriority," and a source of resistant physicalities. In this movement, oppressed bodies are reoriented to configure resistant living. Moreover, this reorientation is not a matter of socialization, of incorporation into historical trajectories, but of being drawn by an *aísthesis* that can be mediated by artworks and that crosses demarcations of the "human" so as to be able to "see" faces.

Interpreting Dussel through Lugones, and an *Aísthesis* of "Pachakuti"

For Dussel the sphere of art can be concretely lived as popular culture, far away from museums:

> The popular . . . is a whole social sector in a nation that is exploited and oppressed, but that holds a certain exteriority at the same time. . . . Oppressed in the state system, in alterity and free in those cultural moments that are simply despised by the dominators, like folklore, music, food, dress, fiestas, the memory of their heroes, emancipatory movements, political and social organizations, etc. (2012: 11)

In this sphere of popular art, "exteriority" involves a mode of *aísthesis* disengaged from future-oriented projections that extend the systemic hold of oppression. It remains, instead, in a heterogeneous present, or in a utopia of the "present" as Dussel puts it: "The one of the peripheral peoples, of the oppressed classes, of the woman and child" (1977: 90). This is an aesthetic "present utopia" because lives that have no place are sensed as presently possible, sustained by excluded lineages yet without significant delimitations. Dussel's utopia of the "present" is close to my notion of ana-topia, a spatio-temporality untethered by the temporal and spatial hierarchies of modern/colonial domination. On this basis, I interpret Dussel (extending his own work in relation to this book) as positing the embodied involvement in popular art as an anachronic or temporally self-less proximity that mobilizes denied experiences, cultures, and socialities, facilitating the epiphenomenon of "dignity" and the sensing of "respect" from exteriority. Popular art elicits the formation of resistant dispositions in an ana-topic present, dispositions oriented toward a present in its heterogeneity and epiphenomenal passing emergence.

At this point I want to mark a shift in emphasis between my path and Dussel's. His orientation is toward liberation and the analectic emergence of a liberated world, so he does not dwell in the physicalities and ways of living that inhabit concrete dimensions of the present, that are "utopically present," in his terms. My orientation in this book is, rather, cosmological and resistive, so I seek to remain with physical dispositions (like those of after-bodies, ana-topic spatializations, bodily mutations, unsociable bodies) that I see as embedded in the cosmos as *pacha*. These dispositions belong to a heterogeneous present and a self-less time, and are ambivalent to the human "world" enforced by modernity/colonialism.

Perhaps putting it too simplistically, Dussel is ultimately interested in an ethical project that includes an aesthetic dimension, homing in on a principle for liberatory praxis. Mine is a cosmological project for which aesthetics traces the manifestation of physicalities interwoven with a sentience that links humans, animals, and landscapes. These physicalities transpire resistantly in the tension between modern/colonial social subjectifications for the sake of global production of capital and cosmological rhythmic movements that attune bodies to possibilities of communal balance within non-objectifiable processes of destruction and regeneration. I am not suggesting that ethics and liberation are not my concern, but that I am looking for a cosmological basis that may allow for a different articulation of them.

In particular, this cosmic repositioning, in my view, is attentive to the ways the difference between the human and not human instantiated with colonialism demands a re-thinking of both ethics and liberation beyond determinations of the "human." My departure from Dussel hinges on this one point, namely, that his liberatory project can still be understood in terms of processes of socialization insofar as it is anchored in the affectivity of a human self in exposure to alterity. Another way of putting this is that the transhuman implications of his ana-lectics have yet to be developed. This development would lead, I suggest, to the cosmos as informing resistance. At the same time, I find that his aesthetic approach to exteriority that I just laid out speaks to my project, and provides an opening toward its cosmological dimension. Lugones and Kusch help me pursue this opening.

Lugones critiques, as I noted earlier, a modern Western conception of agency that "presupposes ready-made hierarchical worlds of sense in which individuals form intentions, make choices, and carry out actions in the ready-made terms of those worlds" (2005: 86). Such an agency has to be differentiated from resistant enactments that assume an oppressed yet "active subjectivity" that "has no such presuppositions, no ready-made sense within which our actions and intentions can be made congruent with our domination" (2005: 86). "Active subjectivity" looks like passivity from modern Western agential perspectives, but it is forming sense beyond the logics of totalized worlds that oppress it (in the ambit of "exteriority," Dussel would say): "The active subject concocts sense away from the encasement of dominant sense. Her intentions, the meaning of her possibilities, is to be fashioned" (2005: 86–7). Lugones calls this formation of sense that is not confined by the closure of totalized worlds "germination."

The Andean notion of *pachakuti*, especially as it is interpreted by Rodolfo Kusch, sheds light on resonances between Lugones and Dussel. *Pachakuti* can be translated as "turning the cosmos upside down" and can constitute a mode of "estar" (in Kusch's terms) as "being toward a cosmic turning" (2010: 112). As a form of *aísthesis*, "estar" senses a possibility of a radical overturning in a field that is not submitted to human objectifying intentions, an overturning like the one granted by sensing the "dignity" of the oppressed. Through it an oppressive world can appear about to turn so that its total structure recedes and affirmative possibilities for excluded lives can become manifest. In this way, irreducible, multiple presents come to pass anachronically and ana-topically—in the cusp of a cosmic turn or *kuty*. This *aesthesis* of *pachakuti* resonates with both Dussel's "epiphenomenality" and "exteriority," and Lugones's "germinative" state.

An aesthetic approach to *pachakuti* brings together these two theorists. Lugones, for example, states that in "germination" the oppressed "is not yet living up to her potentialities; rather, she is fomenting her potential self, the creation of a counter-universe of sense in which she can engage her potential fully" (2003: 95). I connect this to Dussel's assertion that for any negation of an oppressive system: "it is necessary to effectuate beforehand the affirmation of what the oppressed is as exteriority" (1977: 108). This physical, affective "prior affirmation" of possibilities of living that from dominant, especially modern/colonialist, perspectives are immaterial, is possible from exteriority as an aesthetic sensuous affirmation of and through a resistant living in an heterogeneous, "turning" present. Resistance here means the sensing/being sensed of and from epiphenomenal dignity in an exteriority that sustains the passing of social and political orders without closure. Such resistance draws from (and here I am going beyond Dussel) a cosmic movement of radical overturns that physically situates living.

Dussel's Aísthesis and the Art of the Oppressed

The notions of ana-topia and *pachakuti* shed light on Dussel's recent determination of *aísthesis* as uncovering things "possessing real properties that make possible the affirmation of life" (2020: 4). Dussel's *aísthesis* can sense epiphenomenal emerging worlds that sustain the needs of the oppressed. He calls this mode of appearing "disponibilidad," which I translate as "readiness," and considers it to be the "originary phenomena" of beauty.[21] It implies a "modality of the presence of the real thing linked to the possibility of the subject to continue to live in plenitude" (2020: 4). It is important to note that *aísthesis* in Dussel's determination does not submit to a world constituted as a field of dominant interests. It, rather, senses the possibility of the emerging and passing of "worlds" in the suspension of pre-determined hierarchies that deny the plenitude of lives; it can sense a "pachakuti" in my terms.

Dussel's *aísthesis* does not assume, nor is it bound by, a totalized system of significance in order to sense readiness. And I maintain that readiness elicits embodied transfigurations that are not overdetermined by instrumental dispositions. Echoing my discussion in this chapter so far, I find in Dussel's notion of *aísthesis* an emphasis on sensing in an epiphenomenal aperture both the delimitations, emergence, and passing of social and economic orders as totalized "worlds," and the "readiness" of presently utopic worlds. This elicits, borrowing Dussel's description of the experience of beauty (including beauty in art): "astonishment, a spasm, a joy in the face of the real as mediation, as the enabling, for the continuance of life, that is, of life itself" (4).

Elaborating on his discussion of *aísthesis*, Dussel explores the image of the Virgin of Guadalupe in art of the oppressed. He finds in this image simultaneities and mixings of cultural referents and of histories of resistance, and singles out the emergence of the creole national consciousness as having been made possible through its artistic rendition. I find it illuminating to build on this reference to the iconic Virgin by studying a more recent example of art of the oppressed: Yolanda López's *Virgin de Guadalupe* series. In this series the image of the Virgin recedes so as to become the setting for the (epiphenomenal, I propose) appearance of Chicana women. In this recession, the iconic image allows for the needs and demands of excluded women to gain resonance within an aesthetic sphere that breaks through assumed totalized systems of social significance, even overturning the dominant, oppressive meanings related to the Virgin. In this aesthetic movement a margin for the expression of resistance arises in connection with colonized women's silenced history and culture. I note this example because the way in which the image of the Virgin recedes in these artworks resonates with what Dussel means by beauty as "readiness." In the recession (a turning or *kuti*) of the image, the works reach a kind of fulfillment by "ready-ing" the world for the Chicana women that are foregrounded. I see in the recession of the image of the Virgin a *pachakuti*, and the opening of an ambit that triggers *aísthesis* from exteriority, enabling resistance articulated through renewed forms of "dignity" and "respect."

Dussel also analyzes artworks that present the world ready for an act of liberation or rebellion, where "aesthesis and the aesthetic work potentialize the meaning of a political event" (2020: 14). By "potentialize" I understand that an artwork lets such an event appear as *disponible* or "ready," even though it is the expression of a will-to-live that is out of place in the prevailing system. Dussel mentions Chopin's "Heroic Polonaise" as an example of this. It

> expresses the Polish people in a critical political juncture where the genius celebrates the aesthetic perception of the community, and the work of art nourishes the community in order to vitalize (like an *aesthetic hyperpotentia*) the patriotism of a state of rebellion, of the aspiration toward liberation. (2020: 23)

In liberatory junctures Dussel's *aísthesis*, as I have elucidated it in this section, can constitute an "aesthetic hyperpotentia." Political hyperpotentia, in his terms, involves a recovery of the will-to-live on the part of the excluded so that this will "tears down the walls of Totality and opens a space at the limits of the system through which Exteriority bursts into history."[22] I propose here to reread this statement in light of my discussion so far and suggest that this opening of an epiphenomenal space can be performed through an aesthetic enactment of resistance. Returning to the exteriority of the Chicana women presented in López's series, the *kuty* of the image of the Virgin of Guadalupe, and the "readiness" it allows for, open such a space. In this aesthetic spacing, the oppressed can gather in resistance. "Aesthetic hyperpotentia," in my view, is the power of the art of the oppressed to situate a people in ana-topic aesthetic spaces of "readiness" or spaces of "germination."

I qualify, however, Dussel's statement that "exteriority bursts into history." From the point of view of the resistance, ana-topia and self-less time that I have developed so far, there is no "history" to burst into, but rather cosmic entanglements that need to be (k)notted and re-(k)notted. Resistance is not a moment or an irruption, but physical enactments in which the colonially constructed "human" sphere is revealed to be embedded in more expansive movements of destruction and generation of the cosmos, movements larger than fields of human control and where the difference between the human and non-human holds sway. This is how I read Dussel's statement about opening a space "at the limits of the system." Making too neat of a distinction, perhaps, the "bursting into history" may show an emphasis on his part on liberation rather than resistance.

Conclusion
Turns and Departures

"Cosmological aesthetics," as developed in Part I in the Andean context, guides my elucidations of physical (perceptual, memorial, spatio-temporal) modes of embeddedness in the cosmos or *pacha* that assume anticolonial resistant forms without relying on modern/colonial configurations of agency, subjectivity, and sociality. It constitutes a turn away from the framing of aesthetic experiences by colonialist and modernist institutions (such as museums, art galleries, and the academy), and toward the "body of the earth" in Anzaldúa's sense. That is, it is a turn toward a plane in which transhuman connectivity with the cosmos can allow for living socially without submitting to the colonial imposition of the difference between the human and non-human, and the violation of lives it implies. I finish by revisiting this turn in two ways. First, extending the notion of ana-topia developed in Chapter 5, I focus on the relationship between art, space, and resistance. Second, extending the discussion of *aísthesis* in Chapter 6, I bring up Alejandro Vallega's work on aesthetics, and follow his turn toward the earth in a departure from Dussel's philosophy of liberation. These two analyses converge in an ethical dimension of resistance that emerges with the cosmos.[1]

Invoked Art and Space[2]

The Ana-topia of Art

Notions of resistance can assume Western temporalities that return to a self or to a "here/now" as a disclosive moment of decision, and value processes of self-transformation that involve continuity, development, cultivation, and socialization. Yet, when the colonized disempower oppressive structures that deny their humanity, they also dismantle the dominant ways in which they understand themselves. This loss can be paralyzing. It reinforces a sense of worthlessness and incompetency that validates the dehumanization of the oppressed. Anzaldúa finds in this a debilitating sense of shame.[3] Through this paralysis, however, the mendacity of redemptive promises of belonging and socialization is most apparent.

In resistance, the oppressed face physical, psychic, and affective leaps, leading to discontinuities in inhabitations of identity (in terms of social categories, for example), and to embodied metamorphoses that are of a self-less time. I am pointing to a difficulty that assails the self-understanding and physicalities of the resistant-oppressed, as they strive to hold on to the social articulations of their oppression as if they supported their senses of self. This difficulty also points to an edge, to possibilities of transformation, in which fears of loss of self can lead to affects, memorial forms, and spatio-temporal bearings that don't need to abide by socialities based on the difference between the human and non-human, by socialities managed for global capitalist interests born in colonialism. These are resistant physicalities that are accessible from the experience of oppression, yet they are unsociable and irredeemable. An ana-topic aesthetic approach can shed light on this edge of resistance as manifest in the process of artistic creation and in the space of invoked artworks.

Gloria Anzaldúa's description of her experience of writing might as well be a description of resisting:

> When I write it feels like I am carving bone. It feels like I am creating my own face, my own heart—a Nahuatl concept. My soul makes itself through the creative act. It is constantly remaking and giving birth to itself through my body. It is this learning to live with la Coatlicue that transforms living in the Borderlands from a nightmare into a numinous experience. It is always a path/state to something else. (2007: 46)

This statement influenced Lugones's notions of "active subjectivity" and resistance as a (self) creation that does not rely on pre-articulated socialities or identities. It shows the deep affinity between Lugones's account of resistance and Anzaldúa's aesthetics. In this respect, I have already explored and extended Lugones's phenomenology of space (see Chapter 5). Now I continue in this path with an emphasis on the spatiality of "invoked art."

Anzaldúa's "invoked art" (discussed in Chapter 1) does not reside in an object or a finished product. If it did, it would render the process of creation secondary to the creation, and objectify and commodify a work to be hung in a cold museum wall. Anzaldúa, instead, develops an aesthetics that centers on the experience of making art, a process that is never completed and that ceases to be the artist's, since it interacts with an active audience as well. "Invoked art" is housed in homes and other everyday, peopled places, and has an engaging presence beyond its technical accomplishment. As she explains in terms of *Borderlands/La Frontera* as her written creation, the text continues to be alive and to engage her, so that the creative act, like the cosmos I would say, renews and destroys itself, and never ends. The space of these living artworks is not that of museums: they are not meant to be passively witnessed, or to be admired for their technique.

The spatial difference between museums and homes as sites for art can be approached through an "anticipatory aesthetics" that is attentive to the spacing of art as leeway or as ana-topic. Homes as peopled, intergenerational spaces that gather families, neighborhoods, and ghosts, have leeway. This is in contrast to museums having set habitable dimensions that minimize the interaction with artworks, and that suppress their creative force by making them fit within restrictive social and historical frames (see Chapter 1). For "anticipatory aesthetics" the ana-topia of artworks means that they are never outside of the infinite process of their own making and remaking, and continue to involve the artist and audience in self-creation even if beyond their control. This is evident when the artwork is placed in lived-in spaces, where there is no overriding directive as to how it ought to be approached, and where institutionality recedes, opening up leeway for peopled festive and ritual gatherings. In these kinds of spaces of leeway, like plazas, homes, or ritual sites, artworks remain "anticipatory," being about to be, or always at the edge of being something other. In this sense, now using Lugones lexicon, artworks can open liminal sites that allow for world travel.

There is no spatial determination of a clear outside/inside of the invoked artwork, it is always in a border. "Anticipatory aesthetics" attends to this border as sheltering (rather than culminating, objectifying, and externalizing) the creative act. In this interactive spatiality, where the audience is anticipatorily enthralled by the artwork, and by itself, being at an edge, a gathered festive community can become part of its own creation and recreation. The border spacing of the artwork does not let the creativity of the artist, or of the community, return to a sense of identity and mastery supported by dominant socializations, institutionalized histories, and the appreciation of artistic technique.

For "anticipatory aesthetics," the artwork has an ana-topic space that can allow for discontinuous transformations and rebirths in a self-less time, and even at the border of colonial and modern processes of socialization, testing and unsettling their demarcation of the difference between the human and non-human. Thus, I understand the space of Anzaldúa's "invoked art" as leeway or ana-topically, and propose "anticipatory aesthetics" as a dimension of my earlier discussion of "cosmological aesthetics," one that emphasizes the space of art.

Creative Blocks and *Ukhu Pacha*

Anzaldúa is particularly interested in the artist's creative "blocks" as illuminating the nature of artistic creation. Such "blocks" are petrifying because they reveal both the entrapment of the artist's sense of self in dominant social structures, and the necessity for the destruction of such structures for the sake of creating art; in this respect creative blocks converge with the lapses and discontinuities that affect the resistant-oppressed. That is, both the artist and the resistant-oppressed are compelled to undergo destruction as part of (self) creation. This demand is paralyzing and this "block" cannot be worked through by relying on instrumental, subjective, and self-conscious projections of pre-articulated social meanings. Anzaldúa's "invoked art," moreover, emphasizes creative blocks as undermining processes of cultivation and socialization temporalized so that there is always a return to the self or to a resolute moment. It also dispels the view of the artist as owning her creation, since it embeds the artwork in the community and its concrete peopled places.

In the gaps and spacings provided by the spatiality of "invoked art," by lived-in ana-topias rather than by museums and art galleries, the artist/audience is thrust into the depths of their own bodies as sites of destruction and regeneration. Bodies in relation to the artwork become a portal to new bodies. Building on my discussion of after-bodies in Chapter 4, this physical enactment is not of a self, but is the site of transformations and rebirths that involve selves. Moreover, I connect this enactment to a modality of Andean space: *ukhu pacha*, a concrete dimension of the cosmos.

Ukhu pacha is the spatiality of snakes and of the underworld.[4] It is not the metaphoric site of the unconscious, since it is not framed in terms of a subject, therapy, or normalcy. The unconscious is still within the human sphere delineated by modernity and colonialism. *Ukhu pacha*, instead, is a concrete determination of space, such as in atmospheres that put one at the edge, like an entryway into a deep cave; or architectures where the physical hold of socialities loses grip, as if there were only leeway; and other spaces from which a self does not return. In view of my earlier discussion of Inka architecture (Chapter 2), *ukhu pacha* is concretized in buildings that bear a cataclysmic potency, whose relation to the earth renders the demarcations of the human sphere insignificant. I suggest, then, that *ukhu pacha* is the ana-topic space of "invoked art."

Ukhu Pacha, as the palpable space of "invoked art," is often found in homes, cemeteries, and in the frenzied spatialities of plazas, in market places and busy Andean churches. It is the space of streets that sustain protests, strikes, and revolutions. It is also the space of unending aesthetic creation: in which the artist, community, and artwork are held at an ana-topic edge of social intelligibility and values, germinating in the spacing of *ukhu*, anticipating without fulfillment, in bodily transformation. This potential or anticipatory state is apparent in the inability to simply "read," with detachment, the meaning of "invoked art" from available histories, cultures, and institutionalized knowledge, or from its technique. The artwork, instead, is a burst of cosmic space from the underworld that gives leeway to stretch toward surprising inhabitations without them crystallizing in determinate and absolute "human" worlds.

This is why the potency of the artwork is not a falling short of an expected or pre-delineated signification (as if it were incomplete or unfinished). It is, rather, always being ready for its rebirth in unprecedented bodied spaces that do not appear under human control. For this reason, invoked artworks in their potency can provide portals. They offer, through leeway, glimpses and intimations of other places in a way that human interests and projections do not appear definitive in them, as if "humanity" were still to be shaped by them in unfathomable ways, or not to be shaped at all. Their potency and character of portals, of being at an ontological edge, is not something that one gleans from representational "content." It is a spatial presence invoked in them, an emanating atmosphere that enfolds the artist's and community's creative blocks and rebirths.

Anzaldúa's aesthetics turns to artworks as localized ritual presences (she mentions, for example, the relation between artworks and totem poles and cave paintings).[5] I suggest that she begins her analysis of "invoked art" with the experience of the artist as a way to transition and re-visit the emplaced communal enactment of rituals. In rituals people are given to renew themselves and overcome the fear of self-destruction without abiding by an instrumental, linear logic of development, and without falling prey to socializations, redemptive promises, or finalities. Ritual presences—in song, dance, sculpture, architecture—when invoked, are ana-topical portals for communities in destruction/regeneration, in the cosmic realm of *ukhu pacha*, and allow those communities to resist the framings and expectations of enforced modern/colonial socialities and self-centered temporalities of development and progress. In terms of Chapter 3, "invoked art" can come to pass at what Lugones calls the "colonial difference," which is the spacing of anticolonial resistance. I note here, then, the entanglement between the communal and concrete spatiality of invoked artworks, regenerative processes of creation, and resistances to colonialism and modernity. I emphasize that the space of artworks in this sense is not the result of an artwork being "there." This is a cosmic region, a pervasive and defining spatial modality that artworks join.

In-Dreaming/Ensueños[6]

When looking through a portal, the side toward which one is about to cross only appears as a fragment, it refuses to disclose itself, to give one a proper footing and a sense of embeddedness in a habitable place. Portals can physically evoke a way of undermining the possibility of social solidity, and they capture the back and forth between one's identities that never quite leaves each other behind, like in Lugones's discussion of *chachawarmi*. In terms of Chapter 3 and my analysis of Aguilar's photography, the leeway of portals allow for (k)notting, for the emptiness of embodied social interweavings.

Here I underscore the possibility of someone being on the other side of a portal and looking back, or of one looking back at oneself after crossing (having become split and seen through the portal). Such a fragmented looking back, in which an articulated world does not support seeing or being seen, reveals oneself as in transition without continuity, which is reminiscent of my earlier discussion of Aguilar's *clothed/unclothed*. Hovering in discontinuous transit is the ana-topic effect of portals. It solicits a kind of being in a leap between different bodies. It also configures a mode of seeing, of "bearing witness," without the support and expected validations of pre-articulated socialities, values, and modern determinations of the "human." This is a seeing of oneself and others that, in conditions of oppression, does not seek assimilative and socializing processes of recognition, a "bearing witness" that connects the uncanny stillness of Aguilar's photographs and Wilson's paintings.

The spatial, physical enactment of "bearing witness" can be made possible by the anticipatory potency of artworks, and by their ana-topic spatiality. They are at issue in Anzaldúa's account of "bearing witness" as both an aesthetic and resistive enactment. Beyond subjectification or objectification, "bearing witness" is a relation with another, or with oneself as other, that is fragmentary yet intimate; where difference or alterity, rather than being a besieging or productive negation, is an emptiness that allows for transformation, destruction, and rebirth as enmeshed processes. It involves the manifestation of physicalities in transit, dislocated from familiar worlds and from the draw of the familiar. Anzaldúa finds "bearing witness" in the "ensueños" of the paintings of Liliana Wilson (discussed in Chapter 4). Here I return to these works in view of embodied anatopic spatialities.

Anzaldúa notes in Wilson's otherworldly characters a "solidity" and "balance" enduring a "seeing" that looks back and makes us look back at ourselves from differential realities. Seeing and being seen in this way releases us from the strictures of normalcy and fixed social identifications. She explains that this is not a matter of leaving our world behind, but of becoming suddenly aware of the illusory character of the determinacy of the orders of social meanings that hold bodies hostage.

In this respect, Anzaldúa offers *ensueños* as a psychic/embodied enactment to shed light on the possibility of "bearing witness." She writes in an essay on Wilson: "The watching inner eye está viendo como en sueños, in a kind of controlled waking dream" (2015: 31). "Seeing like in dreams," or *ensueños*, which I translate as "in-dreaming," refers to the "bearing witness" of Wilson's paintings that involves the spacing of artworks as portals, and their continuous readiness for rebirthing, and self-creation without socializing investments.

An "ensueño" takes one over when, while awake, one imagines oneself as having wings, as winning the lottery, as being someone else. In it the continuity of these transformations is suspended, allowing for fleeting departures from familiar embodied orders, and a rebirth through which one thinks, craves, hopes, from another body. This is a physical, cosmic event insofar as what shifts are not just things or ideas, but the concrete corporeal relations that give them significance. In this sense, in-dreaming aligns with the memory of afterbodies, and with their in-stilled draw to the cosmic time of *ñaupa pacha* that anachronically releases sedimented corporeal habitations, including those that delimit the human. In *Borderlands* Anzaldúa writes:

> My "awakened dreams" are about shifts. Thought shifts, reality shifts, gender shifts: one person metamorphoses into another in a world where people fly through the air, heal from mortal wounds. I am playing with my Self, I am playing with the world's soul, I am the dialogue between myself and *el espíritu del mundo*. I change myself, I change the world. (2007: 45)

This playing with one's self while shifting entails a proliferation of inhabitations of and dispositions toward oneself. In this dreamy detachment one is prone to fragmentation, transformation, to destruction and rebirth, to creation.

Yet playing in this way is not speculative or ethereal. It happens in the dynamic intimacy between passing bodies and the sensuous passing of the inhabitations that shape them. "In-dreaming" is hard to understand from modern Western perspectives that favor a disembodied imagination, self-returning temporalities, and the split between reality and fiction. Wilson's art challenges these tenets, by drawing our bodies into a spatiality with infinite leeway and depth that is both light and grounded, earthy, bestowing portals for physical rebirth. Such is the aesthetic mystery of the "solidity" and "balance" of her characters, and their concrete spaces.

Ensueño in Wilson's paintings is a modality of physical in-stillness that is transformational. It allows for "bearing witness" through a shamanic seeing that lets go, mourns, destructs, rebirths, and sees the sorrow of the dehumanized without socializing narratives. In this respect, "in-dreaming" in Wilson's paintings as enabling "bearing witness" appears as a physical form of resistance. When the oppressed is perched at the ana-topic edges of social orders that exclude her, without interest in turning back, she risks her life and "bears witness" to others doing the same without promises of redemption.

In some of her paintings the difference between in-dreaming and death is blurred, re-enforcing the fact that those who live in-dreaming, in a self-less time, are most vulnerable to being killed. She finds among immigrants and other border crossers people who are constantly in an *ensueño*, and resisting. In one of her paintings, Rodrigo Rojas, who was killed by the Chilean military, refuses to leave the earth. As if in an *ensueño*, having crossed over, he looks back without transcendence or redemption, "bearing witness." Oscillating between dreaming and dying it is possible to see not just human, but cosmic sorrow and vulnerability.

Ana-topic Spectrality

Edwin Quispecuro Nina's artworks belong to and reflect on the lineage of religious painting of the Cuzco School, which emerged in the early colonial era led by indigenous artists like Diego Quispe Tito. Quispecuro Nina recovers the materials and motifs of this lineage (he sometimes uses discarded wooden frames from colonial churches, for example) to recreate numinous ritual presences. In his "virgin series," contemporary mestiza and indigenous women from Cuzco are portrayed taking up the place of the Virgin Mary, similarly to Yolanda López's *Virgen de Guadalupe* series. He preserves the familiar settings and iconography associated with the virgin, and inhabits them with photographs of cuzqueña women he encounters every day in the streets of the Andean city and surrounding areas.[7]

The effect of the series is not to erase the image of the iconic virgin, but to retain it as a receding presence in tension with the emergence of the photograph. This is a transformative moment in-between two images, an inconclusive and discontinuous moment that reverts the ways Andean women have been dehumanized, covered up, and silenced in their gender, racial, and ethnic identities by renditions of a white, pure virgin. This reversion, however, is not replacement: a tense border is maintained. The result of this is that the difference between the human and non-human is suspended by bordering or edging, rather than being flipped.

The indeterminacy of this moment is amplified by the spatial, specifically layered, character of the artworks; by an ana-topic spectrality that allows for tensions, juxtapositions, mixings, overlaps: something that charges the artwork with an in-stilled movement, as if at the verge of a metamorphosis, giving leeway so that the colonialist meanings attached to the virgin can give way. Quispecuro Nina shared with me the struggle that this series represented for him as a mestizo male confronting his participation in the oppression of indigenous women. He fears that a male gaze is still and always will be apparent in the works, which makes the process of making them unfinished, anticipatory, infinite, as well as neither developmental nor self-centered. The process of (self) creation—and (self) destruction—still haunts him, but it is also his non-redemptive resistance.

There is an Andean lineage of "cosmological aesthetics" that is operative in Quispecuro Nina's work, and it can be traced back to Inka architecture. As I noted in the first chapter, by this term I intend the movement away from art as socialization (that is, as it is enforced by modern/colonial institutions) and the aesthetic turn toward the earth that spectralizes the human, making it lose its center, miniaturizing its significance, as if watching an earthquake from above. "Cosmological aesthetics" is apparent in the play of light and earth in the "Virgin Series" in particular, conjuring Inka elemental stonework. The transparent photographs of the series are held within layers of resin, which make the artwork deep and translucent: as if the bodies of the cuzqueña women held light in, yet letting it shine at the same time. This irradiation is similar to the earthly light in Wilson's paintings. In Quispecuro Nina's case the light is held in a translucent stone-like medium producing an airy atmosphere. In Wilson's case the light is earthy, sustained by bodies that are "solid" and "balanced," as if her paintings were made of a stone that absorbs light while irradiating it. Light shining to and from earth infuses their work. In both cases, the ana-topic space of the artworks irradiates with elemental force, as if letting the cosmological background of life come to the fore.

Alejandro Vallega's Aesthetics of Liberation[8]

Vallega's interpretation of exteriority as "radical exteriority," of analectics as temporally anachronic, and of "life" as the movement of the cosmos, develops the philosophy of liberation beyond the purview of Dussel's work. The departures at stake here complement and illuminate mine in the last chapter. Vallega is a creative scholar of Dussel's work, about which he has written extensively. Important for me are the texts "Exordio/Exordium: For an Aesthetics of Liberation out of a Latin American Experience," *Latin American Philosophy from Identity to Radical Exteriority* (where he develops the notion of "anachrony" I have already mentioned), and "An Introduction to Liberatory Decolonial Aesthetic Thought (a South-South path, from Indigenous and Popular Thought in América and from the Sense of Xu (虛) in Chinese Painting)." Here I will briefly focus on the latter two.

The example of Yolanda López's *Virgin of Guadalupe* series I discussed in light of Dussel's work is about "turns" rather than "turning into." When the virgin recedes, the spacing in which this recession happens has to be understood as leeway or ana-topically, it is not integrative, uni-topic. In other words, there is a leap between the receding virgin and the foregrounded Chicana, the latter does not arise from the former, nor does she negate her. In the painting, borrowing a phrase from Vallega, "no form is transformed into another, but rather many forms remain active and non-dialectically at play without possible resolution" (2014: 112). Virgin and Chicana are there in tension but not in opposition, they also miss each other, and they bring with them lineages and histories that do not blend even if they weave and unweave in the living movement of the canvas. Not only does the presence of the Chicana arise from "exteriority" and analectically, she also is embedded in eventuations of times that are concrete and carried physically, namely, in "ana-chrony."

Vallega's "anachrony" is not "a" time, or a modality of time, or a temporality (as in the volatile relations between past, present, and future). It is the emptiness in which time(s) and temporalities happen without a unifying horizon. Both anachrony and ana-topia name aspects of this emptiness. In a way reminiscent of López's art, Vallega writes of "an overlapping of histories that by virtue of the overlapping of lineages decenter and ultimately disseminate any possible idea of an essential or ontological single origin to which lives must answer" (2014: 115). This absence of an origin is a way of thinking of anachronic emptiness, which reveals the illusion of sedimented historical identities. This emptiness can also be thought of as the irreducible gaps between one time and another, like the time of birds, stones, tides, and people. It also becomes apparent when the illusion of a moment of decision is dispelled, in the anxiety of recognizing that it is impossible not to leave loose ends; when after a betrayal a loved one walks away into the insignificance of the past; or as the memorial force of absence and letting go.

I understand anachrony as akin to *ñaupa pacha*, or the Andean notion of cosmic time that runs throughout this book, in which the past passes by us and undergoes mutations and resignifications ahead of us, being woven and rewoven into a fluid present. Emptiness is this (k)notting which can inform physicalities, and it is the cosmos or *pacha* in its "así" (using Kusch's terms). Emptiness is a way of conceiving of the simultaneous generation and destruction of the cosmos, of its creative force or "seminality," of day/night happening without negation or opposition.

With "anachrony" Vallega delves further into the temporality of Dussel's analectics, showing the cosmic emptiness of the analectic leap between oppressive and liberatory worlds, and the sensibility and physicality of this emptiness. In this respect, he mentions "affectivity, emotion, memorial rather than historical memory (trauma, loss, involuntary memory), concreteness (*con-crescere*), the temporalizing-spacing movement in bodying, which in various configurations we call 'bodily.'"[9] I would add to this sense perception as a sentience of emptiness, like the seeing of cataclysms and of the play of elementals.

Most of this book can be understood as a development of these anachronic, cosmological physicalities suggested in this departure from Dussel. It offers an elucidation of their resistant, cosmic enactments that unsettle a colonially forged "human" world and the corresponding dehumanization of the oppressed. Cosmic physicalities of resistance point to a life that is not only an analectic and ethical transition toward liberation constituting the world as a new totality (as in Dussel's account) but also a sentience of a seminal cosmos seeping into our bodies, a life of corporealities without a "subject" even if they situate senses of self; corporealities that live in a self-less time.

Vallega's notion of "radical exteriority" constitutes a related departure from Dussel. It is important to note that Vallega's "radical exteriority" is a development of Dussel's notion of "exteriority" in a similar way that "anachrony" is a development of Dussel's "analectics." For Dussel, "exteriority" is the manifestation of the oppressed in their distinctness: that is, released from the way they are objectified in the world as a totality. As I suggested in the last chapter, exteriority is not an outside of the world. It entails, rather, the possibility of an aesthetic turn in which one transitions from seeing others and oneself as a phenomenon (overdetermined by the logics of the world) to seeing others and oneself as an epiphenomenon, in the passing of the delimitation of worlds (arising in the ambit of freedom, showing dignity and eliciting respect). For Dussel this aesthetic turn implies the aesthetic affirmation of the plenitude of the life of the oppressed, which is at the core of his material principle of ethics, and leads to the affirmation of a new "liberated" world as a totality. In other words here aesthetics is subsumed under ethics, and ethics is oriented toward a liberatory event.

Vallega's "radical exteriority" is a way of persisting in exteriority. It is not a negation of the ethical, but a way of letting an ethical/aesthetic moment arise from an explicit cosmological (rather than anthropocentric) ground. When he states that radical exteriority is "the difference that is always already operative in the claim to identity," he does not mean that all identities are already mediated by difference, something that is central to Western metaphysics (2014: 116). For Vallega the difference implied in exteriority is not operative as a mediation of the identity of the oppressed (as black, woman, disabled, indigenous, queer). Exteriority does not, then, qualify the oppressed in their epiphany.

Rather, the difference of exteriority, which allows for the distinctness of the oppressed, arises in the transition between phenomenal and epiphenomenal sensing, and is operative in this sensing as the indefinite possibility of making claims about the oppressed. In other words, exteriority happens as a movement of life whose sensuous differing situates one face to face with the oppressed in/from exteriority. In the difference of exteriority, the relations of identity and difference between persons (those that constitute social identities, for example) are not predominantly marked. The difference of exteriority, instead, enables situating those relations in an epiphantic field that releases them from the closure of the worlds that give them a fixed significance, making them ephemeral, light, localized, non-essentializing, and anachronic.

Being face to face with the oppressed, one can identify different planes of relationality. First, one's identity and theirs position each other through difference, carving one another out on the basis of differences related to social structures and embodiments, for example. Second, the social determination of this encounter can lose grip through each other's singularity, and through the recognition of the intersecting lineages that constitute each other's identities, of the difference between them, and of the difference they make when they position identities that elude social classifications. I am referring to openness to border and intersectional identities, for example. Here distinctness can come through in faces not as subjective, individualist gestures, but in their resonance with one's peoples, cultures, genders, and in open and porous determinations.

Third, in the encounter the epiphany of the face can also involve lineages and social embodiments in their "seminality": that is, in non-continuous mutations and disseminations (the face becoming an "interface" in Anzaldúa's terms), in their emptiness (not just open endedness and porosity) of determinations, and in their indifference to the difference that identities make. There is a cosmological aspect in this plane of relationality that, I would argue, is resistant. I suggest that these three planes are implicated in an ethical/liberatory encounter, and articulate important political options, including resistant ones, in different registers. I read Vallega's "radical exteriority" as emphasizing the movement from the second plane to the third, broaching the cosmological, and extending Dussel's ethics of liberation from exteriority (which I see as mostly remaining in the second plane). In "radical exteriority" the sensing of the epiphany of the other is oriented toward the emptiness in which the relations of identity and difference come to pass in cosmic, "seminal" processes. This does not mean, however, that these relations are abstract or politically insignificant.

Vallega notes the concreteness and physicality of "radical exteriority":

> I want to underscore that this "radical exteriority" is found at the affective, concrete and memorial dimensions of the movement of existing. . . . In my view body, as would be gender, or race, are terms that operate as borders, sites of resistance and configuration, ecological attunements, through which one negotiates existing by engaging lineages, transforming, and imagining identities in the process. (2014: 213)

"Radical exteriority" is a physical enactment that is not of a subject but that arises with the "movement of existing." Vallega sees himself departing from Dussel, and following Kusch's articulation of Andean thought, by not centering on the ethical subject at this juncture, but on the *aísthesis* that situates her as a sensing of the other in exteriority, and as the movement of life that in this sensing releases lineages and identities from their enforced socialized configurations. "Radical exteriority," is for Vallega the sentience of life as "a holding-freeing movement, a cosmological germinal dance of livingdying-birthing."

For both Dussel and Vallega *aísthesis* names the sentience of life itself. For Dussel this sentience leads to the ethical enactment of liberation. For Vallega, this sentience also exceeds the confines of subjectivity—and "humanity"—in a physical abandonment into the cosmos in its generating, destructing, and creating, in its anachrony, in its emptiness. I suggest that Vallega in this step does not leave the ethics of liberation, but seeks to articulate it from the cosmos and beyond the constructions of the "human." Perhaps for him, as it was for *Taki Oncoy*, the subject of the revolution is *pacha*. At this juncture, in the departure from Dussel in terms of *aísthesis* as the sentience of life, Vallega joins the Andean aesthetic sense I have developed in this book. He states, for example: "living appears also in a word in Quéchua and Aymara impossible to fully translate or grasp: *Pacha*, which means: space, place, depth, time, the state of affairs, the cosmos, and the living cosmos with the term *Pacha-mama*."[10]

The analyses in this work, especially as they build up to these last sections on Anzaldúa's and Vallega's aesthetics, bring up the question of how to understand an ethics of liberation (the ethical as the possibility for the transformation of conditions of oppression) from physical involvements with the cosmos (at the level of affect, sense perception, memory, and spatio-temporal bearings). I suggest that the cosmological resistance I have been focusing on clarifies this realignment of the ethical, and decenters conceptualities and social formations that are mobilized for the preservation of a modern/colonial order. This realignment is also a step toward developing a theory of anticolonial resistance into a theory of liberation, which I briefly touched on in the introduction—a development that exceeds the purview of this book.

"Bearing witness" to the suffering of the oppressed in Anzaldúa's rendition of Liliana Wilson's paintings relies on "in-dreaming," which I understand to be a concrete, physical inhabitation of an ana-topic spatiality. Quispecuro Nina is left in a transformative border opened up in the tension between the virgin and contemporary Andean women. He offers in his artworks, rather than redemption from racial and gendered oppression, a space of both renewal and destruction, destabilizing the insidiousness of the difference between the human and non-human that undergirds social oppression. These two cases reveal ethical moments that belong in the cosmic region of *ukhu pacha*. Vallega's radical exteriority also emerges from this underworld, the region of serpents shedding their skins, and of cosmic seminality, that is hidden from the sky. There is, perhaps, nothing to see in the underworld, just emptiness as a force of cosmic (k)notting. Yet this (k)notting is always there, enabling an ethical opening toward the oppressed in resistance.

Notes

Introduction

1 The issue of the influence of Andean cosmology in the formation and articulation of movements of resistance is not the focus of this book, but the explanatory power of the notion of "pachakuti" is noteworthy in this regard. See, for example, Gutiérrez Aguilar (2014). Another text at the background of my discussion that analyzes the influence of indigenous traditions on movements of resistance is Flores Galindo (1986). All the translations from Spanish in this book are mine.

2 Cited by Luis Alberto Reyes (2008: 289). I am directly referring to Reyes connecting this quote by Arguedas with *Pachakuti* as a site where "one of the opposites must give up its life so that the other one takes a turn" (Ibid.), but adding my interpretation of this as a challenge to resistance rooted in modern subjective forms of agency, intentionality and deliberation. Reyes's notion of *Pacha* as the subject of the revolution and his related interpretation of *Taki Oncoy* (see immediately below in the notion of a non-reformist or oppositional "propitiation") are constant referents in this work that I study in this introduction.

3 "Decolonization" in its general meaning is not the aim of anticolonial resistance in my discussion. There are many forms of decolonization and my analysis is related to only a few of them. So "decolonization" as an idea/aim is much broader than the scope of this book. Like "decolonial theory" (as I understand it), my discussion has a specific focus: to show how theories of oppression and theories of liberation can be blinded to the pernicious ways in which modes of socialization and exploitation rooted in the colonial era persist under different guises, surviving through contextual transformations and contributing to perhaps more salient manifestations of oppression. I remain within this focus attending to physical inhabitations of socialities with colonial lineages, centering on racial and gendered socialities. I bring forth physical resistances in such inhabitations. With regard to socialities with colonial lineages, I emphasize in my discussion the enforcement of the difference between the human and non-human as an overarching social determination that permeates modern/colonial social formations. I contemplated using the term "decolonial resistance" rather than "anticolonial resistance." Unfortunately the term "decolonial" is losing coherent theoretical framings and has been stretched out in ways that no longer correspond to my analysis. I use the term "anticolonial" as conveying what I understood "decolonial" to mean. With "anticolonial" as

referring to "modern/colonial" social oppressions, my intention is not to single out colonization as the single cause of all oppressions and resistances, but to bring out a dimension of oppression/resistance that has remained undertheorized and that is not necessarily central to the understanding of oppression and resistance in all contexts (even though it can be a factor).

4   Arturo Escobar's work is complementary to mine in this book. Our interests are different, however. My efforts lead to an interpretation of possibilities of resistance at the level of embodiment, drawing from the intersection of cosmology and aesthetics. My intent is not to make a historical point or a sociological analysis of movements of resistance. Escobar focuses on current anticolonial movements and their relation to non-Western cosmologies. See Escobar (2008, 2018).

5   From this perspective, cosmologically informed anticolonial resistance can be discerned as an undercurrent of colonial indigenous "syncretic" art; of the texts and drawings of Felipe Guaman Poma de Ayala (ca. 1615), which argue for an indigenous government in the colonial era; of the heterodox socialism of José Carlos Mariátegui (1894–1930); of the ethnographic and philosophical work of Rodolfo Kusch (1922–1979), which reveals an indigenous cosmological thinking beneath Latin American modernity; and of contemporary theories of resistance put forth by the Bolivian sociologist Silvia Rivera Cusicanqui and María Lugones, a leading decolonial feminist. Through Lugones, this Andean lineage of resistance joins Latinx and Chicana Feminisms, the work of Gloria Anzaldúa in particular, which is itself infused by Mesoamerican indigenous philosophies. My analyses of physical, aesthetic, and cosmological dimensions of resistance are in dialogue with this spreading aesthetic lineage of *Taki Oncoy* mainly in the twentieth and twenty-first centuries.

6   See also Anzaldúa (2009). My approach to cosmology is informed by Blaser and de la Cadena (2018) Marisol de la Cadena's, Verran (2018) and Viveiros de Castro (2018). Her approach to the Andean praxis of politics does not map on the aesthetic sensibilities I trace, but the methodological framing of *Earth Beings: Ecologies of Practice across Andean Worlds* (2015) is similar to mine. Some texts on "decolonial theory" have also informed my approach. See, for example, Castro Gómez (2005, 2017, 2008), Fornet-Betancourt (2002), Grosfoguel (2007), Maldonado Torres (2008), Dina Picotti (1992), Quintero (2014), Schutte (2017) and Walsh (2008, 2010).

7   Antonio Cornejo Polar, in *Writing in the Air* (2013), pays attention to this physical aspect of resistance, especially in the context of rites and festivals. See also chapter six of Rivera (2019).

8   This paralysis appears in the discussion of the "coatlicue state" in Anzaldúa's *Borderlands/La Frontera*. Lugones gives a thorough interpretation of it in "From Within Germinative Stasis: Creating Active Subjectivity, Resistant Agency" (2005).

9   The discussion of "chuyma" and "estar" appear in Kusch (2010).

10 My main source for the meaning of *Ukhu Pacha* is Reyes (2008).

11 I borrow this term from Charles Scott, his article "Livingdying" (2015) in particular. He connects this term with the work of Gloria Anzaldúa, intersecting with my analyses here and in Chapter 4.
12 This point is one of the early intersections between Lugones and decolonial theory and the postcolonial notion of hybridity. See Aníbal Quijano's notion of structural heterogeneity in "The Coloniality of Power" (2008) and Homi Bhabha's foreword in *Debating Cultural Hybridity* (1997).
13 This discussion draws from Alejandro Vallega's notion of sensibility in *Sense and Finitude* (2009), part three in particular.
14 In addition to Vallega's notion of sensibility, I am referring here to Linda Martín Alcoff's hermeneutic epistemology that investigates the bodily situatedness of the understanding. See *Visible Identities* (2006) chapter 4. See also Omar Rivera, "Interpreting Enrique Dussel's Transmodernity" (2017).
15 This difference is an important contribution of decolonial theory. See, for example, Nelson Maldonado-Torres "On the Coloniality of Being" (2007).
16 I draw the coincidence of the social with the human from Lugones "Toward a Decolonial Feminism" (2010). I expand on this point in "Mestizajes and Resistant Alterities" (2020).
17 I expand on the issue of space and the difference between the human and non-human in Chapter 5. The configuration of space as "neutral" is a colonial enforcement that works in tandem with an unrecognized determination of global space in terms of labor and race. See Aníbal Quijano "The Coloniality of Power" (2008).
18 See especially Al-Saji (2003, 2014).
19 Here Fanon is an important referent in terms of the destabilization of the body schema in chapter five of *Black Skin, White Masks* (2008).
20 This discussion of the ugly appears in relation to the notion of fetishism in *Philosophy of Liberation* (1977).
21 Certainly Nietzsche's The Birth of Tragedy offers tools within Greek Tragedy to approach the physical enactment of *Taki Oncoy*, especially in relation to the Dyonisian. Yet the issue of colonialism and dehumanization requires a different framework than the classical one here.
22 This is a term that has become central in decolonial and indigenous epistemologies. See Escobar (2018).
23 The "así" is the way Kusch conveys the culmination of Andean indigenous cosmological knowledge in *Popular and Indigenous Thinking in America* (2010).
24 This entrapment is at the core of the notions of modernization and development. A telling example of this entrapment is exemplified by Mario Vargas LLosa's "Questions of Conquest" (1990). A rebuttal of this from within the field of Peruvian anthropology is Carlos Iván Degregori and Pablo Sandoval "From Otherness to a Shared Diversity" (2008).
25 I will develop this account of resistance in Chapter 3.

Chapter 1

1 The term "world" is used by some of the main figures in this book in different senses. Heidegger's sense of "world" is, however, present in all of them. "World" in *Being and Time* is a totality of references that sustains the usefulness of things, determining their handiness, but the references themselves do not appear as things do (*Being and Time*, p. 71). At the same time, "world" only has meaning as constitutive of a being, Dasein, "which is essentially concerned *about* this being itself in its being." In this way, Heidegger posits the referential totality of world to be ultimately articulated from and for a being that cares, and that always already makes things relevant (cf. 79). The inclusion of Dasein in the analysis of world means that "world" is linked to the understanding, which "frees" things in their relevance in a moment of interpretation. In a more nuanced sense, the "world" appears as the site in which the understanding takes place as a moment of Dasein's being. From this perspective, the "world" does not appear as a totality in the sense of a static system, since the understanding is temporally determined. But Heidegger, however, leaves underdetermined, at least in *Being and Time*, the possibility that a sense of totality (an emphasis in referential closure, or finitude, perhaps) continues to be operative as a condition for understanding. Enrique Dussel (whom I discuss in the last chapter of this book) builds on Heidegger's notion of "world" just described, but also critically departs from it. He emphasizes the role of referential totality in the determination of world, as well as in the ultimate self referentiality (even if a temporalized one) operative in Heidegger's account of the understanding. In this way, he offers a notion of world as a totality that allows for instrumental, calculative, and instrumental dispositions anchored in a dominant, colonially informed self (a patriarchal, racist self). Dussel, in *Philosophy of Liberation*, mobilizes the notion of world to articulate a totalized form of oppression and exclusion, as well as the possibility of sensing an "other" from exteriority (not an outside of the world but the suspension of its referential systematicity) in dignity. This sensing of the other is an aesthetic and ethical moment that allows for projects of liberation. In other words, he rethinks Heidegger's "world" from the perspective of the oppressed in order to show its colonialist entanglements. María Lugones, in *Pilgrimages/Peregrinajes* preserves both the relational character of Heidegger's "world" and Dussel's intent to mobilize this term to articulate anti-colonial resistance. Her notion of world is open ended and multiple, non-totalizing, even if relational. She is not attached to secure the understanding as anchored in a self. Worlds (not world) are her focus, interfacing worlds, simultaneous worlds, dominant and non-dominant worlds. Her intent is to show the formation of intents across worlds, or from limina, intents that are not articulatable within the logic of particular worlds but that nevertheless can re-constitute their dominant sense. She is concerned with the notion of traveling through worlds not as an activity of a self that accumulates understanding, but of

a self that is "playful" with worlds and discloses possibilities of resistance. In this way she emphasizes embodied, memorial, perceptive, and affective orientations of praxical possibilities that are not pre-articulated by a world. In this book, I use the term "human world" to extend Dussel's colonial determination of this term, and emphasize the coincidence between an instrumental referential totality submitted to a dominant self with the demarcation of what counts as human and as having human value. I draw from Lugones throughout this work, her notion of traveling in particular. In Chapter 6 I explicitly interpret her notion of "world."

2 I am referring here to the decolonial determination of modernity/coloniality. The main source for this is Aníbal Quijano's "Coloniality of Power, Eurocentrism and Latin America," where colonialism and modernity are historical processes that cannot be disentangled (Quijano 2008). See also, "Modernity, Utopia and Latin America" (Quijano 1993)," Coloniality and Modernity/Rationality" (Quijano 2010). My interpretation of Quijano is informed by Rita Segato's work, which also introduces feminist critiques to the coloniality of power. See *La crítica de la colonialidad en ocho ensayos; Y una antropología por demanda* (2018). My work is also in dialogue with Walter Mignolo's determination of the decolonial on the basis of Quijano's work. See, "Introduction: Coloniality of Power and De-Colonial Thinking" (2010), "The Geopolitics of Knowledge and the Colonial Difference" (2008), and *Local Histories and Global Designs: Essays on the Coloniality of Power, Subaltern Knowledges and Border Thinking* (2000). This last book offers a similar methodology to mine in relation to "border thinking" (which also draws from Anzaldúa), and there is also a connection between this concept and pluritopic hermeneutics. See Linda Martín Alcoff's "Mignolo's Epistemology of Coloniality" (2007) for further background on my methodological approach and its relation to hermeneutics and decolonial theory.

3 I draw from Sylvia Wynter to inform this idea, specifically the relationship of colonialism/modernity with the determination of the human. See Wynter, "The Ceremony Must Be Found" After Humanism" (1984).

4 The way in which modernity narrows down the framings of liberation and resistance is a focus of Latin American philosophy. See for example Bolívar Echevarría, *Modernity and "Whiteness"* (2019).

5 At the background of this discussion is Mariátegui's relation to the avant-garde. Some of my interlocutors here are Beigel (2003), Hanneken (2012), Löwy (2009, 1993). I have also published on this (2008, 2007, 2014).

6 This is the discussion of aesthetics in *Borderlands/La Frontera* (2007).

7 The critique of museums as colonialist institutions has become an important aspect of decolonial theory. See Walter Mignolo "Museums in the Colonial Horizon of Modernity: Fred Wilson's Mining the Museum (1992)."

8 See also the chapter "Border Arte." A related set of critical conceptualities related to mine, from the perspective of "Decolonial Theory," is behind the movement of "decolonial aesthesis." See Walter Mignolo (2010).

9 I have a longer discussion of "borrowing" in the conclusion of *Delimitations of Latin American Philosophy* (2019: 178–83).
10 See the chapter "Border Arte" in (Anzaldúa 2015).
11 Anzaldúa tackles this theme in the chapter "Border Arte" in (2009).
12 The following discussion of Mariátegui centers on his relationship with the avant-garde that has recently garnered attention. Noteworthy is the exhibit *The Avant-Garde Networks of Amauta*. Related to this exhibit, see Natalia Majluf "*The Left and Latin American Avant-Gardes José Carlos Mariátegui and the Art of His Time*" (2019). I connect my discussion of Mariátegui's avant-garde with his investments in indigenismo. My interlocutors in this respect are Marisol de la Cadena (2004), Antonio Cornejo Polar (2004, 2004, 2013), Jorge Coronado (2009, 2009), Alvaro Campuzano Arteta (2017), Fernanda Beigel (2001), Javier San Jinés (2017) and Aníbal Quijano (1993). I am bridging in this section the political and aesthetic aspects of Mariátegui's work. I am elaborating from Mariátegui's texts (1988, 2011, 2005, 2012, 1996, 1996, 2012), and from the work of Ofelia Schutte (1993).
13 This struggle between creative and decadent spirits is the topic of Mariátegui's *Art, Revolution and Decadence* (2011).
14 This point resonates with Sallis discussion of the elemental dimensions of landscape in relation to the viewer. As noted in the introduction, his sense of the elemental is not articulated in its dissemination of the human world. See especially chapters one and three of *Senses of Landscape* (2015).
15 The basis for my study of the relationship between Mariátegui and Pettoruti is Patricia Artundo, "José Carlos Mariátegui and Emilio Pettoruti: Between Europe and América, 1920-1930" (2019).
16 I develop Mariátegui's relation to futurism in Rivera (2019).
17 Mariátegui develops this notion of temporality in the *Seven Essays* (2012). Later Quijano appropriates it as part of the notion of the "Coloniality of Power." Alejandro Vallega also develops this temporality in his aesthetics of liberation; especially in *Latin American Philosophy from Identity to Radical Exteriority* (2014).
18 I develop this theme in chapter 3 of *Delimitations* (2019).
19 I draw this from Quijano's *Coloniality of Power* (2008).
20 I am not engaging in the kind of telluric fabrication of indigenous identities that emerges in indigenismo as a creole strategy of domination. I, rather, emphasize that now it is possible to have a more nuanced understanding of pre-colonial and contemporary Andean cosmologies that are not "telluric," but, rather, shed light on complex social mixings in conditions of colonialism and modernity. It is this elaborate relationship between cosmology and sociality that I (and others, like Lugones) find to elude colonialist gazes. See also, Rivera Cusicanqui (2018).
21 The dangers of representation in indigenismo are developed by Jorge Coronado in *The Andes Imagined* (2009). An early critique of indigenismo along the same lines is

Luis Alberto Sánchez's *Indigenismo e Indianismo en la Literatura Peruana* (1981). I address these two critiques in *Delimitations* (2019: 119–40).
22 This discussion is found in the seventh essay of Mariátegui's *Seven Essays* (2012).
23 The main secondary sources informing my discussion are Natalia Majluf, "Indigenism as Avant-Garde. The Graphic Arts" (2019) and Roberto Amigo, "Modern Encounters. José Sabogal in Buenos Aires" (2019).
24 See Dean (2010: 23–6).
25 In "An Archeological Perspective on the Andean Concept of Camaquen" (2000), Tamara Bray develops philosophically a notion of animism that informs my discussion here.
26 Josef Estermann develops this in (Estermann 1998, 2008).
27 See (Estermann 1998).
28 See my discussion of Andean epistemologies in "Resistant Epistemologies from the Andes" (Rivera 2020).
29 See (Cummins and Manheim 2011: 6).
30 Dean analyzes this aspect of Inka built environments in *A Culture of Stone* (2010: 65–103).
31 As I explained in the introduction, this emphasis on recession differentiates my notion of the elements from Sallis's.

Chapter 2

1 The most rigorous and comprehensive analysis of the aesthetics of Inka stonework, including its differences from Western aesthetic frames, is Carolyn Dean's *A Culture of Stone*, especially chapter 1 (2010). Also see Dean, "The Inka Married the Earth: Integrated Outcrops and the Making of Place" (2007). I am very influenced by Constance Classen's study of perception in the pre-colonial Andes (1993). I am also indebted to the work of Rodolfo Kusch (2010).
2 See Dean, "Rocks and Reverence: Inka and Spanish Perceptions of Stonework in the Early Modern Andes" (2015).
3 The question of miniaturization in Inka architecture is extensively developed by Nadine Gavazzi in *Microcosmos* (2012). This text allowed me to begin to explore the notion of scale in Inka aesthetics that permeates this chapter.
4 For the relationship of Inka stonework with its settings, see Dean, "The Inka Married the Earth: Integrated Outcrops and the Making of Place" (2007). See also, D'Altroy and Wilkinson "The Past as Kin: Materiality and Time in Inka Landscapes" (2018).
5 For a study of the relationship between built environments and the cosmos, see Seoane and Culchicón-Venegas, "Hitching the Present to the Stars: The

Architecture of Time and Space in the Ancient Andes" (2018). See also, D'Altroy's *The Incas*, Chapters 5 and 8 (2015).

6   See Kusch (2010: 31).
7   See Kusch, *Indigenous and Popular Thinking in América* (2010) chapters 2,3,16, and 17.
8   For knowledge and "pointing," see *Indigenous and Popular Thinking in América* (2010), chapters 2, 3, and 4.
9   I am here referring to Vallega's reading of Sallis in "Freeing the Eyes" (forthcoming).
10 There are intersections between my discussion here and Merleau-Ponty's, "Cezanne's doubt" (1993) and "Ontology and Painting: Eye and Mind" (1993).
11 I stay close to Gadamer here because I am interested in critiquing his notion of historical consciousness as developed in *Truth and Method* (2004). I try to challenge its rootedness in a determination of the "human."
12 This point is worked out phenomenologically in Merleau-Ponty's "Cezanne's Doubt" (1993). In my view, the turn to the cosmos is suggested there but not pursued.
13 Dean gives an analysis of echo stones in "The Inka Married the Earth" (2007).
14 See also Sallis work on the elemental in (2018, 2015, 2016). Stone in particular is discussed in (1994).
15 Interest in Gadamer's notion of architecture is usually focused on its relation to ornamentation, culture, and history. I am taking it in another direction, toward the elemental. See Lucy Elvis, "Hermeneutics, Architecture and Belonging."
16 I am thinking of Gadamer's attention to festivals and play, for example. See Gadamer (1998: 57–65) and (2007).
17 I am drawing here from Heidegger's discussion of the hammer and world disclosure in *Being and Time* (1996).
18 Architecture has an essential role in *Truth and Method* as the text transitions toward the discussion of historical consciousness.
19 See Gadamer (2004: 102–71).
20 I am assuming an able-bodied perspective that my discussion will implicitly undermine in later chapters. I am led here by the work of Allison Kafer (2013), her discussion of disability and nature in particular.
21 See Gadamer (1998: 44–5).
22 For Western frameworks it would be tempting to compare Inka architecture with the work of Frank Lloyd Wright in terms of the inclusion of the natural settings in buildings. This would be, however, a limited comparison, especially in terms of "cataclysmic potency." One of my interlocutors in terms of phenomenological approach to architecture in view of Gadamer and Lloyd Wright is Günter Figal. I question the role that tradition and the notion of nature play in his texts, such as *Ando: Space Architecture Modernity* and *Aesthetics as Phenomenology* (2020).
23 The three Inka cosmological dimensions are *Hanan Pacha* (sky), *Uku Pacha* (earth/underworld), and *Kay Pacha* (the world here and now).

24 See Cummins and Manheim (2011).
25 This is the same prayer I discussed in Chapter 1, but translated by me in this case.
26 I draw the notion of *purin* from Cummins and Manheim (2011: 8).
27 I am referring to my discussion of Petorutti in the previous chapter.
28 At this point I mean by "world" a non-objectifiable expanse of relations that provide significance to things. It is not static and proffers meaning as that from which things are understood.
29 I draw the notions of envelopment and encompassing from Sallis (2018).
30 See Gavazzi, *Microcosmos* (2012), for a discussion of toys and scale in Inka aesthetics.
31 In *The Incas*, Terence D'Altroy offers a detailed account of Inka time that does not fit within linear or cyclical temporalities (2015: 123–33).
32 Alia Al-Saji suggested to me that I consider Andean temporalities in relation to Henri Bergson. See Alia Al-Saji (2020: 99–106).
33 See Rivera Cusicanqui (2015: 142).
34 This is developed in Josef Estermann (1998).
35 This point refers back to my earlier discussion of architectural integrity in Gadamer.

Chapter 3

1 See D'Altroy's elucidation of Inka time in (2015).
2 See Dean (1999: 33–45).
3 See Hajovsky (2018: 34).
4 Estermann "Apu Taytaku" (1998).
5 I am drawing from Alia Al-Saji's work on the phenomenology of race.
6 Here my approach to Chambi departs from Jorge Coronado's in *The Andes Imagined*.
7 In a private conversation, the Director de Patrimonio of the Archivo Martín Chambi, Oscar Chambi, differentiated between the Western inspired chiaroscuro techniques that Chambi used in his portraits, and the lighting that appears in the photographs of Inka ruins and landscapes. I think this differentiation is helpful and revealing of the point I am making here. I here approach Chambi's use of light in the tension between the two.
8 María Lugones and Silvia Rivera Cusicanqui introduced me to this aesthetic possibility. Here I focus on Lugones. Rivera's Cusicanqui's relevant text would be *Un Mundo Ch'ixi es Posible* (2018).
9 The reference to the eyes here resonates with Alia Al-Saji's work on the perception of race. See Al-Saji (2003).

10 This problem is taken up in *Defensa del Marxismo* (1988).
11 See Rivera, *Delimitations* (2019) and Quijano, *Reencuentro y Debate* (1979).
12 This is developed by Ofelia Schutte in the introduction to *Cultural Identity and Social Liberation in Latin American Thought* (1993).
13 I discuss this aesthetic operation in *The Image of the "Indio" in a Non-representative Economy* (2007).
14 The question on myth in Mariátegui has been extensively discussed. See J Hanneken, *José Carlos Mariátegui and the Time of Myth* (2012) and Christopher D. Tirres, *At the Crossroads of Liberation Theology and Liberation Philosophy: José Carlos Mariátegui's "New Sense" of Religion* (2017).
15 Here Mariátegui's proximity to Georges Sorel is important to consider. See Rivera (2019: 141–70) and (2014).
16 Here Mariátegui's editorial work in the journal *Amauta* is essential to understand his view of the relationship between aesthetics and revolution. In this journal he included the work of many Latin American avant-garde artists.
17 Cornejo Polar in *Writing in the Air* has a non-representative approach to Mariátegui's *indigenismo* that influences my work (2013). See also, Omar Rivera, "Approaching Racial Embodiment, Aesthetics, and Liberation in José Carlos Mariátegui's *Seven Essays*" (2019).
18 Here I point to a limitation of my analysis in terms of an explicit treatment of gender in this image and more generally in my discussion. I find Rivera Cusicanqui's *Sociología de la Imagen* (2015), her discussion of *miserabilismo* and of the resistance of Andean women, to be helpful in this respect.
19 I pursue the representative commitments in Mariátegui in "Hermeneútica, Representatividad y Espacio en Filosofías de LIberación Social: Una Perspectiva Latinoamericana" (2018). I emphasize here that there are many different Mariáteguis, and that his works show a number of tensions, which I explore in chapters four, five, and six of *Delimitations* (2019). I am following Martín Alcoff's focus on racial embodiment. See Martín Alcoff (2001).
20 Stephanie Rivera Berruz also mobilizes Lugones in view of the ways Latinas test other Latinas politically. See "Stylized Resistance: Boomerang Perception and Latinas in the Twenty-First Century" (2020).
21 See Lugones "Purity, Impurity, Separation" and "Hablando Cara a Cara/Speaking Face to Face: An Exploration of Ethnocentric Racism" (2003).
22 In *Sociología de la Imagen* (2015), Rivera Cusicanqui emphasizes that colonialism makes race take multifarious shapes as part of a larger set of dehumanizing perceptual practices. Al-Saji also extends the visualization of race into clothes and cultural artifacts. See "A Phenomenology of Hesitation" and "Too Late: Racialized Time and the Closure of the Past" (2014).
23 My discussion is informed by Martín Alcoff (2020); and Lugones (2019, 2003, 2012, 2020, 2020, 2010, 2010).

24 There are a number of important and recent critiques of Lugones's decolonial feminism that I am responding to in this section. See Ofelia Schutte "Border Zones, In-Between Spaces, and Turns: On Lugones, the Coloniality of Gender, and the Diasporic Peregrina" (2020) and Kathryn Sophia Belle," Interlocking, Intersecting, and Intermeshing: Critical Engagements with Black and Latina Feminist Paradigms of Identity and Oppression" (2020).

25 One of the main sources of the decolonial approach to race Quijano (2008).

26 See Emma Velez, "Decolonial Feminism at the Intersection: A Critical Reflection on the Relationship Between Decolonial Feminism and Intersectionality" (2019).

27 Maldonado Torres's "On the Coloniality of Being" (2007) is one source for theorizing the colonial determination of lives as dispensable.

28 See Lugones (2015: 34).

29 Alejandro Vallega offers an analysis of oppressing-resisting in Lugones in "The Aisthetic and Cosmological Dimension of María Lugones' Decolonial Feminism" (2020).

30 For an analysis of the meaning of *ayni* and reciprocity, see Reyes (2008: 171–82) and Josef Estermann (1998: 207–12).

31 See Martín Alcoff (2020) in relation to non-dominant differences in Lugones.

32 The notion of active subjectivity as released from social hierarchies can be traced to Anzaldúa (2007).

33 Jorge Eielson is my source for my notion of knots in relation to emptiness, in *El Diálogo Infinito* (2011).

34 I pursue a phenomenological account of this disruption in "Stillness, Aesthesis, Resistance" (2020).

35 See Lugones (2003: 112).

36 My analysis of clothed/unclothed draws from *Laura Aguilar, Show and Tell* (2017: 156–70).

Chapter 4

1 Here Mariana Ortega's interview of Lugones (2020) is a key referent.

2 I am relying here on Lugones's analysis of *chachawarmi* I discussed in the previous chapter.

3 There is an intersection here with disability studies. My sources are Melanie Yergeau (2018) and Kafer (2013).

4 Viveiros de Castro (2015) is my referent here.

5 Tamara Bray links Viveiros de Castro and Andean cosmologies *in An Archelogical Perspective on the Andean Concept of Camaquen* (2000).

6 Viveiros discusses the limitations of Western notions of perspectivism in light of Amerindian ontologies in *The Relative Native* (2015).

7. This point is also developed in "Cosmological Deixis" (1988).
8. This discussion refers to Frantz Fanon's analysis of the experience of the Black man in *Black Skin, White Masks* (2008). See also Helen Ngo, *Habits of Racism* (2017).
9. Vallega calls this temporal displacement the "Coloniality of Time." See *Latin American Philosophy From Identity to Radical Exteriority* (2014).
10. This discussion is in dialogue with Lugones's notion of "germinative stasis."
11. Kusch's analysis of "estar" in *Indigenous and Popular Thinking in América* (2010) is my source here.
12. I am trying to problematize the modernist discourse on indigenous passivity that took shape in indigenismo. Mariátegui wrestles with this passivity in the *Seven Essays*. See Omar Rivera, "The Image of the Indio in a Non-representative Economy" (2007).
13. See Rivera (2020).
14. I explore the theme of stillness in relation to praxis in "Stillness, Aesthesis, Resistance" (2020).
15. See Viveiros de Castro (1988) and Anzaldúa (2015).
16. This dynamic of attachment/detachment appears in the chapter "Border Arte" in *Light in the Dark/Luz en lo Oscuro* (2015).
17. I explore this idea of detachment in the conclusion to *Delimitations* (2019).
18. She draws from Mesoamerican philosophies in this regard. See Maffie (2013).
19. I expand on this memory as "exilic memory" and a related "exilic love" in the introduction to *Delimitations* (2019).
20. D'Altroy (2015: 143).
21. This whole chapter is in dialogue with Charles Scott's work on memory and indifference, in particular with *Living with Indifference* (2007).
22. Ibid.
23. I develop this reading of Kusch in *Resistant Epistemologies from the Andes* (2020).
24. Vallega has a helpful interpretation of this story in "The Descent of Thought and the Beginning of World Philosophies" (2020).
25. I also discuss *manchariska* in "Resistant Epistemologies from the Andes" (2020).

Chapter 5

1. See Lugones (2010); (2010) and (2007).
2. I will remain within the purview of Anzaldúa's understanding of "bearing witness" and put aside engagements with other related philosophical treatments of witnessing.

3 My interpretation of gesture is a critical departure from Gadamer's. See Hans Georg Gadamer (2007).
4 I am using the notion of limen found in Lugones (2003: 53–64).
5 At the background of this discussion is the decolonial account of race found in Nelson Maldonado-Torres (2007) and Aníbal Quijano (2010: 533–80).
6 Lugones (2010: 217).
7 Carlos Monsiváis (2000: 96).
8 Carlos Monsiváis (2000: 96).
9 See the notion of "colonial difference" in Walter Mignolo (2012).
10 Lugones analysis of complex communication (2006) sheds light on Cantinflas's language.
11 See Rivera (2017).
12 Following Lugones, memory can be the transition from fragmentation to multiplicity. See Lugones "On the Logic of Pluralist Feminism" (2003).
13 See Lugones (2006).
14 This new inclusive socialities, I have indicated, can be rooted in pre-colonial lineages. See Lugones "Toward a Decolonial Feminism" (2010).
15 See Lugones (2003: 151–66).
16 I am working here with the notion of the shadow beast in Anzaldúa (2007).
17 See Anzaldúa (2009: 124).
18 Italics mine.
19 For a thorough treatment of *kamay*, see Dean (2010).
20 I discuss this term in Chapter 1.
21 Anzaldúa includes reflections on shamanism in *Luz en lo Oscuro* (2015). Also see Eduardo Viveiros de Castro (1988).
22 See (2015: 31–4).
23 See Rivera (2020).

Chapter 6

1 Don Deere gives a complementary analysis to mine in "Coloniality and Disciplinary Power: On Social Techniques of Ordering" (2019).
2 In *Visible Identities* (2006) Linda Martín Alcoff gives an account of racial embodiment and space that informs this chapter. I am also drawing from Vallega's recent essay on Lugones (2020), and Pitts (2020).
3 I expand on this kind of spatiality in Rivera (2018).
4 I am referring here to Lugones's essay "Playfulness 'World'-Traveling and Loving Perception" (2003).
5 See Lugones (1998, 2005) and Rivera (2018, 2020) for an analysis of this variance.

6 See Lugones (2003: 88).
7 Alison Kafer's *Feminist, Queer, Crip* (2013) chapter 6 in particular, offers the kind of bodily spatiality that I am exploring here, without investments in able bodies.
8 See Chapter 3.
9 I draw from the discussion of Andahuaylillas in MacCormack, *Religion in the Andes* (1991).
10 This architectural analysis is based on *Religion in the Andes* (1991).
11 This is a non-essentialist approach developed by Rivera Cusicanqui (2010, 2018).
12 For an analysis of Andean Catholic Religiosity as its own religious form, see Estermann (2008).
13 This notion of *ch'ixi* is elucidated by Rivera Cusicanqui in *Ch'ixinakax Utxiwa: Una Reflexión Sobre Prácticas y Discursos Descolonizadores* (2010).
14 I understand Lugones here as implicitly critiquing Gadamer's notion of play in *Truth and Method* (2004).
15 See Lugones (2005: 93).
16 Space is almost always at play in Lugones's work. This particular point refers to "Playfulness" (2003); another relevant text is "Tactical Strategies of the Streetwalker/ Estrategias Tácticas de la Callejera" (2003).
17 The influence of Kusch (2010) is important here, as well as a turn to cosmology.
18 Lugones most sustained engagement with Andean thought is with the work of Kusch. She also studied art historical and anthropological texts, as it is evident in "Toward a Decolonial Feminism" (2010).
19 I am referring here to Pablo Oyarzún's (2007) and María de Acosta's (2018) work on trauma in Latin American contexts.
20 See Lugones, "Tactical Strategies of the Streetwalker/Estrategias Tácticas de la Callejera" (2003).
21 See Rivera Cusicanqui (2018: 67).

Chapter 7

1 The main sources for me in terms of this aesthetic approach are Alejandro Vallega (2014), Enrique Dussel, and Frantz Fanon. I understand these aesthetic explorations to be different from Walter Mignolo's notion of "decolonial aesthesis." I also draw from Linda Martín Alcoff's interpretations of Dussel (2011, 2012, 2000). There is some important current work on Dussel's aesthetics. See Christian Soazo Ahumada (2020), Alejandro Vallega (2020), and Enrique Tellez (2020).
2 I find this distinction in Lugones (2005). I develop some of these themes in (2017).
3 Dussel tackles this issue in "Transmodernity and Interculturality" (2012).

4   I am influenced by George Ciccarello-Maher's (2017) reading of Dussel in this respect, and by the role of analectics in the ethics of liberation (Dussel 2013).
5   See Lugones (2003: 40).
6   Maria Elena García discusses this in *Making Indigenous Citizens* (2005).
7   She develops this point in "On the Logic of Pluralist Feminism" (2003).
8   In the Andean context, Mariátegui begins a discussion of the embodiment of oppression that informs my work. See the last essay of his *Seven Essays* (2012).
9   The notion of exteriority is carefully elucidated in *Philosophy of Liberation* (1977).
10 Linda Martín Alcoff develops this point in "Enrique Dussel's Transmodernism" (2012).
11 Dussel develops the notion of the *Ego conquiro* in "The Invention of the Americas" (1995), see also (2014).
12 See Rivera (2020).
13 See Dussel (1977: 35).
14 See (1977: 38–9).
15 See (1977: 16).
16 See (1977: 42).
17 See (1977: 47).
18 See (1977: 43).
19 See (1977: 43).
20 See (1977: 41).
21 See (2020: 1).
22 See (2008: 78–9).

Conclusion

1   This chapter is deeply indebted to the work of Chicanx artists and scholars who are developing the field of Chicanx aesthetics at the margins of academic discourse. See in particular Elicia Facio and Irene Lara (2014), Martha Gonzalez (2020), Ralph Rugoff (2019), Tomás Ybarra-Frausto (2019), and Víctor Zamudio-Taylor (2019).
2   Intend this title to provoke a dialogue with Heidegger's "Art and Space" (2009).
3   I am referring to chapter four of *Borderlands/La Frontera* (2007).
4   Mesoamerican and Andean indigenous philosophies have a similar conception of the underworld as a place of destruction and rebirth. This relationship has not been adequately studied, especially as instigating modes of resistance.
5   See (2007: 25–6).
6   This section draws from Turner (2015).
7   See Hajovsky and Rivera (2020), and Rivera (2020).

8 I develop some of these themes in Rivera (2017).
9 Alejandro Vallega, "An Introduction to Liberatory Decolonial Aesthetic Thought (a South-South path, from Indigenous and Popular Thought in Américan and from the Sense of Xu (虛) in Chinese Painting)" (forthcoming).
10 "An Introduction to Liberatory Decolonial Aesthetic Thought (a South-South path, from Indigenous and Popular Thought in Américan and from the Sense of Xu (虛) in Chinese Painting)" (forthcoming).

Bibliography

Acosta López, María del Rosario. "Gramáticas de la escucha: descolonizar la historia y la memoria." In *Sujeto, decolonización, transmodernidad: Debates filosóficos Latinoamericanos*. Edited by Mabel Moraña, 159–80. Madrid: Iberoamericana, 2018.

Aguilar, Laura. *Laura Aguilar: Show and Tell*. Edited by Rebecca Epstein. California: University of California Press, 2017.

Al-Saji, Alia. "A Phenomenology of Hesitation: Interrupting Racializing Habits of Seeing." In *Living Alterities: Phenomenology, Embodiment and Race*. Edited by Emily Lee, 133–72. New York: SUNY Press, 2014.

Al-Saji, Alia. "Durée." In *50 Concepts for a Critical Phenomenology*. Edited by Gail Weiss, Ann V. Murphy, and Gayle Salamon, 99–106. Evanston, IL: Northwestern University Press, 2020.

Al-Saji, Alia. "Too Late: Racialized Time and Closure of the Past." *Insights* 6, no. 5 (2003): 1–13.

Amigo, Roberto. "Modern Encounters. José Sabogal in Buenos Aires, 1928." In *The Avant-Garde Networks of Amauta*, Edited by Beverly Adams and Natalia Majluf, 164–9. Lima: MALI, 2019.

Anzaldúa, Gloria E. "Bearing Witness: Their Eyes Anticipate the Healing." In *Ofrenda: Liliana Wilson's Art of Dissidence and Dreams*. Edited by Norma E. Cantú, 31–3. College Station, TX: Texas A&M University Press, 2015.

Anzaldúa, Gloria E. "Border Arte: Nepantla, el Lugar de la Frontera." In *The Gloria Anzaldúa Reader*. Edited by Analouise Keating, 176–85. Durham, NC: Duke University Press, 2009.

Anzaldúa, Gloria E. *Borderlands/ La Frontera: The New Mestiza*. 3rd ed. San Francisco: Aunt Lute Books, 2007.

Anzaldúa, Gloria E. "Creativity and Switching Modes of Consciousness." In *The Gloria Anzaldúa Reader*. Edited by Ananlouise Keating, 103–10. Durham, NC: Duke University Press, 2009.

Anzaldúa, Gloria E. *Light in the Dark: Luz En Lo Oscuro: Rewriting Identity, Spirituality, Reality*. Edited by Analouise Keating. Durham, NC: Duke University Press, 2015.

Anzaldúa, Gloria E. "The New Mestiza Nation: A Multicultural Movement." In *The Gloria Anzaldúa Reader*. Edited by Ananlouise Keating, 203–15. Durham, NC: Duke University Press, 2009.

Anzaldúa, Gloria E. "Speaking in Tongues: A Letter to Third World Women Writers." In *The Gloria Anzaldúa Reader*. Edited by Ananlouise Keating, 26–34. Durham, NC: Duke University Press, 2009.

Artundo, Patricia. "José Carlos Mariátegui and Emilio Pettoruti. Between Europe and America, 1920–1930." In *The Avant Garde Networks of Amauta*. Edited by Beverly Adams and Natalia Majluf, 90–103. Lima: MALI, 2019.

Beigel, Fernanda. *El Itinerario y la brújula: el vanguardismo estético-político de José Carlos Mariátegui*. Buenos Aires: Biblos, 2003.

Beigel, Fernanda. "Mariátegui y las antinomías del indigenismo." *Utopía y Praxis Latinoamericana* 6, no. 13 (2001): 36–57.

Belle, Kathryn Sophia. "Interlocking, Intersecting and Intermeshing: Critical Engagements with Black and Latina Feminist Paradigms of Identity and Oppression." *Critical Philosophy of Race* 8, no. 1–2 (2020): 165–98.

Bemis, Raye. "March to an Aesthetic of Revolution." In *Chicano and Chicana Art: A Critical Anthology*. Edited by Jennifer A. González, C. Ondine Chavoya, Chon A Noriega, and Terecita Romo, 420–22. Durham, NC: Duke University Press, 2019.

Blaser, Mario and Marisol de la Cadena. "Pluriverse: Proposals for a World of Many Worlds." In *A World of Many Worlds*. Edited by Marisol de la Cadena and Mario Blaser, 1–22. Durham, NC: Duke University Press, 2018.

Bray, Tamara L. "Archaeology, Temporal Complexity, and the Politics of Time." In *Constructions of Time and History in the Pre-Columbian Andes*. Edited by Edward Swenson and Andrew P. Roddick, 263–78. Boulder, CO: University Press of Colorado, 2018.

Bray, Tamara L. "An Archeological Perspective on the Andean Concept of Camaquen: Thinking Through Late Pre-columbian Ofrendas and Huacas." *Cambridge Archeological Journal* 1, no. 3 (2000): 357–66.

Cadena, Marisol de la. *Earth Beings: Ecologies of Practice Across Andean Worlds*. Durham, NC: Duke University Press, 2015.

Cadena, Marisol de la. *Indígenas mestizos: raza y cultura en el Cusco*. Lima: IEP, 2004.

Campuzano Arteta, Alvaro. *La modernidad imaginada: arte y literatura en el pensamiento de José Carlos Mariátegui (1911–1930)*. Madrid: Iberoamericana/Vervuert, 2017.

Carastathis, Anna. "Beyond the 'Logic of Purity': 'Post-Post-Intersectional' Glimpses in Decolonial Feminism." In *Speaking Face to Face: The Visionary Philosophy of María Lugones*. Edited by Pedro J. DiPietro, Jennifer McWeeny, and Shireen Roshanravan, 85–102. Albany, NY: State University of New York Press, 2019.

Castro, Augusto. *Filosofía y política en el Perú*. Lima: Fondo Editorial de la Pontificia Universidad Católica del Perú, 2006.

Castro Gómez, Santiago. *La hybris del punto cero: ciencia, raza e ilustración en la Nueva Granada (1750–1816)*. Bogotá: Pontificia Universidad Javeriana, 2005.

Castro Gómez, Santiago. "(Post)Coloniality for Dummies: Latin American Perspectives on Modernity, Coloniality, and the Geopolitics of Knowledge." In *Coloniality at Large: Latin America* 84. Durham, NC: Duke University Press, 2008.

Castro Gómez, Santiago. "Qué hacer con los universalismos occidentales? Observaciones en torno al giro decolonial." In Moraña, *Sujeto, decolonización, transmodernidad*, 181–208. Madrid: Iberoamericana, 2018.

Ciccariello-Maher, George. *Decolonizing Dialectics*. Durham, NC: Duke University Press, 2017.

Cisneros, Natalie. "Borderlands and Border Crossing." In *50 Concepts for a Critical Phenomenology*. Edited by Gail Weiss, Ann V. Murphy, and Gayle Salamon, 47–52. Evanston, IL: Northwestern University Press, 2020.

Classen, Constance. *Inca Cosmology and the Human Body*. Salt Lake City, UT: University of Utah Press, 1993.

Cornejo Polar, Antonio. "Indigenismo and Heterogeneous Literatures: Their Double Sociocultural Statue." In *The Latin American Cultural Studies Reader*. Edited by Ana del Sarto, Alicia Ríos, and Abril Trigo, 100–15. Durham, NC: Duke University Press, 2004.

Cornejo Polar, Antonio. "*Mestizaje*, Transculturation, Heterogeneity." In *The Latin American Cultural Studies Reader*. Edited by Ana del Sarto, Alicia Ríos, and Abril Trigo, 116–19. Durham, NC: Duke University Press, 2004.

Cornejo Polar, Antonio. *Writing in the Air*. Durham, NC: Duke University Press, 2013.

Coronado, Jorge. *The Andes Imagined*. Pittsburgh, PA: Pittsburgh University Press, 2009.

Coronado, Jorge. "El periódico *Labor* (1928–1929) entre indios y obreros: el indigenismo ante la prensa operaria." In Moraña and Podestá, *José Carlos Mariátegui y los estudios latinoamericanos*. Pittsburgh, PA: Instituto Internacional de Literatura Latinoamericana, 2009

Cummins, Tom and Bruce Manheim. "The River Around us, the Stream Within Us: The Traces of the Sun and Inka Kinetics." *RES: Anthropology and Aesthetics*, 59/60 (spring/autumn 2011): 5–21.

D'Altroy, Terence. *The Incas*. 2nd ed. London: Blackwell, 2015.

Dean, Carolyn. *A Culture of Stone: Inka Perspectives on Rock*. Durham, NC: Duke University Press, 2010.

Dean, Carolyn. *Inka Bodies and the Body of Christ: Corpus Christi and Colonial Cuzco, Peru*. Durham, NC: Duke University Press, 1999.

Dean, Carolyn. "The Inka Married the Earth: Integrated Outcrops and the Making of Place." *The Art Bulletin* 89, no. 3 (2007): 502–18.

Deere, Don. "Coloniality and Disciplinary Power: On Spatial Techniques of Ordering." *Interamerican Journal of Philosophy* 10, no. 2 (2019): 25–42.

Degregori, Carlos Iván, and Pablo Sandoval. "Peru: From Otherness to a Shared Diversity." In *A Companion to Latin American Anthropology*. Edited by Deborah Poole, 150–73. Malden, MA: Blackwell Publishing, 2008.

Dussel, Enrique. "Anti-Cartesian Meditations: On the Origin of the Philosophical Anti-discourse of Modernity." *Journal for Culture and Religious Theory* 13, no. 1 (2014): 11–52.

Dussel, Enrique. *Ethics of Liberation: In the Age of Globalization and Exclusion*. Translated by Alejandro Vallega, Eduardo Mendieta, Camilo Pérez Bustillo, Yolanda Angulo, and Nelson Maldonado-Torres. Durham, NC: Duke University Press, 2013.

Dussel, Enrique. *Filosofía de la Liberación*. México: Edicol, 1977.

Dussel, Enrique. *The Invention of the Americas: Eclipse of "the Other" and the myth of Modernity*. Translate by Michael D. Barber. New York: Continuum, 1995.

Dussel, Enrique. "Transmodernity and Interculturality: An Interpretation from the Perspective of the Philosophy of Liberation." *Transmodernity* 1, no. 3 (2012): 29–55.

Dussel, Enrique. "Siete hipótesis para una estética de la liberación." In *Para una estéica de la liberación decolonial*. Edited by Enrique Téllez, 17–54. Iztapalapa, CDMX: Ediciones del lirio, 2020.

Dussel, Enrique. *Twenty Theses on Politics*. Translated by George Ciccariello-Maher. Durham, NC: Duke University Press, 2008.

Echevarría, Bolívar. *Modernity and "Whiteness"*. Cambridge: Polity Press, 2019.

Eielson, Jorge Eduardo. *El Diálogo Infinito: Una Conversación Con Martha L. Canfield*. Spain: Sibilina S.L., 2011.

Escobar, Arturo. *Designs for the Pluriverse: Radical Interdependence, Autonomy, and the Making of Worlds*. New Ecologies for the Twenty-First Century. Durham, NC: Duke University Press, 2018.

Escobar, Arturo. *Territories of Difference: Place, Movements, Life, Redes*. Durham, NC: Duke University Press, 2008.

Estermann, Josef. "Apu Taytayku: Theological Implications of Andean Thought," *Studies in World Christianity* 4, no. 1 (1998): 1–20.

Estermann, Josef. *Filosofía andina*. Quito: Abya Yala, 1998.

Estermann, Josef. *Si el sur fuera el norte: chakanas interculturales entre Andes y Occidente*. Quito, Ecuador: Ediciones Abya Yala, 2008.

Facio, Elisa, and Irene Lara. *Fleshing the Spirit: Spirituality and Activism in Chicana, Latina, and Indigenous Women's Lives*. Tucson, AR: University of Arizona Press, 2014.

Fanon, Frantz. *Black Skin, White Masks*. Translated by Richard Philcox. New York: Grove, 2008.

Flores Galindo, Alberto. *Buscando un Inca: identidad y utopía en los Andes*. Cuba, La Habana: Casa de las Américas, 1986.

Fornet-Betancourt, Raúl. "An Alternative to Globalization: Theses for the Development of an Intercultural Philosophy." In *Latin American Perspectives on Globalization*. Edited by Mario Sáenz, 230–6. Lanham, MD: Rowman and Littlefield, 2002.

Gadamer, Hans-Georg. "The Festive Character of Theater." In *The Relevance of the Beautiful and Other Essays*. Edited by Robert Bernasconi. Translated by Dan Tate, 57–65. Cambridge: Cambridge University Press, 1998.

Gadamer, Hans-Georg. *The Gadamer Reader: A Bouquet of the Later Writings*. Edited by Richard E Palmer. Translation of the 1997 Gadamer Lesebuch. Evanston, IL: Northwestern University Press, 2007.

Gadamer, Hans-Georg. *The Relevance of the Beautiful and Other Essays*. Edited by Robert Bernasconi. Translated by Dan Tate. Cambridge: Cambridge University Press, 1998.

Gadamer, Hans-Georg. *Truth and Method*. 2nd rev. ed. Translation revised by Joel Weinsheimer and Donald G. Marshall. London: Continuum, 2004.
García, Maria Elena. *Making Indigenous Citizens: Identities, Education and Multicultural Development in Peru*. Stanford: Stanford University Press, 2005.
Gavazzi, Adine. *Microcosmos*. Lima: Apus Graph Ediciones, 2012.
Gonzalez, Martha. *Chican@ Artivistas: Music, Community, and Transborder Tactics in East Los Angeles*. Austin: University of Texas Press, 2020
Grajeda, Erika. *On the Corner: Gender, Race and the Making of Informal Day Labor Markets in New York City and San Francisco*. Unpublished Dissertation in Sociology, UT Austin, 2016.
Grosfoguel, Ramón. "The Epistemic Decolonial Turn: Beyond Political Economy Paradigms." *Cultural Studies* 21, no. 2–3 (2007): 211–23.
Gutiérrez Aguilar, Raquel. *Rhythms of the Pachakuti: Indigenous Uprising and State Power in Bolivia*. Translated by Stacey Alba D. Skar. Durham, NC: Duke University Press, 2014.
Hajovsky, Patrick. "Shifting Panoramas: Contested Visions of Cuzco's 1650 Earthquake." *The Art Bulletin* 100, no. 4 (2018): 34–61.
Hajovsky, Patrick, and Omar Rivera. "Visual Epistemologies of Resistance: Imaging Virgins and Saints in Contemporary Cusco." *Revista de Estudios Globales y Arte Contemporáneo* 7, no. 1 (2020): 237–66.
Hanneken, Jamie. "José Carlos Mariátegui and the Time of Myth." *Cultural Critique* 81 (Spring 2012): 1–30.
Heidegger, Martin. "Art and Space." *The Heidegger Reader*. Edited by Figal Günter. Translated by Jerome Veith. Bloomington, IN: Indiana University Press, 2009.
Heidegger, Martin. *Being and Time: A Translation of Sein Und Zeit*. Translated by Joan Stambaugh. Albany, NY: State University of New York Press, 1996.
Hernández, Robb. "Drawing Offensive/Offensive Drawing: Toward a Theory of Mariconógraphy." In *Chicano and Chicana Art: A Critical Anthology*. Edited by Jennifer A. González, C. Ondine Chavoya, Chon A Noriega, and Terecita Romo, 194–207. Durham, NC: Duke University Press, 2019.
Kafer, Alison. *Feminist, Queer, Crip*. Bloomington, IN: Indiana University Press, 2013.
Keating, Analouise. *The Gloria Anzaldúa Reader*. Durham, NC: Duke University Press, 2009.
Kusch, Rodolfo. *Indigenous and Popular Thinking in América*. Translated by María Lugones and Joshua M. Price. Durham, NC: Duke University Press, 2010.
Latorre, Guisela. "Exiled Creativity and Immigrant Aesthetics: The Politically Transformative Work of Liliana Wilson." In *Ofrenda: Liliana Wilson's Art of Dissidence and Dreams*. Edited by Norma E. Cantú, 83–5. College Station, TX: Texas A&M University Press, 2015.
León-Portilla, Miguel. *Aztec Thought and Culture: A Study of the Ancient Nahuatl Mind*. Translated by Jack Emory Davis. Norman, OK: University of Oklahoma Press, 1963.

Llorente, Renzo. "The Amauta's Ambivalence: Mariátegui on Race." In Gracia, *Forging People*, 228–47. Indiana: Notre Dame Press.

Löwy, Michael. "Marxismo romántico." *Anuario Mariateguiano* 5 (1993): 155–9.

Löwy, Michael. *Morning Star: Surrealism, Marxism, Anarchism, Situationism, Utopia*. Austin, TX: University of Texas Press, 2009.

Lugones, María. "Boomerang Perception and the Colonizing Gaze: Ginger Reflections on Horizontal Hostility." In *Pilgrimages/Peregrinajes*, 151–66. Lanham, MD: Rowman and Littlefield, 2003.

Lugones, María. "Carnal Disruptions: Mariana Ortega Interviews María Lugones." In *Speaking Face to Face: The Visionary Philosophy of María Lugones*. Edited by Pedro J. DiPietro, Jennifer McWeeny, and Shireen Roshanravan, 273–84. Albany, NY: State University of New York Press, 2019.

Lugones, María. "The Coloniality of Gender." In *Globalization and the Decolonial Option*. Edited by Walter Mignolo and Arturo Escobar, 369–91. London: Routledge, 2010.

Lugones, María. "From within Germinative Stasis: Creating Active Subjectivity, Resistant Agency." In *Entre Mundos/among Worlds*. Edited by Analouise Keating. New York: Palgrave Macmillan, 2005.

Lugones, María. "Gender and Universality in Colonial Methodology." *Critical Philosophy of Race* 8, no. 1–2 (2020): 25–46.

Lugones, María. "Hablando Cara a Cara/Speaking Face to Face: An Exploration of Ethnocentric Racism." In *Pilgrimages/Peregrinajes*, 41–52. Lanham, MD: Rowman and Littlefield, 2003.

Lugones, María. "Heterosexualism and the Colonial/Modern Gender System." *Hypatia* 22, no. 1 (2007): 186–209.

Lugones, María. "Methodological Notes Toward a Decolonial Feminism." In *Decolonizing Epistemologies: Latina/o Theology and Philosophy*. Edited by Ada María, Isasi-Díaz, and Eduardo Mendieta, 68–86. New York: Fordham University Press, 2012.

Lugones, María. "Motion, Stasis, and Resistance to Interlocked Oppressions." In *Making Worlds: Gender, Metaphor, Materiality*. Edited by Susan Hardy Aiken, Ann Brigham, Sallie A. Marston, and Penny Waterstone, 49–52. Tucson, AZ: University of Arizona Press, 1998.

Lugones, María. "On Complex Communication." *Hypatia* 21, no. 3 (2006): 75–85.

Lugones, María. "On the Logic of Pluralist Feminism." In *Pilgrimages/Peregrinajes*, 65–76. Lanham, MD: Rowman and Littlefield, 2003.

Lugones, María. "Playfulness, "World"-Traveling, and Loving Perception." In *Pilgrimages/Peregrinajes*, 77–102. Lanham, MD: Rowman and Littlefield, 2003.

Lugones, María. "Purity, Impurity, and Separation." In *Pilgrimages/Peregrinajes*, 121–50. Lanham, MD: Rowman and Littlefield, 2003.

Lugones, María. "Revisiting Gender: A Decolonial Approach." In *Theories of the Flesh: Latinx and Latin American Feminisms, Transformation, and Resistance*. Edited by Andrea J. Pitts, Mariana Ortega, and Medina José, 29–37. New York: Oxford University Press, 2020.

Lugones, María. "Tactical Strategies of the Streetwalker / Estrategias Tácticas de la Callejera." In *Pilgrimages/Peregrinajes*, 207–37. Lanham, MD: Rowman and Littlefield, 2003.

Lugones, María. "Toward a Decolonial Feminism." *Hypatia* 25, no. 4 (2010): 742–59.

MacCormack, Sabine. *Religion in the Andes*. Princeton, NJ: Princeton University Press, 1991.

Maffie, James. *Aztec Philosophy : Understanding a World in Motion*. Boulder, CO: University Press of Colorado, 2013.

Majluf, Natalia. "The Left and The Latin American Avant-Gardes. José Carlos Mariátegui and the Art of his Time." In *The Avant Garde Networks of Amauta*. Edited by Beverly Adams and Natalia Majluf, 20–34. Lima: MALI, 2019.

Maldonado Torres, Nelson. *Against War: Views from the Underside of Modernity*. Durham, NC: Duke University Press, 2008.

Maldonado Torres, Nelson. "On the Coloniality of Being: Contributions to the Development of a Concept." *Cultural Studies* 21, no. 2–3 (March–May 2007): 240–70.

Mariátegui, José Carlos. "Art, Revolution and Decadence." In *José Carlos Mariátegui. An Anthology*. Edited by Harry Vanden and Marc Becker, 145–0. New York: Monthly Review Press, 2011.

Mariátegui, José Carlos. *Cartas de Italia*. Lima: Amuata, 1975.

Mariátegui, José Carlos. *Defensa del Marxismo: polémica revolucionaria*.14th ed. Lima: Amauta, 1988.

Mariátegui, José Carlos. *El artista y la época*. Peru: Empresa Editora Amauta, 1970.

Mariátegui, José Carlos. "The Final Struggle." In *José Carlos Mariátegui. An Anthology*. Edited by Harry Vanden and Marc Becker, 123–6. New York: Monthly Review Press, 2011.

Mariátegui, José Carlos. "Heterodoxia de la tradición." In *Invitación a la vida heroíca: José Carlos Mariátegui; textos esenciales*. Edited by Alberto Flores Galindo and Ricardo Portocarrero Grados, 34–40. Lima: Fondo Editorial del Congreso del Perú, 2005.

Mariátegui, José Carlos. *La Escena Contemporánea*. 5th ed. Lima: Amauta, 1950.

Mariátegui, José Carlos. "Man and Myth." In *Mariátegui, Heroic and Creative Meaning of Socialism: Selected Essays of José Carlos Mariátegui*. Edited and Translated by Michael Pearlman, 70–8. Amherst, NY: Humanity, 1996.

Mariátegui, José Carlos. "Pessimism of the Real and Optimism of the Ideal." In Mariátegui, *Heroic and Creative Meaning of Socialism: Selected Essays of José Carlos Mariátegui*. Edited and Translated by Michael Pearlman, 57–64. Amherst, NY: Humanity, 1996.

Mariátegui, José Carlos. *7 ensayos de interpretación de la realidad peruana: ideología y política*. 2nd ed. Lima: Minerva, 2012.

Marinetti, Filippo Tommaso. "The Futurist Manifesto," 1909. Retrieved from: https://www.societyforasianart.org/sites/default/files/manifesto_futurista.pdf

Martí, José. "Coney Island." In *José Martí: Selected Writings*. Translated by Esther Allen, 89–94. New York: Penguin Books, 2002.

Martí, José. "Our America." In *Latin American Philosophy for the 21st Century: The Human Condition, Values, and the Search for Identity*. Edited by Jorge J. E. Garcia and Elizabeth Millán-Zaibert, 245–52. Amherst, NY: Prometheus, 2004.

Martín Alcoff, Linda. "An Epistemology for the Next Revolution." *Transmodernity* 1, no. 2 (2011): 67–78.

Martín Alcoff, Linda. "Educating with a (De)Colonial Consciousness." *Latin American Philosophy of Education Journal* 1 (2014): 4–18.

Martín Alcoff, Linda. "Enrique Dussel's Transmodernism." *Transmodernity* 1, no. 3 (2012): 60–8.

Martín Alcoff, Linda. "Decolonizing Feminist Theory: Latina Contributions to the Debate." In *Theories of the Flesh: Latinx and Latin American Feminisms, Transformation, and Resistance*. Edited by Andrea J. Pitts, Mariana Ortega, and Medina José, 11–28. New York: Oxford University Press, 2020.

Martín Alcoff, Linda. "Lugones's World Making." *Critical Philosophy of Race* 8, 1–2 (2020): 199–211.

Martín Alcoff, Linda. "Mignolo's Epistemology of Coloniality." *New Centennial Review* 7, no. 3 (2007): 79–102.

Martín Alcoff, Linda. "Power/Knowledges in the Colonial Unconscious: A Dialogue between Dussel and Foucault." In *Thinking from the Underside of History: Enrique Dussel's Philosophy of Liberation*. Edited by Linda Martín Alcoff and Eduardo Mendieta, 249–68. Lanham, MD: Rowman and Littlefield, 2000.

Martín Alcoff, Linda. "Toward a Phenomenology of Racial Embodiment." In *Race*. Edited by Robert Bernasconi, 267–83. Malden, MA: Blackwell, 2001.

Martín Alcoff, Linda. *Visible Identities: Race, Gender, and the Self*. New York: Oxford University Press, 2006.

Medina, José, Ortega, Mariana and Pitts, Andrea. *Theories of the Flesh: Latinx and American Feminisms, Transformation and Resistance*. Oxford: Oxford University Press, 2020.

Merleau-Ponty, Maurice. "Cézanne's Doubt." In *The Merleau-Ponty Aesthetics Reader: Philosophy and Painting*. Edited by Galen A. Johnson. Translation by Michael B. Smith, 121–50. Evanston, IL: Northwestern University Press, 1993.

Merleau-Ponty, Maurice. "Ontology and Painting: 'Eye and Mind.'" In *The Merleau-Ponty Aesthetics Reader: Philosophy and Painting*. Edited by Galen A. Johnson. Translation by Michael B. Smith, 35–57. Evanston, IL: Northwestern University Press, 1993.

Mignolo, Walter D. "Aisthesis decolonial: artículo de reflexión." *Calle* 14, no. 4 (2010): 13.

Mignolo, Walter D. *The Darker Side of Western Modernity*. Durham, NC: Duke University Press, 2011.

Mignolo, Walter D. "The Geopolitics of Knowledge and the Colonial Difference." In *Coloniality at Large: Latin America and the Postcolonial Debate*. Edited by Mabel

Moraña, Enrique Dussel, and Carlos A. Jáuregui, 225–58. Durham, NC: Duke University Press, 2008.

Mignolo, Walter D. "Introduction: Coloniality of Power and De-Colonial Thinking." In *Globalization and the Decolonial Option*. Edited by Walter Mignolo and Arturo Escobar, 1–21. London: Routledge, 2010.

Mignolo, Walter D. *Local Histories/Global Designs: Essays on the Coloniality of Power, Subaltern Knowledges and Border Thinking*. Princeton, NJ: Princeton University Press, 2012.

Monsivais, Carlos. *Mexican Postcards*. London: Verso, 2000.

Moreno, S. Hugo and, Elizabeth Millán. "Introduction: The Aesthetic Tradition of Hispanic Thought." *Symposium* 18, no. 1 (2014): 1–21.

Ngo, Helen. *The Habits of Racism: A Phenomenology of Racism and Racialized Embodiment*. Lanham: Lexington, 2017.

Oliver, Kelly. "Witnessing." In *50 Concepts for a Critical Phenomenology*. Edited by Gail Weiss, Ann V. Murphy, and Gayle Salamon, 337–42. Evanston, IL: Northwestern University Press, 2020.

Ortega, Mariana. "*Cámara* Queer: Longing, the Photograph, and Queer Latinidad." In *Theories of the Flesh: Latinx and Latin American Feminisms, Transformation, and Resistance*. Edited by Andrea J. Pitts, Mariana Ortega, and Medina José, 264–80. New York: Oxford University Press, 2020.

Oyarzún, Pablo. "Memory, Moment and Tears: A Speculative Approach to the Problem of Latin American Singularities." *New Centennial Review* 7, no. 3 (2007): 1–20.

Pérez, Laura E. *Chicana Art: The Politics of Spiritual and Aesthetic Altarities*. Durham, NC: Duke University Press, 2007.

Pérez, Laura E. *Eros Ideologies: Writings on Art, Spirituality, and the Decolonial*. Durham, NC: Duke University Press, 2019.

Pérez, Laura E. "The Inviolate Erotic in the Paintings of Liliana Wilson." In *Ofrenda: Liliana Wilson's Art of Dissidence and Dreams*. Edited by Norma E. Cantú, 83–5. College Station, TX: Texas A&M University Press, 2015.

Pérez, Laura E. "Writing on the Social Body: Dresses and Body Ornamentation in Contemporary Chicana Art." In *Chicano and Chicana Art: A Critical Anthology*. Edited by Jennifer A. González, C. Ondine Chavoya, Chon A Noriega, and Terecita Romo, 219–36. Durham, NC: Duke University Press, 2019.

Perpich, Diane. "The Face." In *50 Concepts for a Critical Phenomenology*. Edited by Gail Weiss, Ann V. Murphy, and Gayle Salamon, 135–40. Evanston, IL: Northwestern University Press, 2020.

Petorutti, Emilio. "Letter from Emilio Petorutti." 1927. [Archivo José Carlos Mariátegui. 1926-01-17].

Picotti, Dina V. "Colonialidad y modernidad/racionalidad." *Perú Indígena* 13, no. 29 (1992): 11–20.

Pitts, Andrea J. "World-Traveling." In *50 Concepts for a Critical Phenomenology*. Edited by Gail Weiss, Ann V. Murphy, and Gayle Salamon, 343–50. Evanston, IL: Northwestern University Press, 2020.

Poole, Deborah. *Vision, Race, and Modernity : A Visual Economy of the Andean Image World*. Princeton: Princeton University Press, 1997.
Portocarrero, Gonzalo Maisch. *Razones de Sangre: Aproximaciones a la violencia política*. Lima: Pontifica Universidad Católica del Perú, 2012.
Quijano, Aníbal. "Coloniality and Modernity/Rationality." In *Globalization and the Decolonial Option*. Edited by Walter Mignolo and Arturo Escobar, 22–32. London: Routledge, 2010.
Quijano, Aníbal. "Coloniality of Power, Eurocentrism, and Latin America." In *Coloniality at Large: Latin America and the Postcolonial Debate*. Edited by Mabel Moraña, Enrique Dussel, and Carlos A. Jauregui, 181–224. Durham, NC: Duke University Press, 2008.
Quijano, Aníbal. "Modernity, Identi and Utopia in Latin America." *boundary 2* 20, no. 3 (1993). Reprinted in Aníbal Quijano. *The Postmodern Debate in Latin America*. Durham, NC: Duke University Press, 1995.
Quijano, Aníbal. "'Raza,' 'Etnia' y Nación' en Mariátegui: cuestiones abiertas." In *José Carlos Mariátegui y Europa: El Otro Aspecto del Descubrimiento*. Edited by Roland Forgues, 130–45. Lima, Perú: Empresa Editora Amauta, 1993.
Quijano, Aníbal. *Reencuentro y Debate: una introducción a Mariátegui*. Lima: Mosca Azul, 1979.
Quintero, Pablo. "Notas sobre la teoría de la colonialidad del poder y la estructuración de la sociedad en América Latina." In *Des/Colonialidad Y Bien Vivir: Un Nuevo Debate En América Latina*. Primera edición. Edited by Aníbal Quijano, 193–216. Lima, Perú: Universidad Ricardo, Editorial Universitaria, Cátedra América Latina y la Colonialidad del Poder, 2014.
Reyes, Luis Alberto. *El pensamiento indígena en América: Los antiguos andinos, mayas y nahuas*. Luis Alberto Reyes; con prólogo de Arturo Andrés. 1st. ed. Buenos Aires: Biblos, 2008.
Rivera Berruz, Stephanie. "Stylized Resistance: Boomerang Perception and Latinas in the Twenty-First Century." In *Theories of the Flesh: Latinx and Latin American Feminisms, Transformation, and Resistance*. Edited by Andrea J. Pitts, Mariana Ortega, and Medina José, 239–50. New York: Oxford University Press, 2020.
Rivera Cusicanqui, Silvia. *Ch'ixinakax utxiwa: On Practices and Discourses of Decolonization*. Translated by Molly Geidel. Cambridge: Polity Press, 2020.
Rivera Cusicanqui, Silvia. *Ch'ixinakax utxiwa: Una reflexión sobre prácticas y discursos descolonizadores*. 1st ed. Buenos Aires: Tinta Limón, 2010.
Rivera Cusicanqui, Silvia. *Sociologia de la imagen: ensayos*. 1st ed. Ciudad Autónoma de Buenos Aires: Tinta Limón, 2015.
Rivera Cusicanqui, Silvia. *Un mundo ch'ixi es posible. Ensayos desde un presente en crisis*. 1st ed. Ciudad Autónoma de Buenos Aires: Tinta Limón, 2018.
Rivera, Omar. "Approaching Racial Embodiment, Aesthetics and Liberation in José Carlos Mariategui's Seven Essays." *APA Newsletter for Hispanics in Philosophy* 19 (2019): 8–12.

Rivera, Omar. *Delimitations of Latin American Philosophy: Beyond Redemption.* Bloomington, IN: Indiana University Press, 2019.

Rivera, Omar. "Epistemological and Aesthetic Aspects of Transmodernism: Linda Martín Alcoff's and Alejandro Vallega's Readings of Enrique Dussel." *Interamerican Journal of Philosophy* 8, no. 2 (2017): 42–57.

Rivera, Omar. "From Revolving Time to the Time of Revolution: Mariátegui's Encounter with Nietzsche." *APA Newsletter on Hispanic/Latino Issues in Philosophy* 8, no. 1 (2008): 22–6.

Rivera, Omar. "Hermenéutica, representatividad y espacio en filosofías de la liberación social: una perspectiva latinoamericana." In *Sujeto, Decolonización, Transmodernidad: Debates Filosóficos Latinoamericanos.* Edited by Mabel Moraña, 69–84. Madrid: Iberoamericana, 2018.

Rivera, Omar. "The Image of the "Indio" in a Non-representative Economy: Meditations on Peruvian Marxism." *New Centennial Review* 7, no. 3 (2007): 131–48.

Rivera, Omar. "Inversiones Estéticas y Visualidad Andina." In *Para una estéica de la liberación decolonial.* Edited by Enrique Téllez, 183–200. Iztapalapa, CDMX: ediciones del lirio, 2020.

Rivera, Omar. "Mariátegui's Avant-Garde and Surrealism as Discipline." *Symposium* 18, no. 1 (2014): 102–24.

Rivera, Omar. "Reading Alejandro Vallega toward a Decolonial Aesthetics." *Comparative and Continental Philosophy* 9, no. 2 (2017): 162–73.

Rivera, Omar. "Resistance as Alterity in Borderlands Aesthetics" *Interamerican Journal of Philosophy* 11, no. 1 (2020): 26–43.

Rugoff, Ralph. "Resisting Modernism: Chicano Art: Retro Progressive or Progressive Retro?" In *Chicano and Chicana Art: A Critical Anthology.* Edited by Jennifer A. González, C. Ondine Chavoya, Chon A Noriega, and Terecita Romo, 423–26. Durham, NC: Duke University Press, 2019.

Rivera, Omar. "Stillness, Aesthesis, Resistance." *Critical Philosophy of Race* 8, 1–2 (2020): 84–100.

Sallis, John. *Elemental Discourses: The Collected Writings of John Sallis.* Bloomington, IN: Indiana University Press, 2018.

Sallis, John. *Logic of imagination: The Expanse of the Elemental.* Bloomington, IN: Indiana University Press, 2012.

Sallis, John. *Senses of Landscape.* Evanston, IL: Northwestern University Press, 2015.

Sallis, John. *Stone.* Bloomington, IN: Indiana University Press, 1994.

Sallis, John. *The Return of Nature: Coming As If from Nowhere.* Bloomington, IN: Indiana University Press, 2016.

San Jinés, Javier. "Between Doubt and Hope: The Religious Disjunction of José Carlos Mariátegui." In Moraña and Podestá, *José Carlos Mariátegui*, 115–38.

San Jinés, Javier. "The Nation: An Imagined Community?" In *Globalization and the Decolonial Option.* Edited by Walter Mignolo and Arturo Escobar, 149–62. London: Routledge, 2010.

Sánchez, Luis Alberto. *Indianismo e indigenismo en la literatura peruana*. Lima: Mosca Azul, 1981.

Sandoval, Chela. *Methodology of the Oppressed*. Minneapolis: University of Minnesota Press, 2000.

Sanin Cano, Baldomero. "Emilio Petorruti." *Amauta, Lima* I, no. 2 (1926): 21–4.

Schutte, Ofelia. "Border Zones, In-Between Spaces and Turns: On Lugones, the Coloniality of Gender and the Diasporic Peregrina." *Critical Philosophy of Race* 8, no. 1–2 (2020): 102–18.

Schutte, Ofelia. "Crossroads and In-Between Spaces: A Meditation on Anzaldúa and Beyond." In *Theories of the Flesh: Latinx and Latin American Feminisms, Transformation, and Resistance*. Edited by Andrea J. Pitts, Mariana Ortega, and Medina José, 123–34. New York: Oxford University Press, 2020.

Schutte, Ofelia. "Cultural Alterity: 'Cross-Cultural Communication and Feminist Theory in North-South Contexts." *Hypatia* 13, no. 2 (1998): 53–72.

Schutte, Ofelia. *Cultural Identity and Social Liberation in Latin American Thought*. Albany: State University of New York Press, 1993.

Schutte, Ofelia. "De la colonialidad del poder al feminismo decolonial en América Latina." In Moraña, *Sujeto, decolonización, transmodernidad*, 137–58.

Scott, Charles E. "Livingdying." *Mosaic: An Interdisciplinary Critical Journal* 48, no. 2 (2015): 211–17.

Scott, Charles E. *Living with Indifference*. Studies in Continental Thought. Bloomington, IN: Indiana University Press, 2007.

Scott, Charles E. *The Time of Memory*. Albany, NY: State University of New York Press, 1999.

Segato, Rita. *La crítica de la colonialidad en ocho ensayos: Y una antropología por demanda*. 2nd ed. Ciudad Autónoma de Buenos Aires: Prometeo Libros, 2018.

Seoane, Francisco, and María José Culquichicón-Venegas. "Hitching the Present to the Stars: The Architecture of Time and Space in the Ancient Andes." In *Constructions of Time and History in the Pre-Columbian Andes*. Edited by Edward Swenson and Andrew P. Roddick. Boulder, CO: University Press of Colorado, 2018. 239–62.

Silverblatt, Irene. *Moon, Sun, and Witches: Gender Ideologies and Class in Inca and Colonial Peru*. New Jersey: Princeton University Press, 1987.

Soazo Ahumada, Christian. "Estética analéctica a Aesthesis descolonial." In *Para una estéica de la liberación decolonial*. Edited by Enrique Téllez. Iztapalapa, CDMX: ediciones del lirio, 2020. 55–87.

Stern, Steve J. *Shining and Other Paths: War and Society in Peru, 1980–1995*. Durham, NC: Duke University Press, 1998.

Strathern, Marilyn. "Opening Up Relation." In *A World of Many Worlds*. Edited by Marisol de la Cadena and Mario Blaser. Durham, NC: Duke University Press, 2018. 23–52.

Swenson, Edward, and Andrew P. Roddick. "Introduction: Rethinking Temporality and Historicity from the Perspective of Andean Archaeology." In *Constructions of Time and History in the Pre-Columbian Andes*. Edited by Edward Swenson and Andrew P. Roddick, 3–43. Boulder, CO: University Press of Colorado, 2018.

Téllez Fabiani, Enrique. "El arte de la política, o la aísthesis de la imposibilidad." In *Para una estéica de la liberación decolonial*. Edited by Enrique Téllez, 87–118. Iztapalapa, CDMX: ediciones del lirio, 2020.

Tirres, Christopher D. "At the Crossroads of Liberation Theology and Liberation Philosophy: Mariátegui's "New Sense" of Religion." *Interamerican Journal of Philosophy* 8, no. 1. (2017): 1–16.

Tuana, Nancy, and Charles E. Scott. *Beyond Philosophy: Nietzsche, Foucault, Anzaldúa*. Bloomington, IN: Indiana University Press, 2020.

Turner, Kay. "Liliana Wilson: Learning to Live Finally." In *Ofrenda: Liliana Wilson's Art of Dissidence and Dreams*. Edited by Norma Cantú, 41–52. Texas: Texas A&M University Press, 2015.

Vallega, Alejandro A. "The Aisthetic-Cosmological Dimension of María Lugones's Decolonial Feminism." *Critical Philosophy of Race* 8, no. 1–2 (2020): 61–83.

Vallega, Alejandro A. "The Descent of Thought and. A Beginning of World Philosophies." *Journal of World Philosophies* 1, no. 5 (2020): 61–75.

Vallega, Alejandro A. "El Pensamiento Sentido: Introducción a un Pensamiento Estético Decolonial Liberatorio (Desde un Dialogo Sur-Sur con Sentido de Xu en la Pintura Clásica China)." In *Para una estéica de la liberación decolonial*. Edited by Enrique Téllez, 223–56. Iztapalapa, CDMX: ediciones del lirio, 2020.

Vallega, Alejandro A. "Exordio/Exordium: For an Aesthetics of Liberation out of Latin American Experience." *Symposium* 18, no. 1 (Spring 2014): 125–40.

Vallega, Alejandro A. "Exterioridad radical, estética y liberación decolonial." In Moraña, *Sujeto, decolonización, transmodernidad*, 121–36. 2009.

Vallega, Alejandro A. "Freeing the Eye." In *Philosophy, Art, and the Imagination: Essays on the Work of John Sallis*. Edited by James Risser. Bloomington, IN: Indiana University Press, 2021.

Vallega, Alejandro A. *Latin American Philosophy: From Identity to Radical Exteriority*. Bloomington, IN: Indiana University Press, 2014.

Vallega, Alejandro A. *Sense and Finitude: Encounters at the Limit of Art, Language and the Political*. New York: SUNY, 2009.

Velez, Emma. "Decolonial Feminism at the Intersection: A Critical Reflection on the Relationship Between Decolonial Feminism and Intersectionality." *Journal of Speculative Philosophy* 33, no. 3 (2019): 309–406.

Verran, Helen. "The Politics of Working Cosmologies Together While Keeping Them Separate." In *A World of Many Worlds*. Edited by Marisol de la Cadena and Mario Blaser, 112–30. Durham, NC: Duke University Press, 2018.

Viveiros de Castro, Eduardo, and Déborah Danowski. "Cosmological Deixis and Amerindian Perspectivism." *The Journal of the Royal Anthropological Institute* 4, no. 3 (1988): 469–88.

Viveiros de Castro, Eduardo, and Déborah Danowski. "Humans and Terrans in the Gaia War." In *A World of Many Worlds*. Edited by Marisol de la Cadena and Mario Blaser, 172–204. Durham, NC: Duke University Press, 2018.

Viveiros de Castro, Eduardo, and Déborah Danowski. *The Relative Native: Essays on Indigenous Conceptual Worlds*. Chicago, IL: Hau Books, 2015.

Walsh, Catherine. "(Post) Coloniality in Ecuador: The Indigenous Movement's Practices and Politics of (Re)Signification and Decolonization." In *Coloniality at Large: Latin America and the Postcolonial Debate*. Edited by Mabel Moraña, Enrique Dussel, and Carlos A. Jáuregui. Durham, NC: Duke University Press, 2008. 506–18.

Walsh, Catherine. "Shifting the Geopolitics of Critical Knowledge: Decolonial Thought and Cultural Studies 'Other' in the Andes." In *Globalization and the Decolonial Option*. Edited by Walter Mignolo and Arturo Escobar. London: Routledge, 2010. 78–93.

Wilkinson, Darryl, and Terence D'Altroy. "The Past as Kin: Materiality and Time in Inka Landscapes." In *Constructions of Time and History in the Pre-Columbian Andes*. Edited by Edward Swenson and Andrew P. Roddick, 107–32. Boulder, CO: University Press of Colorado, 2018.

Winter, Sylvia. "The Ceremony Must Be Found: After Humanism." *boundary 2* 12, no. 3 (1984): 19–70.

Yergeau, Melanie. *Authoring Autism: On Rhetoric and Neurological Queerness*. Durham, NC: Duke University Press, 2018.

Ybarra-Frausto, Tomás. "Rasquachismo: A Chicano Sensibility." In *Chicano and Chicana Art: A Critical Anthology*. Edited by Jennifer A. González, C. Ondine Chavoya, Chon A Noriega, and Terecita Romo, 85–90. Durham, NC: Duke University Press, 2019.

Zamudio-Taylor, Victor. "Inventing Tradition, Negotiating Modernism: Chicano/a Art and the Pre-Columbian Past." In *Chicano and Chicana Art: A Critical Anthology*. Edited by Jennifer A. González, C. Ondine Chavoya, Chon A Noriega, and Terecita Romo, 123–34. Durham, NC: Duke University Press, 2019.

Index

NOTE: Page references in *italics* refer to figures.

action/passivity dichotomy 7–8, 9–10
active subjectivity 7, 110, 154–7, 174, 179, 203 n.32
activity, and playfulness 153–4
aesthetic hyperpotentia 176–7
aesthetics 19–20
　anticipatory 180–1
　avant-garde 56
　of colonized bodies 95, 96, 99–100
　cosmological (*see* cosmological aesthetics)
　Dussel's 161, 167–8, 173–4
affects 30, 32, 116, 117, 118
　of after-bodies 124, 125–7
after-bodies 4, 123–5
　affects of 124, 125–7
　notion of 115
agency 13, 33, 110, 154, 174
agony, in Sabogal's works 54–5
Aguilar, Laura 95
Clothed/Unclothed #16 112–14, 115, 183
aisthesis 18–20, 78, 161
　of after-bodies 125, 127
　of Dussel 175–7, 190–1
　earthly 57
　and epiphenomena 167–8, 169, 172
　of ethical 169
　of *pachakuti* 172–5
　stillness as 121
　of Vallega's 190–1
Alcoff, Linda Martín 195 n.14
Al-Saji, Alia 17, 201 n.9
Amauta (periodical) 31, 43–4, 45, 202 n.16
anachrony 162, 187–8
analectics 162, 163, 173–4, 188
ana-topic imagination 147–9, 152–3, 154–5
ana-topic memory 155–7

ana-topic space 146–7, 172–3, 191
　of church 150–2
　and invoked art 178–81
　marketplaces as 158–9
ana-topic spectrality 185–6
Andean cosmological aesthetics 3, 56–61, 112–14
　lineages 31, 32, 78, 79
Andean cosmologies 3, 4, 193 n.1, 200 n.23
　Kusch's 64–7
　of sky and earth 28–9
animacy 57–8
　prayer to Wiraqucha 60
anticipatory aesthetics 180–1
anticolonialism 107
anticolonial resistance 1, 3, 31, 95, 105, 193 n.3
　and cosmological aesthetics 38, 161
　Kutsch's example 126–7
　led by women 160
　marginal theories 4
anti-object 66
Anzaldúa, Gloria 31, 105, 117, 203 n.32
　on artist's creative blocks 181–2
　on bearing witness 139, 141–2, 183–5, 191
　on colonialism 3
　on experience of writing 179
　on faces of border witness 136–9
　geo-aesthetics and elemental poetics in 38–42
　on invoked art 38–9, 179–81
　on "*mestizaje* theories" 3
　notion of imagination 32, 128–30
　on shamanism 120–1
　on space 147
architecture
　cataclysmic 23–4

coloniality of 75, 149–52
  hermeneutic identity and
    functionality 71–5
  Inka (*see* Inka architecture)
  integrity of 69, 72–4, 76–7
Arguedas, José Maria 1, 2
art and artworks
  hermeneutic identity of 70–1
  institutionalization of 39, 43–4, 48
  of oppressed 175–7
  reduction to "-isms" 40, 42, 43–4
así 20, 22, 24, 25, 126
  sensing of 82–3
Atahualpa, Inka emperor 10–11
attachment/detachment 118–19, 123
  shamanic detachment 120–1
auspiciousness/inauspiciousness 125–7
avant-garde. *See* Latin American
    avant-garde
ayni 109–10, 112, 126

Barrios de Chungara, Domitila 164–5
bearing witness 32, 134
  in Wilson's paintings 139–42, 183–5,
    191
being and not being 20–1, 153
Bocanegra, Pérez 150, 151, 152
Bocioni, Umberto: *Dynamism of a
    Cyclist* 51
body
  bodily aesthetics 95, 96, 99–100
  body of the earth 138–9, 178
  dreaming 129–30
  Dussel on 167–8
  racialization of 91–4
  as sites for colonial violence and
    resistances 127
  traveling bodies 117–18, 145, 148
  Viveiros de Castro's notion of 116, 117
border miming 132–5
borrowed/borrowing art 40, 41, 54
Bray, Tamara 84

Cano, Sanin 45–6
Cantinflas, Mario Moreno 128
  impersonation of *pelados* 132–5
capitalism 158–9
cataclysmic potency 75–6
  and Inka architecture 77, 200 n.22
  in Navarrete's painting 79

cataclysmic sense 64, 80–4
Chambi, Martín 93–4, 201 n.7
Chopin, Frederic 176
Church of Andahuaylillas, spatial aspects
    of resistance in 32, 145, 149–52
chuyma 9, 126
Ciccarello-Maher, George 207 n.4
colonial didactic paintings 91–3
colonial difference 111, 149, 167
  and bearing witness 14
  and invoked arts 182–3
  notion of 110
colonialism/modernity 197 n.2
  and bearing witness 141
  elemental poetics on 37–8
  as *pachakuti* 25–6
  and race 202 n.22
  social architectures of 15–16
  space enforced by 145–6
  violence of 52–3
coloniality of gender 106–8, 110–11
community 109–10, 112, 114
Coricancha (Cusco) 74–5
Cornejo Polar, Antonio 164
Coronado, Jorge 198 n.21
corporeal imagination 32, 128–30, 132,
    134–5, 147–8, 154–5
cosmic past. *See ñaupa pacha*
cosmological aesthetics 2–3, 4, 28, 178
  Andean 56–61
  decolonial feminism as 111–14
  Inka architecture as 75–6
  in Quispecuro Nina's works 186
  and resistance 31, 32, 38, 105–14,
    161
cosmological identity 77
cosmological resistance 1, 2
  and decolonial feminism 110
  delimitations of 12–14
  physicality of 30–2
  through *aísthesis* 18–20
cosmos. *See pacha*
creative sensibility 47–8
creativity 43
  creative blocks 181–3
crucifix 92
Cummins, Tom and Bruce Manheim,
    "The River around Us, the Stream
    Within Us: The Traces of the Sun
    and Inka Kinetics" 57, 58–60, 86

decolonial feminism   31–2, 95, 105–6, 128
   as cosmological aesthetics   111–14
   and *pacha*   108–11
decolonization   193 n.3
dignity   171–2, 173, 174–5
distinctness   170–2, 189–90
Dussel, Enrique   17, 18, 32
   aesthetics of   161, 167–8
   aísthesis of   175–7
   notion of exteriority   162–3, 169–71, 174, 175–6, 188–9
   notion of phenomena   168
   notion of world   168, 196 n.1
   on oppressed   167–8
   views on liberation   161, 169–70, 173–4

earth   24, 26–30, 59. *See also ukhu pacha*
   body of the earth   138–9, 178
   "invoked art's" relation to   42
   turn to   56–7
earthquake   81, 82, 92–3
economic value   158–9
Eielson, Jorge   203 n.33
elemental(s)
   as aesthetic form   57–8, 59
   and Latin America   52
   rhythmic dimension of   63–4, 68–9, 198 n.14
   and spatialization   150–1
elemental poetics   37
   in Anzaldúa   42
   in Pettoruti   45–7
elemental reliance   75, 76–7
elements   18, 37
   difference between things and   26–8
   as elementals   58–60
   recession of   59
emptiness   20–1
   anachronic   187–8
   and knots   25, 110–11, 183, 188, 191, 203 n.33
epiphenomena   167–8
   of distinctness   169–71
   of face   171–2
Escobar, Arturo   194 n.4
estar   9–10, 13, 64–5, 66, 82, 119, 120, 125, 174

ethics/ethical
   aísthesis of   169
   of liberation   33, 173, 178, 189, 190–1, 207 n.4
everyday
   and invoked art   41, 119, 179–80
   rhythms of   32, 155, 158–60
exteriority   54, 162–3, 174, 188–9
   and *aísthesis*   172–3, 175–6
   and epiphenomenon of distinctness   169–71
   Vallega's interpretation of   187, 188, 189–90, 191
externalization   9

face
   aesthetic epiphenomenon of   171–2
   of border witness   135–9
   and distinctness   189–90
   gestures   129–30
Fanon, Frantz   117, 118, 195 n.19
Figal, Günter   200 n.22
functionality, and hermeneutic identity in architecture   71–5
futurism, and Latin American avant-garde   50

Gadamer, Hans-Georg   200 n.11
   aesthetics of   69–75, 200 n.15
   and Inka architecture   76–8, 200 n.22
   on rhythm   65, 72, 73–4
Gavazzi, Nadine   199 n.3
gender
   dimorphic register of   106
   and miming   133–4
   roles   103
   and socialities   130–1
geo-aesthetics   56–7
   in Anzaldúa   38–42
   notion of   40
germinative stasis   118, 120
gestures   32
   facial   129–30
   interfacial   136–9
   in Wilson's bearing witness paintings   140–1
Guaman Poma de Ayala, Felipe   194 n.5

Hajovsky, Patrick   92
hanan pacha (sky)   22, 23, 26, 200 n.23

Index

chora as the space of   30
   as the elemental source of light   27–9
   stillness of   24
Heidegger, Martin: notion of
   world   195 n.1
hermeneutic aesthetics   69–75, 77
hermeneutic identity   70–1, 76
   and functionality in architecture 71–5
hermeneutic understanding   69–70
historical consciousness   82–5, 200 n.11
home
   immigrant's   101, 103–5
   as site for art   179–80, 182
human/non-human dichotomy   15–16, 31, 32, 193 n.3
   and elemental poetics   37
   and epiphenomena   168
   and immigrants   101, 133–4
   and modern social   130–2, 135–6
   physical parsing of   16–17
   and racial visual construction   94, 106–7
   and subjectification   110, 153
human world   39–41, 162, 197 n.1
Husserl, Edmund   29, 30

imagination   30
   ana-topic   147–9, 152–3
   Anzaldúan   32, 128–30
   and body of the earth   138
   and border miming   132, 134–5
immigrants. *See* Latina immigrants
indigeneity, racial visual constructions of   92–4, 99–100
indigenismo   52, 95, 96, 97–100, 107, 198 nn.20–1
   as avant-garde   53–5, 198 n.12
   and passivity   204 n.12
in-dreaming/*ensueños*   183–5, 191
Inka architecture   31, 57, 59, 62–3
   as cosmological aesthetics   75–6, 200 n.22
   and Gadamer   76–8
   obtrusiveness and incommensurability   62–4
   portals   147
   rhythmic sensuousness in   64–6, 67–8, 69

Inka stonework   31, 57, 59
   as cosmological aesthetics   60, 62–4
   and Gadamer's aesthetics   70, 74–5, 76–7
intihuatana   21–6, 37
in-stilled bodies   32
   of *pacha*   118–19
in-stilled movement   78–9, 85, 125
institutional buildings   72–3
institutionalization of art   39, 43–4
   rejection of   48
integrity   69, 72–4, 76–7
intellectual leadership   165, 166–7
interfaces   136–9, 190
   Wilson's paintings as   142
intihuatana (sundial stone)   21–6, 37
invoked art   38–9
   and ana-topia space   178–81
   and body of the earth   139
   and creative blocks   181
   as geo-aesthetic notion   41–2
   and *ukhu pacha*   182–3
Italian landscapes   56
   elemental poetics in   44–7
   trees in and as   48–50

Jesus Christ   92

kamay (creative force)   58, 78, 85, 137–8
katharsis   19–20
kay pacha (the world here and now) 77–8
Kenko (Peru)   86–8
kinesis   60–1
knots/knotting   25, 110–11, 112, 115, 125, 128, 183, 188, 191, 203 n.33
knowing (*sentipensar*)   14–15
Kusch, Rodolfo
   on Andean cosmologies   64–7
   on crisis   9
   example of rejection of water pump by indigenous man   126–7
   notion of *así*   20
   notion of *estar*   9, 13, 64, 119, 120, 125, 174
   on rhythmic knowledge   64
   on seminality   24
   on *ukhu pacha*   23
   on visibility   65–6

labor 159
landscape: mountainous skylines 67–8
landscape paintings, elemental poetics in 44–50
language 32, 118–19
   double 133–4
Latina immigrants
   pelados 130, 132–5
   socialization of 101–5
Latin America 52
Latin American avant-garde
   futurism and 50–2
   in Mariátegui's works 31, 44–5, 198 n.12
leeway 145–7, 148, 155, 160, 180, 183
liberation
   analytic distinction between resistance and 13–14
   and Dussel's *aísthesis* 169–70, 176–7
   and ethics 33, 173, 178, 189, 190–1, 207 n.4
   notion of 161
   and oppression 101
   pedagogical efforts of 165
   and resistance 162
   Vallega's aesthetics of 187–91
light 27–9, 37
   Chambi's use of 93–4, 201 n.7
   convergence of stone, water and 67–8, 69
   in Pettoruti's works 46–7
   in Quispecuro Nina's Virgin series 186
López, Yolanda: *Virgin de Guadalupe* 175–7, 185, 187
Lugones, María 7, 12–13, 17
   ana-topical imagination in 147–9
   and Anzaldúa 179
   decolonial feminism of 31–2, 95, 105–14, 128
   and Dussel 174–5
   on inescapability of oppression 163–4
   notion of agency 13, 110, 154, 174
   notion of world 32, 146, 148, 156–7, 158, 196 n.1
   notions of play, playfulness and activity 153–4, 206 n.16

   phenomenology of space of 145, 146–7
   on social, human and non-human 130–2, 135–6
   on traveling bodies 117–18, 145
   on world traveling 146–7, 148, 155–7

MacCormack, Sabine 150–1, 152
Machu Picchu 21–2, 68
   cataclysmic potency 76
manchariska 127
manchaytimpu (the time of fright) 96, 101–5
marginal (*mestizaje*) theories
   anticolonial resistance 4
   Anzaldúa on 3
Mariátegui, José Carlos
   avant-garde in 31, 43–4, 198 n.12
   editorial work of 202 n.16
   indigenista aesthetics of 95, 96, 97–100, 111
   and Pettoruti 47–8, 56
   on Pettoruti's landscape paintings 44–7
   on Pettoruti's landscapes paintings as refuge 48–50
   on picturesque style 54
   on Sabogal's paintings 54
   views on Italian futurism 50–2, 198 n.17
Marinetti, Filippo Tomaso 50–1
markets, rhythms of 32, 157–60
Marti, José 52, 80–1
memory 30, 32, 115, 123–5
   ana-topic 155–7
   of *ñaupa pacha* 157–8
Mignolo, Walter 197 n.2
mime 131–2
   by Cantinflas of *pelados* 132–5
mimesis 19
miniaturization 62, 81–2, 83–4, 86–7, 199 n.3
modernity/colonialism. *See* colonialism/modernity
Monsivais, Carlos, on Cantinflas's body and mime 132–5
moon 60–1
mosaics 55–6
multinaturalism 116–17
museums 38–40, 50, 180, 197 n.7

ñaupa pacha (cosmic past)   31, 78, 83–5, 91
  and anachrony   188
  and ana-topic space   151–2
  colonial rendition of   92–3
  embodiment of   121–3
  memory of   157–8
  Rivera Cusicanqui's notion of   157
Navarrete, Julia   88
  Sín Título   79, 87
The New York Times   103–4
Nisenbaum, Aliza: *La Talaverita, Sunday Morning NY Times*   103–5
non-human. *See also* human/non-human dichotomy
  faces of   136–9
  oppressed as   18–19, 131
  pelados as   130
numinous margins   66–7

oppression/oppressed
  appearances of   9–10
  art of   175–7
  dehumanization of   95, 103
  double   101–2
  dreaming and gestural body of   129–30
  Dussel on   167–8
  of indigenous women   185–6
  inescapability of   163–7, 172
  and intellectual leadership   165, 166–7
  as non-human   18–19, 131
  oppressed oppressing the oppressed   31–2, 96
  and *pacha*   6
  pain and sorrow of   11–12
  and resistance   101–5, 111, 164–6
  and socialities   18–19
  solidity of   111–14, 135
  suffering of   32, 137
othering   72–3

pacha (cosmos)   3
  in colonial context   92
  and decolonial feminism   108–11
  and elemental poetics   58
  in-stilled bodies of   118–19
  as kinetic   60–1
  phenomenology of   5, 21–6
  seminality and emptiness   20–1, 25
  and sensing   80, 86–8, 121
  as subject of the revolution/resistance   5–6, 12
pachakuti (cosmic turn)   2, 23, 29–30
  aísthesis of   172–5
pain (*dolor*)   10–12, 138
paintings
  of bearing witness   139–42, 183–5
  of earthquake   92–3
  futurism in   50–1
  Italian landscape in   44–7, 49–50, 51–2
  portrait of Mariátegui   47
passivity   7–8, 9–10
  indigenous   96, 99–100, 204 n.12
  and stillness   119
  of witness   39, 41
past
  aesthetic burden of the past   44–7, 50–1
  cosmic (*see ñaupa pacha*)
  futuristic rejection of   51
  in the present   82–3
perspectivism   116, 117
Pettoruti, Emilio
  Día Tranquilo   45, 46, 48
  José Carlos Mariátegui   47
  landscape paintings of   45–52, 56
  mosaics of   55–6
  Temporal   46–7, 48
  Vieja Puerta   49
phenomena   168
phenomenology
  of elementals   28–30
  of oppressed   167–8
  of *pacha*   5, 21–6
  of space   145, 146–7
  of visibility   65–6
photography
  of Aguilar   95, 112–14, 115
  of Chambi   93–4, 201 n.7
  Quispecuro Nina's Virgin series   185–6
physicality   2, 14–20
  and after-bodies   127
  ancient Greek notion of   19
  of cosmological resistance   30–2
  and *estar*   125–6

physical sentience 14–15, 115
  and Anzaldúan imagination 128–30
  and bearing witness 139–42
  and human/non-human
    dichotomy 17–18
  of liminal bodies 118
  and *Taki Oncoy* 7, 12
  and *ukhu pacha* 10–11
Plato: allegory of cave 30
playfulness 152–5, 157, 206 n.16
portals 147, 182, 183
prayer to Wiraqucha 60, 78–9, 80, 85
propitiatory resistance 1–2, 6–8, 102, 103–5, 110, 126–7

Quijano, Aníbal 106, 197 n.2, 198 n.17
Quispecuro Nina, Edwin 185–6, 191

race
  and colonialism 202 n.22
  embodiment of 117–18
  and human/non-human
    dichotomy 94, 106–7
racialization, of resistant bodies 31, 91–4, 111
radical exteriority 187, 188, 189–90, 191
Ramos, Samuel 132
readiness, as beauty 175, 176–7
religious conversion 149, 150, 152
representation 164–5
resistance 33–4
  active subjectivity as a mode of 154–5
  analytic distinction between liberation and 13–14
  and ana-topic memory 155–7
  Arguedas on 2
  and bearing witness 141–2
  colonialist perspective 5–6
  and cosmological aesthetics 31–2, 105–14
  Lugones's views on 12–13, 110
  notion of 161–2, 167
  as opposition 5
  and oppression 101–5, 111, 164–6
  pacha as physical force of 6
  physical dimension of 8, 9–10
  as propitiation 1–2, 6–8, 102, 103–5, 110, 126–7

  as socialization 102–3, 104, 105, 107
  through *Taki Oncoy* 5–14
respect 171–2, 173
revolutionary aesthetics 99–100
revolutionary Indian 96, 97–100, 111
Reyes, Luis Alberto
  on *Taki Oncoy* 5–6, 7, 8
  on Western tragedy 20
rhythms
  and active subjectivity 154–5
  elemental seeing 66–9
  and memory 155–7
  and playfulness 152–5, 157
  of San Pedro Market 157–60
  sensuous experiences of 64–6, 69, 71–2
rituals 12, 34, 125, 166, 182
Rivera Cusicanqui, Silvia
  on colonialism and race 202 n.22
  on *miserabilismo* 93, 202 n.18
  notion of *ch'ixi* 109, 112, 153, 158, 159
  notion of *ñaupa pacha* 157
Rojas, Rodrigo 185

Sabogal, José
  India del Collao 53, 54, 100
  Procesión de Taitacha Temblores 54, 55
Sallis, John 26–7, 29, 59
  on elementals 68–9, 198 n.14
Sánchez, Luis Alberto 199 n.21
San Pedro Market (Cusco) 157–60
scenography 44–5, 52–3
Scott, Charles 123–4, 125, 195 n.11
self 109
  disembodied 164–5
  fear/love of 130
  notion of 33
self-less time 149–52, 162
self-reflection 130
seminality 9, 18, 20–1
  Kusch on 24
sense perception 17, 19, 30, 64–5
  cataclysmic sensing 64, 80–3
  intihuatana as site of 22–3
  and invoked art 139
  pacha 80, 86–8, 121
  as a resistant physicality 31, 94–5

sensible time   78–80
sensuousness   31
    and elements   59–60
    of rhythms   64–6, 69, 71–2
sequential temporality   91–4
Seven Essays for the Interpretation of the Peruvian Reality (Mariátegui)   97–8, 100, 105, 204 n.12
shamanism   120–1, 123
Shining Path Rebellion (Peru)   95, 96, 99, 100, 105, 111
silence   32, 81
    and mime   132, 134
sky. *See hanan pacha*
social   106–7
    and human & non-human   130–2, 135–6
social architectures   8, 14
    of modernity/colonialism   15–16
social closure of the political   107, 110, 111
    and *manchaytimpu*   101–5
    notion of   95
social identity
    chachawarmi/manwoman   109, 111, 136, 153
    and interfaces   136–9
    mobilization of   4
    nepantla   135
socialist indigenismo   52–5, 107
socialities   1–2, 3, 7
    and *ayni*   109–10, 112
    and cosmology   198 n.20
socialization   34
    in anticolonial resistance movements   165
    and human/non-human dichotomy   15–16, 17–18
    and resistance   102–3, 104, 105, 107
solidity   111–14, 135
    in Wilson's paintings   183–5
sorrow (*pena*)   10–12
space
    decolonizing   145, 147
    as neutral   195 n.17
    phenomenological   32, 145, 146–7
    as vehicle for religious conversion   149, 150

stillness
    of after-bodies   125
    embodiment of   32, 120–1
    as physical sentience   119
    of sky   22, 24, 25
    of stone/earth   24, 25, 29, 77
stone
    convergence of light, water and   67–8, 69
    stillness of   24, 25, 29, 77
    and *ukhu pacha*   23–4
structural oppression   9–10, 97, 166
subjectification   110, 153
suffering
    modes of   10–12
    of oppressed   32, 137
sun   60–1

Taki Oncoy (sickness of song and dance)   1, 30
    colonial context   19
    meaning of   12
    non-reactive stance of   5–6
    propitiatory character of   1–2
    resistance through   5–14
Tambomachay site (Peru)   63
    echo stones   67–8, 76–7
    elemental reliance in   75
technique   39–40
temporality   198 n.17. *See also ñaupa pacha*
    of architecture   74
    of past   82–5, 91
trees, in Italian landscapes   48–50
tribal art, "borrowing" of   40, 41, 54

ugly   18, 195 n.20
ukhu pacha (the underworld)   10–12, 22, 23, 191. *See also* earth
    and creative blocks   181–3
    and stone   23–4
the underworld. *See ukhu pacha*
uni-topic space   150, 151, 152
unsociable bodies   2, 30–1, 32. *See also* after-bodies
    shadow beast as   136, 137

Vallega, Alejandro   19–20, 27–8, 198 n.17

aísthesis of   190–1
　　departure from Dussel   32, 191
　　notion of anachrony   162, 187–8
　　philosophy of liberation   187–91
Virgin Mary   175–7, 185–6, 187
visibility
　　and cataclysm   81–2, 83–4
　　Kusch's views on   65–6
　　of race   92–4, 111
　　and rhythm   66–9
Viveiros de Castro, Eduardo
　　notion of body   116, 117
　　on shamanism   120

water: convergence of light, stone and   67–8, 69
Western art, and "invoked art" distinguished   38–9
Western phenomenology   29–30
Western tragedy   20
Wilson, Liliana   128

bearing witness in   139–42, 183–5, 191
witness. *See also* bearing witness
　　face of border witness   135–9
　　passive   39
women
　　empowerment of   101–2
　　indigenous anticolonial movements led by   160
　　indigenous women   185–6, 187
　　and social   131
world
　　Dussel's notion of   168, 196 n.1
　　Heidegger's notion of   196 n.1
　　human world   162, 197 n.1
　　Lugones's notion of   32, 146, 148, 156–7, 158, 196 n.1
　　notion of   201 n.28
world traveling   146–7, 148
　　as active subjectivity   155–7
Wright, Frank Lloyd   200 n.22
Wynter, Sylvia   197 n.3

www.ingramcontent.com/pod-product-compliance
Lightning Source LLC
Chambersburg PA
CBHW062214300426
44115CB00012BA/2055